IMAGES
of America

LITHUANIAN CHICAGO

On the Cover: Students at St. Casimir Academy make miniature traditional Lithuanian wayside crosses in art class. Such crosses are a common sight along the rural roads of Lithuania. (Sisters of St. Casimir.)

IMAGES
of America

LITHUANIAN CHICAGO

Justin G. Riskus

ARCADIA
PUBLISHING

ISBN 978-0-7385-9854-3

Published by Arcadia Publishing
Charleston, South Carolina

Printed in the United States of America

Library of Congress Control Number: 2012946647

For all general information, please contact Arcadia Publishing:
Telephone 843-853-2070
Fax 843-853-0044
E-mail sales@arcadiapublishing.com
For customer service and orders:
Toll-Free 1-888-313-2665

Visit us on the Internet at www.arcadiapublishing.com

To the Lithuanians of Chicago, especially Lukas

Contents

ACKNOWLEDGMENTS

I thank my wife, Jennifer, whose endless patience and support through many long days made Images of America: *Lithuanian Chicago* a reality. I am grateful for my upbringing, courtesy of my parents George and Rita, that made me an American proud of my Lithuanian heritage. I thank my father, George, for listening, for his advice and insight, and for hunting down many contacts and phone numbers from back in the day. My grandparents Vladas and Maryte and Kazimieras and Stase have always been my link to Lithuania, and I thank them for the risks they took and sacrifices they made to establish a life in the United States.

Numerous individuals were indispensable to my work. I am especially grateful for Kristina Lapienyte's helpfulness at the Lithuanian Research and Studies Center and am indebted to the Sisters of St. Casimir for their kindness, hospitality, and willingness to open their archive of historical treasures. Sr. Margaret Petcavage served as an essential guide to this collection.

Many of the older images of the Lithuanian neighborhoods in Bridgeport and Back of the Yards would have been harder to find had it not been for Jeannette Swist, author of *Back of the Yards*, and her contacts. I would like to especially thank Loretta and her brother Michael Ezerski, as well as Cary Stack, whose trove of family photographs added an extra vintage touch to the book. The following individuals were also of great help to me in my research: Rev. Dr. Valdas Ausra, Grazina Biciunas-Santoski, Eugenijus Butenas, Richard Chorba, Dave Gaidas, Annette "Cookie" Gerger-Palubin, Juozas Kapacinskas, Sheri Klabish, Danguole Kviklyte, Skirmante Migliniene, Rodney Pavilionis, Vince Pavilionis, Val Ramonis, Nijole Riskus-Gierstikas, Antanas Riskus, and Donna Riskus.

The images in *Lithuanian Chicago* appear courtesy of the Lithuanian Research and Studies Center (LRSC), the Sisters of St. Casimir (SSC), and numerous other organizations and individuals.

INTRODUCTION

Outside of Lithuania, there is perhaps no city more Lithuanian than Chicago, which has had a significant Lithuanian presence for nearly 150 years. Lithuanians came to the Windy City from a small country on the Baltic Sea in three major waves of immigration seeking economic and political opportunities that their homeland could not offer. A mighty power in the Middle Ages, Lithuania was occupied by the Russian Empire from 1795 to 1918 and later the Soviet Union from 1940 to 1990. The country's occupation shaped the activities of its émigré community in Chicago; Lithuanians were determined to preserve their culture and work towards the independence of their native land. As Lithuania became victim to foreign occupation for most of the 20th century, Lithuanian Chicago flourished as the vibrant capital of Lithuanian culture in the western hemisphere.

At the turn of the 20th century, Lithuanians first migrated to Chicago from the Eastern United States (many from the anthracite coal mines of Pennsylvania) seeking greater opportunities in Chicago's burgeoning meatpacking industry. Although conditions were harsh, such employment provided enough opportunity to convince Lithuanians to continue coming to the city. Word quickly traveled from the New World to the Old, and Chicago soon became a major destination for Lithuanian immigrants. In the stockyards, Chicago's Lithuanians were immortalized through the work of a young, muckraking journalist aspiring to write the *Uncle Tom's Cabin of the Labor Movement*. Based on his research in Back of the Yards and Bridgeport, Upton Sinclair made the protagonist of his novel a Lithuanian, Jurgis Rudkus. Like Jurgis, most of these first wave Lithuanians came from rural farms. The sprawling jungle of turn of the century Chicago was entirely alien to their old lives, and they coped by settling in tightly knit communities, the center of which was a Roman Catholic parish. The early 1900s were a formative time for Chicago's Lithuanian community; much of its energies were dedicated to creating an infrastructure that catered to and supported the needs of its people. During this time, the majority of Lithuanian Roman Catholic parishes in the city were built with the generous donation of vast sums of time and money on the part of immigrants. These parishes were uniquely Lithuanian, with churches such as St. George's in Bridgeport incorporating Lithuanian cultural motifs with religious ones. As the presence of Lithuanians increased, the Sisters of St. Casimir, a Lithuanian order founded in Pennsylvania, moved their headquarters to Chicago. Such feats required great quantities of energy and wealth provided in part by hardworking laborers, religious laymen and women, and numerous Lithuanian businesses. As they became established, Lithuanian settlement spread to the neighborhoods of Brighton Park and Chicago Lawn, centering on the Sisters of St. Casmir Motherhouse near Marquette Park. The first two decades of the 20th century also saw a great assertion of Lithuanian national identity in Chicago. As the Russian Empire collapsed in the aftermath of World War I, Lithuanians in Chicago mobilized and dedicated their efforts to supporting Lithuanian independence, achieving their goal in 1918. As American immigrant quotas increased and Lithuania flourished under its newfound independence, Lithuanian Chicago saw fewer new arrivals until after World War II.

Lithuania's independence was short lived, lasting only 22 years until the Soviet invasion of 1940. Briefly occupied by Nazi Germany from 1941 to 1944, Lithuania again fell prey to Russian aggression in 1945 and was forcibly incorporated into the Soviet Union. Once again, Lithuanian Chicago devoted its efforts to securing Lithuanian independence and preserving its culture, bolstered by the arrival of political refugees starting in 1948 through the Displaced Persons Act. These refugees constituted the second wave of Lithuanian immigration to Chicago who, fearing persecution, fled the Soviet occupation of their country. Unlike the Lithuanians of the first wave, who came from a rural background, these new Lithuanians were well educated and left their homeland for political reasons. Their arrival to Chicago sometimes highlighted the differences between old and new generations. While older Lithuanians tended to be more assimilated into American culture and followed antiquated traditions and customs, newer Lithuanians came from a more educated background and were focused on retaining their national identity. This sometimes resulted in a cultural rift between those who had arrived at the turn of the century and those who had arrived after the war. However, each generation needed the other. The older generations had devoted their efforts and wealth to creating a thriving Lithuanian community in Chicago while the newer generation provided fresh energy and passion directed towards Lithuanian independence and a preservation of culture. Thus, the differences of these two generations were reconciled in the struggle for regaining Lithuanian independence throughout the post–World War II period. The result was that Chicago solidified its role as the capital of Lithuanian culture abroad as its community focused on making their homeland's plight known. Centering on Marquette Park's Lithuanian Plaza, Chicago became a home to these new Lithuanians where their politically and culturally orientated activities could flourish. Lithuanian institutions that had existed prior to World War II continued to thrive with the support of the second wave. This time period saw an increase in efforts to preserve Lithuanian culture and the history of the community.

Starting in the 1970s and continuing in the decades that followed, the Lithuanian community of Chicago experienced a shift to the suburbs. The move to the suburbs for Lithuanians was not new, as significant numbers had left the city as early as the 1920s and created communities in suburbs such as Cicero. During this time, however, more and more Lithuanians migrated to Chicago's suburbs as the communities of traditionally Lithuanian neighborhoods aged. Many of the communities' institutions continued to prosper in the city itself, but the focus of Chicago's Lithuanian community shifted. The impetus of this can largely be attributed to the foundation of the Lithuanian World Center in Lemont, Illinois. Purchased in 1988, the center has served as the focal point of the Lithuanian community of the Chicagoland area and is used for numerous athletic, religious, and cultural events. It was also home to two key organizations related to Lithuania's independence from the Soviet Union in 1990, Lithuanian Hotline and Lithuanian Mercy Lift. The fall of the Soviet Union and the restoration of Lithuania's independence resulted in the third wave of Lithuanian immigration to Chicago. Unlike their ancestors, Chicago's most recent wave of Lithuanian immigration was motivated primarily by economic factors. Upon arriving, they too became integrated into Chicago's extensive Lithuanian community and have begun to reconcile any cultural differences and contribute to Chicago's rich Lithuanian history. The Lithuanian community of Chicago has persevered for nearly one and a half centuries and certainly has the capability to continue to do so.

The American melting pot undoubtedly carries with it many benefits. It has, however, often resulted in people drifting away from their ethnic identities. While about 100,000 people are primarily of Lithuanian descent in the Chicago area, many more come from Lithuanian ancestors who they likely do not know much about. My hope is that this book will provide them with a closer connection to their past and culture while instilling within them a sense of pride for what their hardworking forbearers accomplished. The sheer scope of Lithuanian activities in Chicago has made it difficult to be inclusive of all the community's achievements, and I apologize for any omissions.

One

Neighborhoods and Churches

Lithuanians began arriving to Chicago in large numbers around the turn of the 20th century. What drew Lithuanians to Chicago from other areas of the country, namely the anthracite coal mines of Pennsylvania, was the growth of Chicago's meatpacking industry. Thus, the first Lithuanian enclaves in the city were near the Union Stockyards, specifically in the Back of the Yards and Bridgeport neighborhoods. For much of the first half of the 20th century, these two areas were home to a large Lithuanian presence. As many residents of the area recalled, one could get by here knowing Lithuanian alone and frequenting only Lithuanian-owned banks, stores, taverns, and restaurants. In addition to settling near the stockyards, other smaller Lithuanian enclaves grew in areas such as Roseland, North Side, and West Side. Eventually, they began moving in large numbers to the more spacious environs of Marquette Park and Brighton Park. As in Bridgeport and the Back of the Yards, Lithuanians flourished here, establishing themselves in business and forming numerous cultural and social organizations. Much of the efforts of Chicago's early Lithuanians sprang from their religion.

Since its conversion to Christianity from paganism in the Middle Ages, Lithuania's population has been mostly Roman Catholic. Religion was particularly important to the first wave of Lithuanian immigrants in Chicago, and significant energy and treasure was expended in the creation of religious institutions. Driving through Chicago's Lithuanian neighborhoods today, one can easily find the numerous religious institutions built by these immigrants. Lithuanians in Chicago made the creation of a parish a priority, donating money and time to realize their desires. Once built, parishes provided newly arrived immigrants with a sense of familiarity and comfort. They were a place to worship, to socialize, and to educate oneself or one's children. In addition, Lithuanian parishes in Chicago often promoted Lithuanian nationalism and culture through schools and political activities.

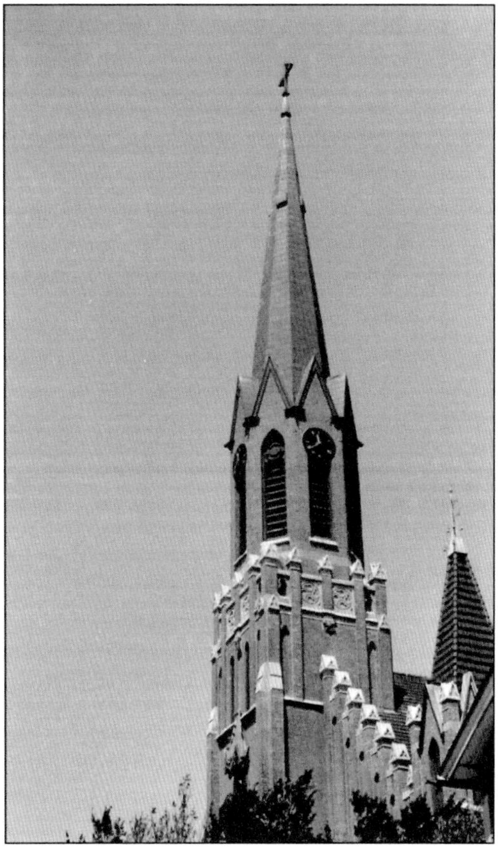

The first Lithuanian parish in Chicago was St. George, established in 1892 in Bridgeport. The original structure had been purchased and moved to a plot of land at Thirty-third Street and Auburn Avenue (later renamed Lituanica). It was one of the largest Lithuanian parishes in the United States, and in 1902, a new church was built in the neo-Gothic style accompanied by a rectory and school. (Eugenijus Butenas.)

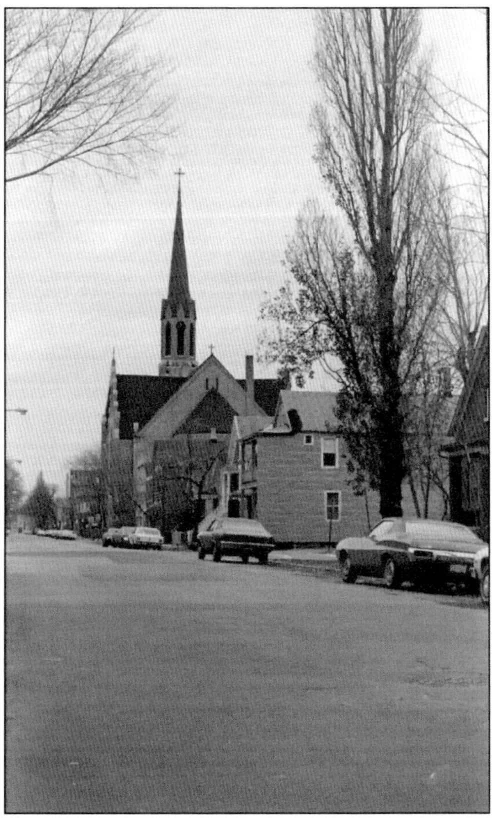

Seen here is the view of St. George's from near Halsted Street in Bridgeport. Halsted Street boasted a significantly large population of Lithuanians in the first half of the 20th century. (Eugenijus Butenas.)

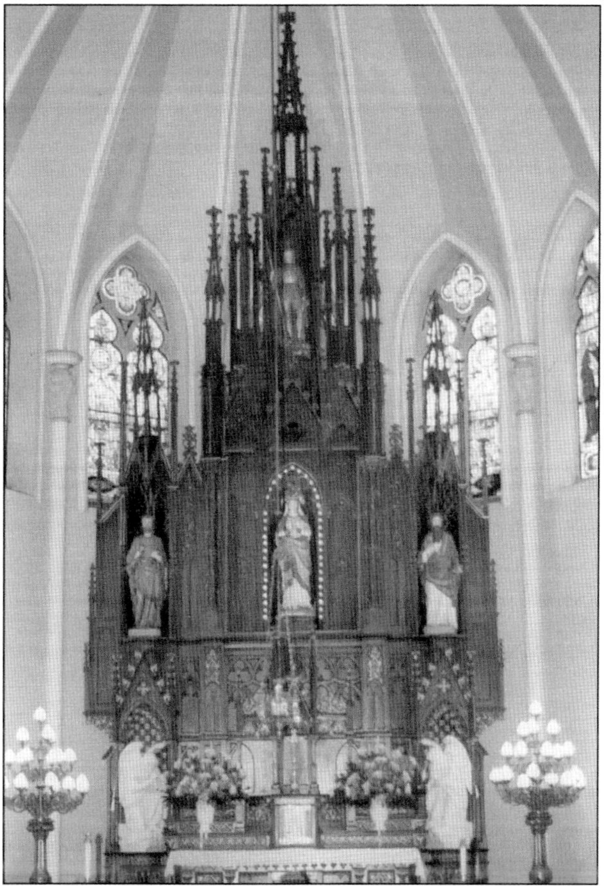

Of all Lithuanian churches in the United States, St. George in Bridgeport was considered the most beautiful. More than 1,500 parishioners could attend mass within its walls. Pictured at right is the interior of the church. By 1916, St. George had become one of the most successful Lithuanian parishes in the country, with an estimated wealth of more than $300,000 and a large number of parishioners, many who had large families. Pictured below is the school building. (Right, Grazina Biciunas-Santoski; below, Eugenijus Butenas.)

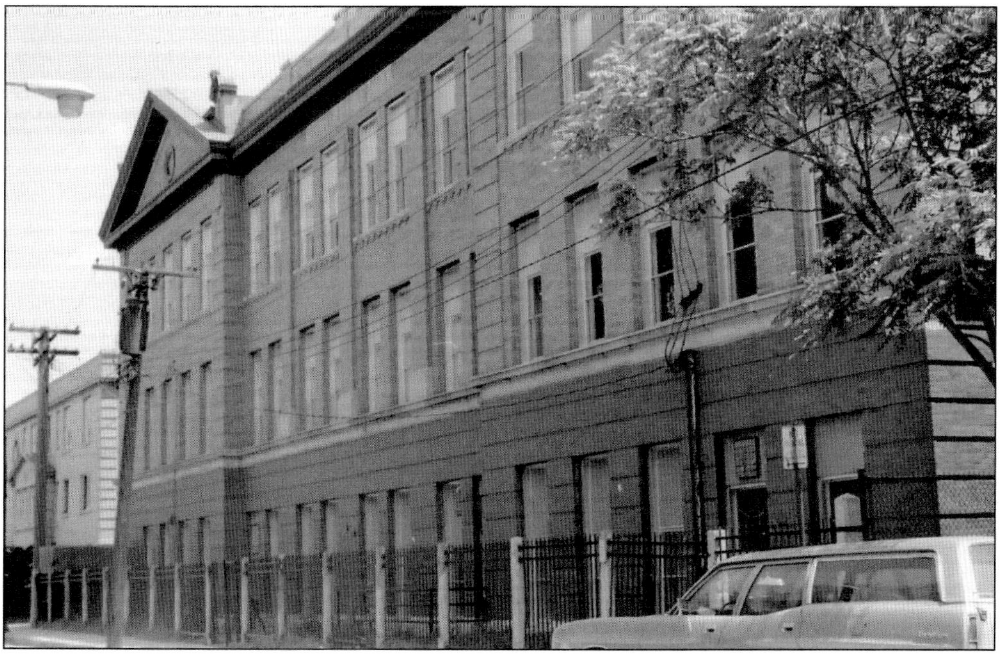

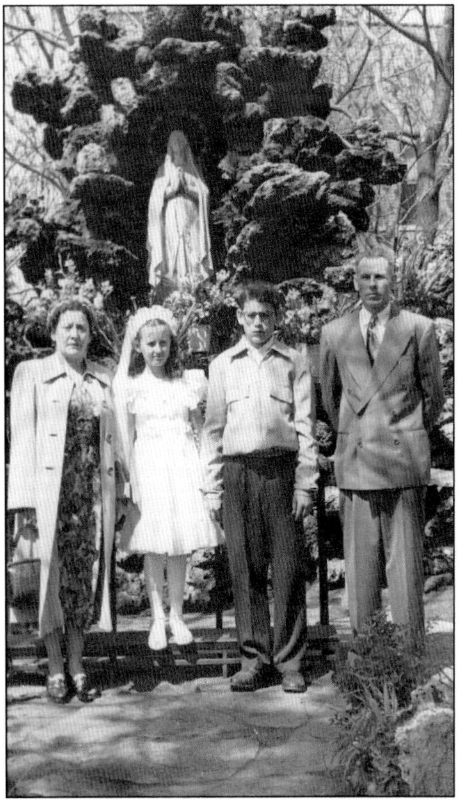

The grounds of St. George included a grotto, a popular spot for quiet reflection or prayer. The Riskus family is pictured here commemorating Nijole's First Communion in 1952. Pictured are, from left to right, Anastasija, Nijole, Vytas, and Stepas Riskus. (Nijole Riskus-Gierstikas.)

St. George's Parish, like the other Lithuanian parishes that followed it, was not only for worship but also provided immigrants a place where they could perpetuate their language and culture. The majority of Lithuanian parishes in Chicago included schools. Shown here are students of St. George School in 1957 posing for a group photograph ahead of their participation in the Lithuanian Song Festival. (SSC.)

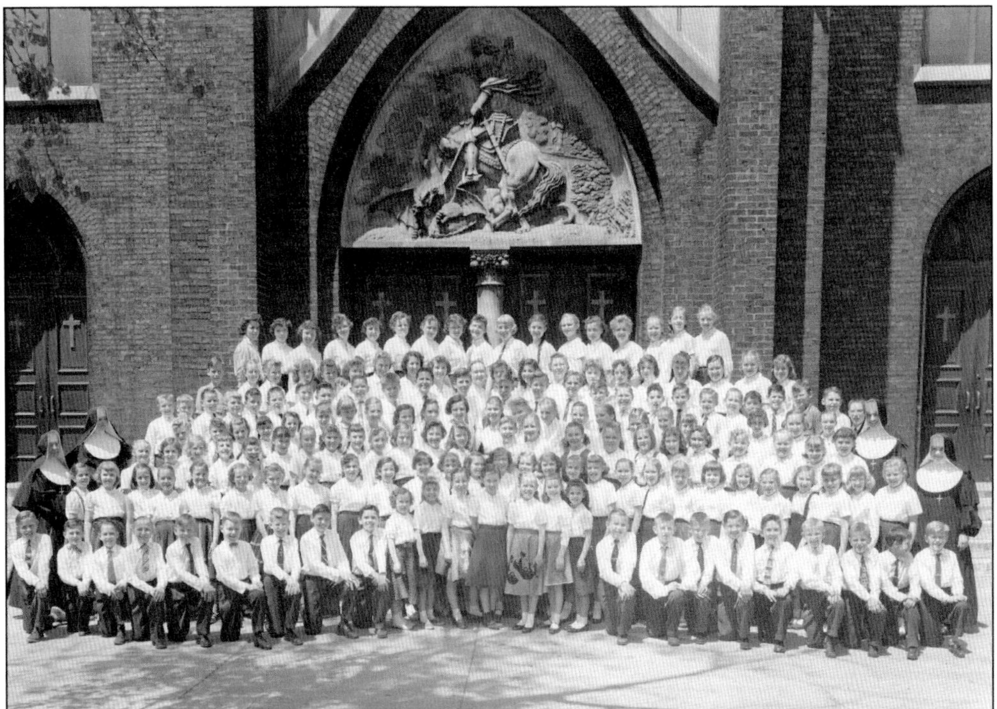

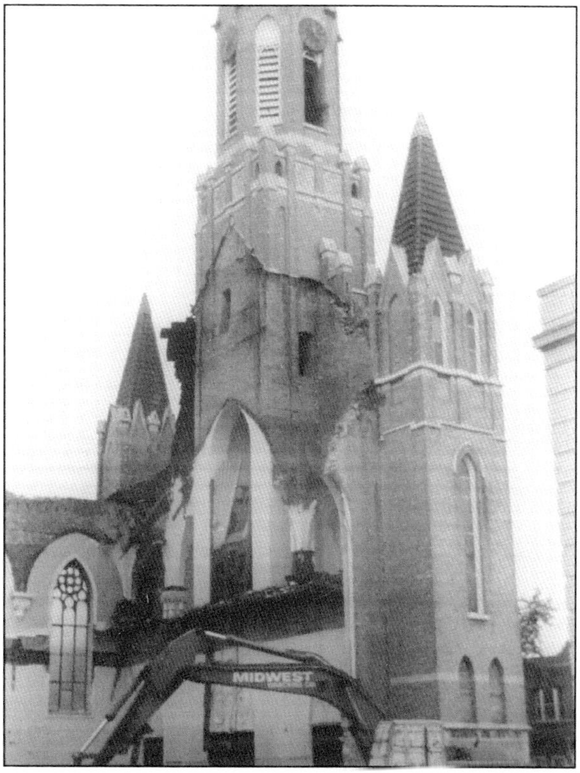

Bridgeport is no longer home to a significant Lithuanian population as it once was. This undoubtedly played a role in the Archdiocese of Chicago's decision to have the church demolished, pictured here, in 1993. As the parish was still home to numerous active Lithuanian parishioners, the decision proved to be a painful one and resulted in the loss of a historic and architectural treasure. (Both, LRSC.)

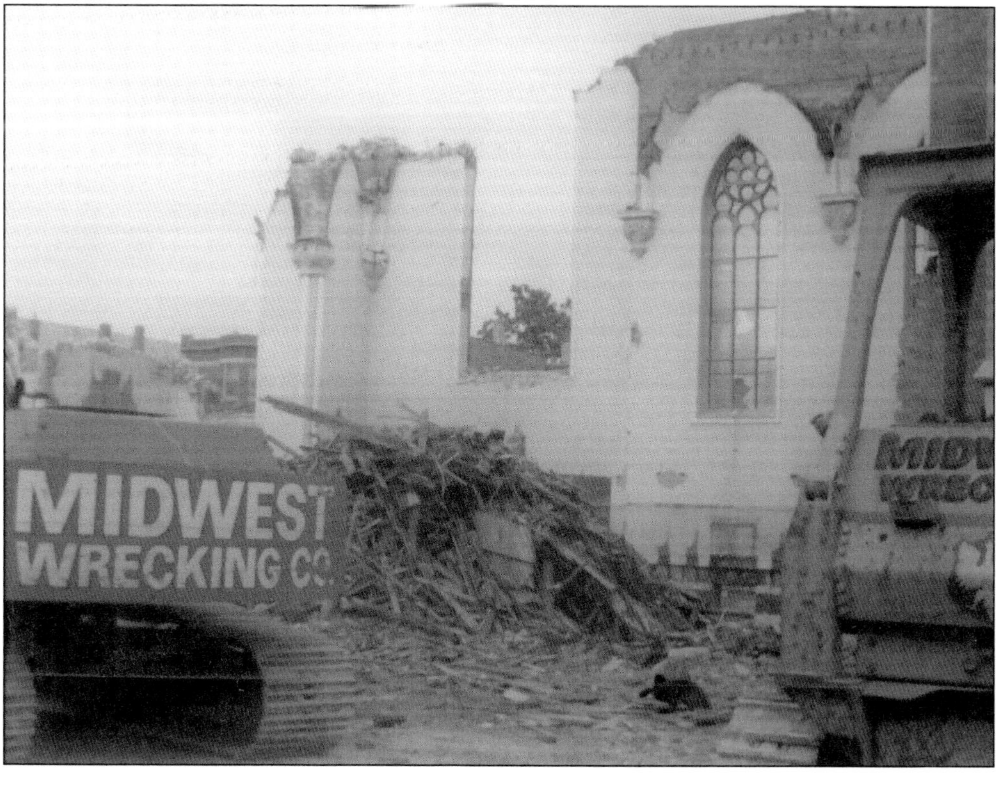

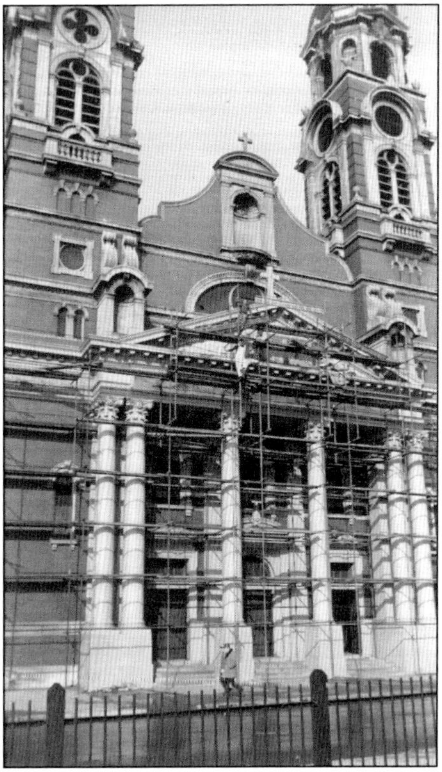

Close to Bridgeport, Holy Cross was another example of a thriving Lithuanian parish. Built among the swampland of the town of Lake (later incorporated into the Back of the Yards neighborhood), the construction of the church was said to have cost more than $185,000. Although a great sum for the time, donations were considerable and came quickly, an impressive feat when considering how many of these Lithuanian immigrants were struggling financially. Pictured at left is the impressive facade of the church (under renovation at time of photograph), adorned by Lithuanian ornamentation and two massive bell towers. Lithuanian-built parishes almost always included living quarters for its resident priests. Shown below is the one attached to Holy Cross. (Both, LRSC.)

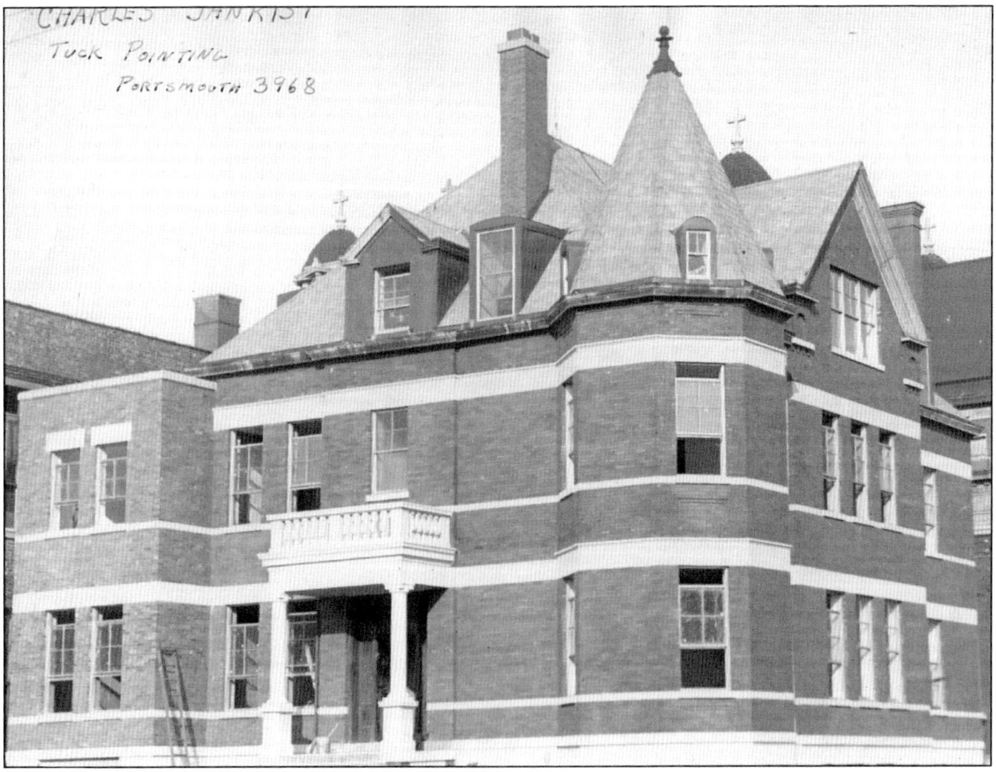

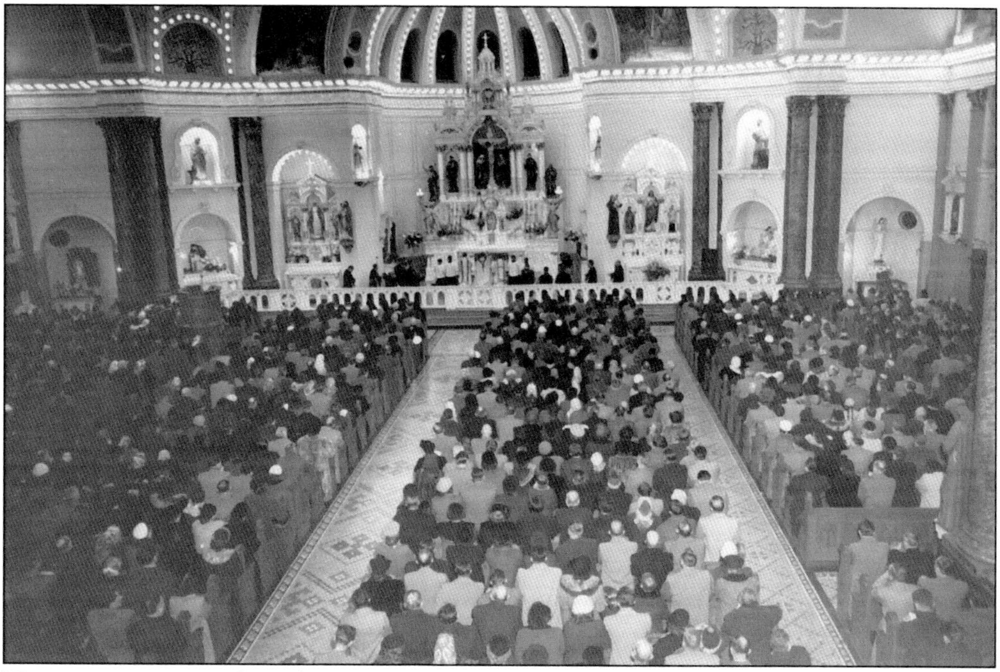

No expense was spared in adorning the inside of these churches. Seen here is the interior of Holy Cross during mass. The altar and floor patterns included Lithuanian-themed ornamentation. (LRSC.)

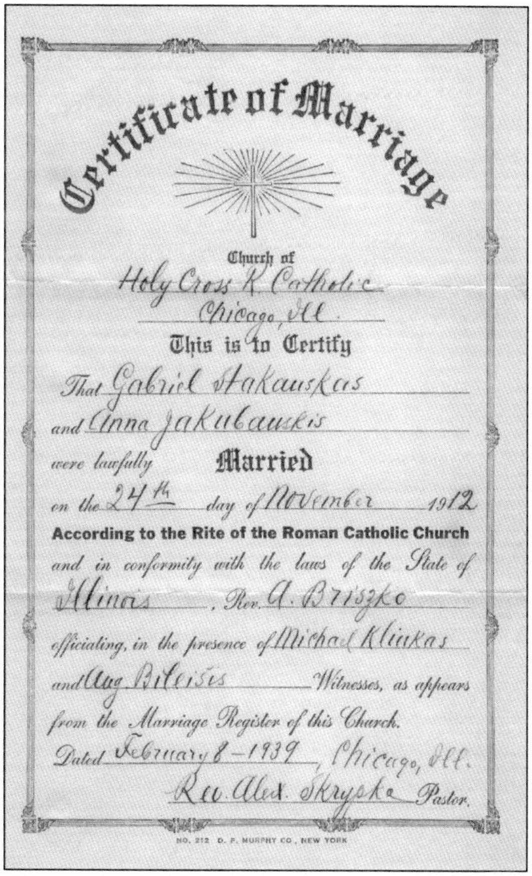

Certificate of Marriage

Church of
Holy Cross R. Catholic
Chicago, Ill.

This is to Certify

That Gabriel Stakauskas
and Anna Jakubauskis
were lawfully Married
on the 24th day of November 1912
According to the Rite of the Roman Catholic Church
and in conformity with the laws of the State of
Illinois, Rev. A. Briszko
officiating, in the presence of Michael Klinkas
and Aug. Bileišis Witnesses, as appears
from the Marriage Register of this Church.
Dated February 8 – 1939, Chicago, Ill.
Rev. Alex. Skrypka Pastor.

NO. 212 D. F. MURPHY CO., NEW YORK

The number of Lithuanians in the Back of the Yards was so great that couples often met each other in the neighborhood rather than back in their native land. Here is the marriage certificate of Gabriel Stakauskas and Anna Jakubauskis, who were married at Holy Cross Church on November 24, 1912. (Stack family.)

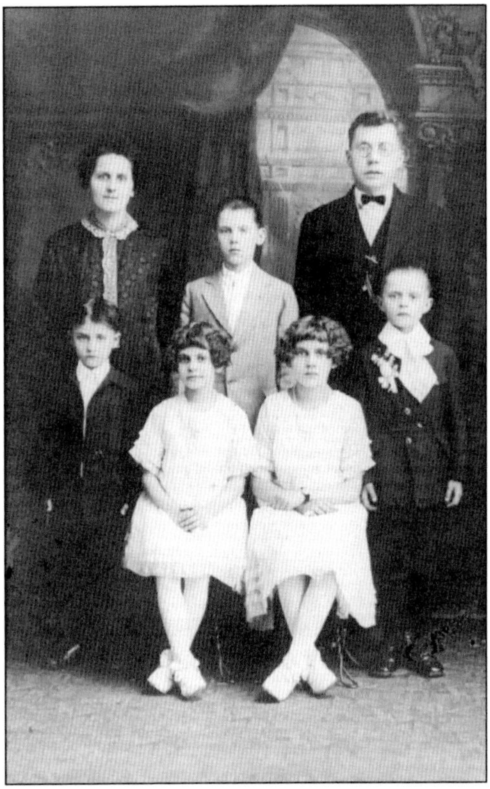

After marrying, Gabriel and Anna Stakauskas had a large family and raised them in the Back of the Yards. Pictured here is the Stakauskas family in 1926. From left to right are (first row) Frank J., Anna T., Helen, and Gabriel C.; (second row) Anna B., Joseph L., and Gabriel J. (Stack family.)

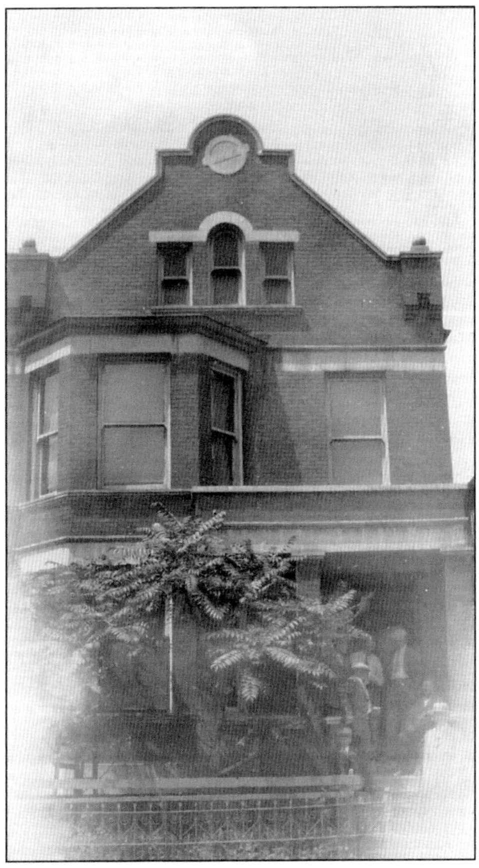

Most Lithuanian families in the Back of the Yards and neighborhoods like it lived in two or four unit apartment buildings with relatives or friends. Ethnic communities tended to stick together. If someone sold a building or apartment, it was expected that the structure was to be sold to either a family member or another Lithuanian. This four flat at 4644 South Hermitage Avenue, owned by relatives of Cary Stack, was less than a block away from Holy Cross church and was less common in that its exterior was all brick opposed to wood. (Stack family.)

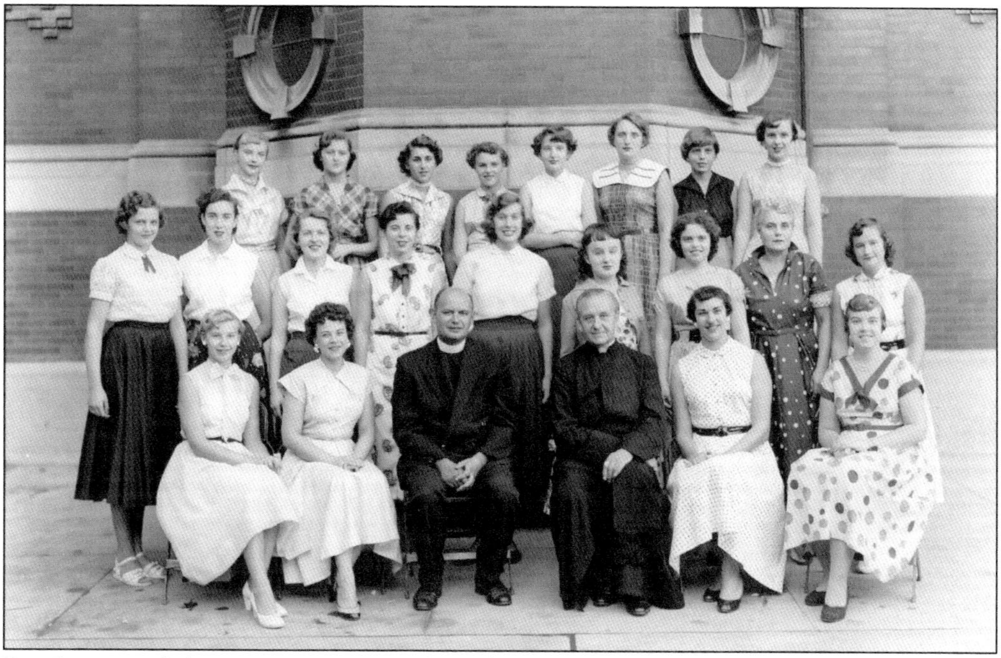

Parishes provided many opportunities for Lithuanians to become involved. Those musically inclined often joined the parish choir. At churches such as Holy Cross, the choir was often quite large, as shown here. This group photograph, likely taken before World War II, includes the parish priests. (LRSC.)

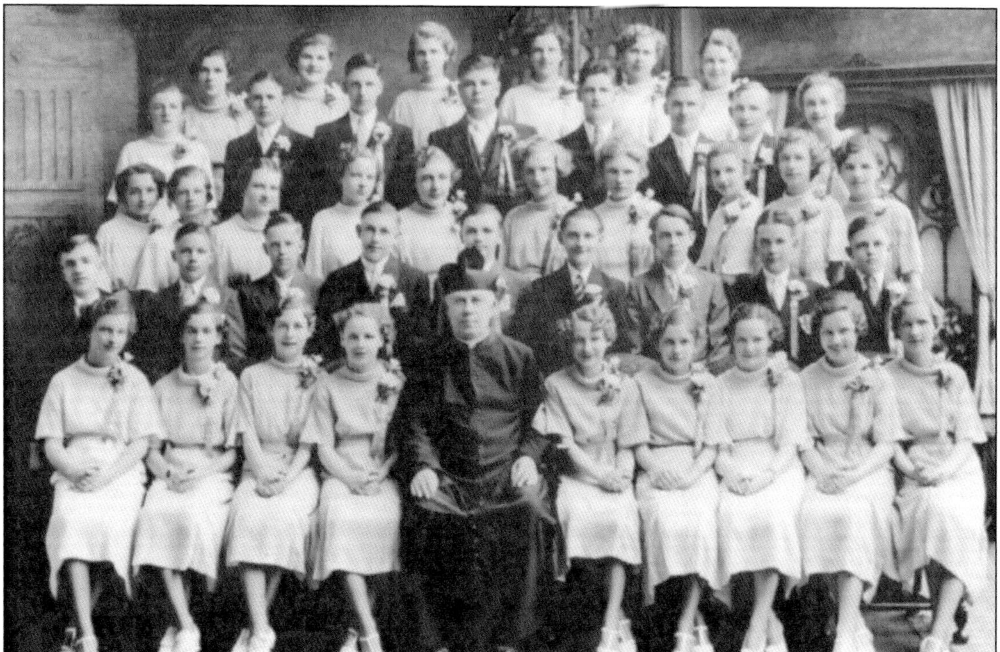

Holy Cross School was where many Lithuanian children in the Back of the Yards were educated. This eighth grade graduation class from 1935 is presided over by Father Skripa, seated in the front center. In the row behind him to the right is Frank Stack. (Stack family.)

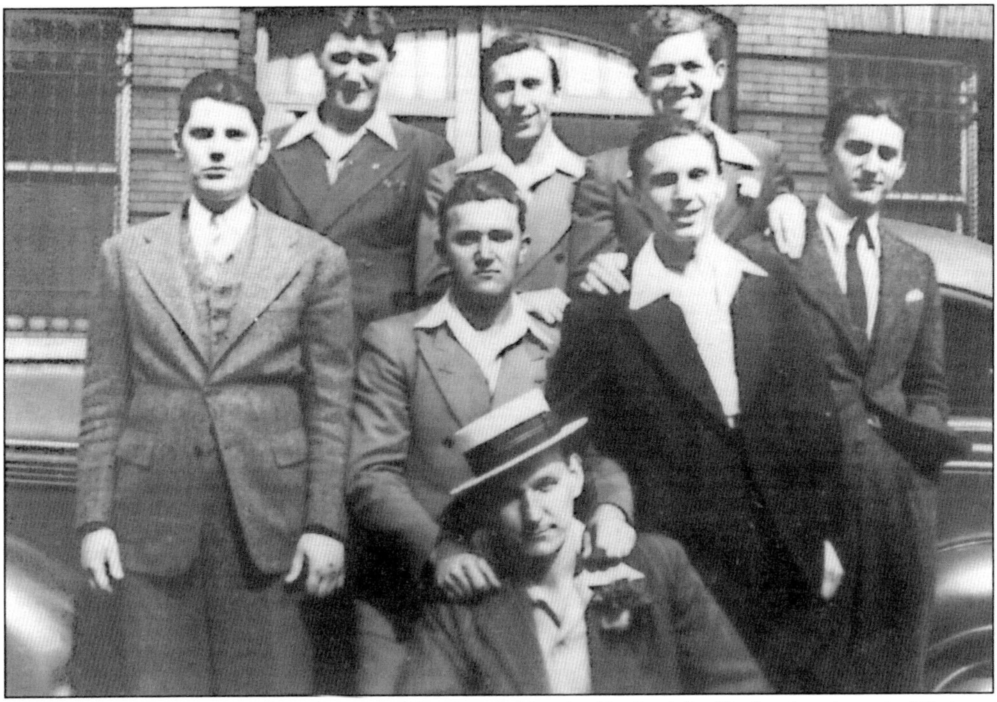

The bonds made between friends in neighborhoods like the Back of the Yards often lasted a lifetime. This group photograph from the 1930s includes Joseph Stakauskas (left), Walter Wozniczka (left, back row), and Frank J. Stack (far right). The rest are unidentified. (Stack family.)

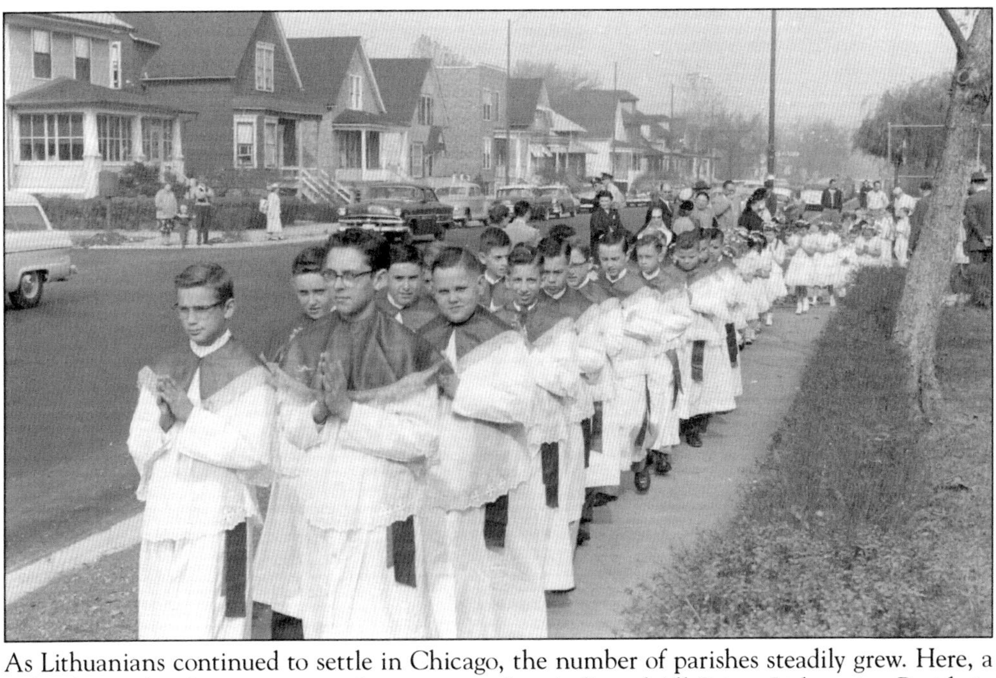

As Lithuanians continued to settle in Chicago, the number of parishes steadily grew. Here, a rather large altar boy procession demonstrates the vitality of All Saints Lithuanian Parish in Roseland. (LRSC.)

All Saints Lithuanian Church in Roseland was built in 1906. Pictured at right, the church boasted a steeple in a traditional Lithuanian design. (LRSC.)

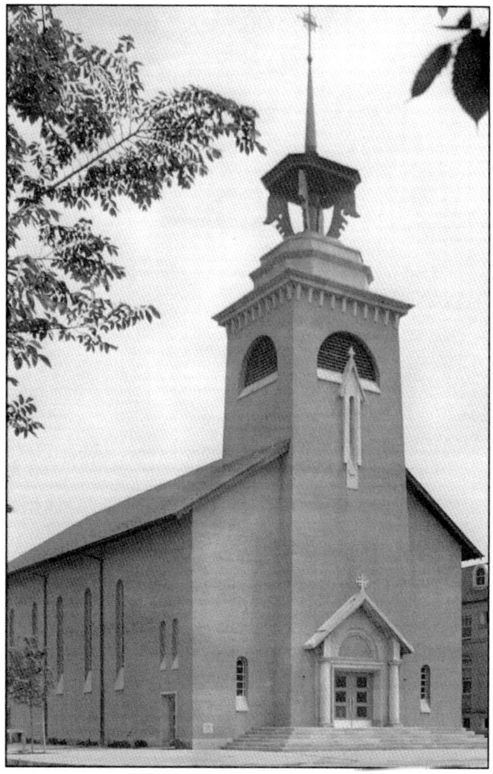

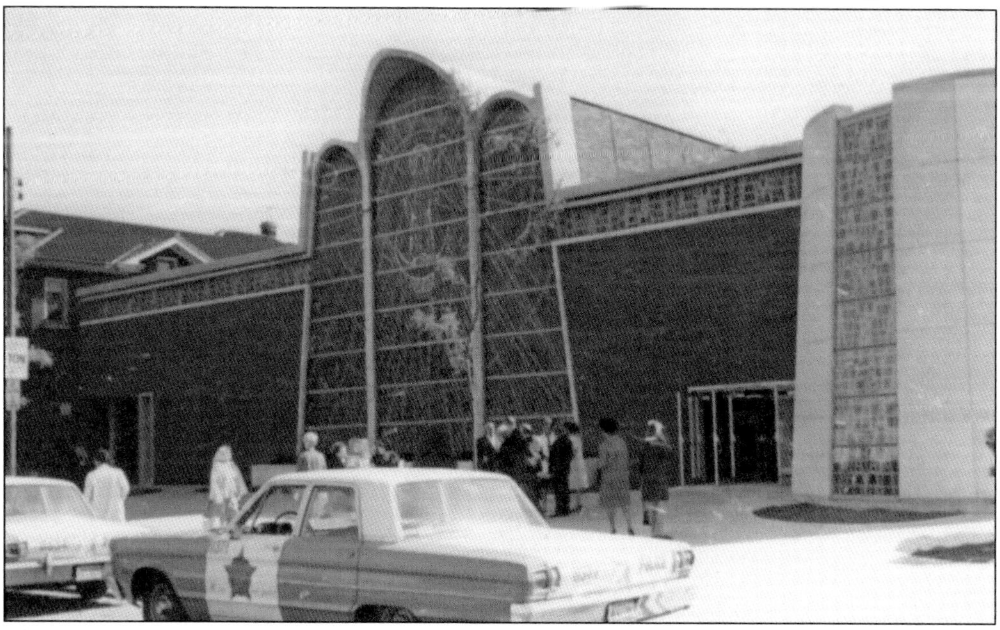

The founding of Immaculate Conception Parish in the Brighton Park neighborhood was a sign of the area's quickly growing Lithuanian population. At the time of its construction in 1915, the area was still rural in character, dominated by swamps and prairies. By 1917, it was a thriving parish to more than 260 families and had a school with more than 221 students. Pictured here is the newer church building finished in 1966. (LRSC.)

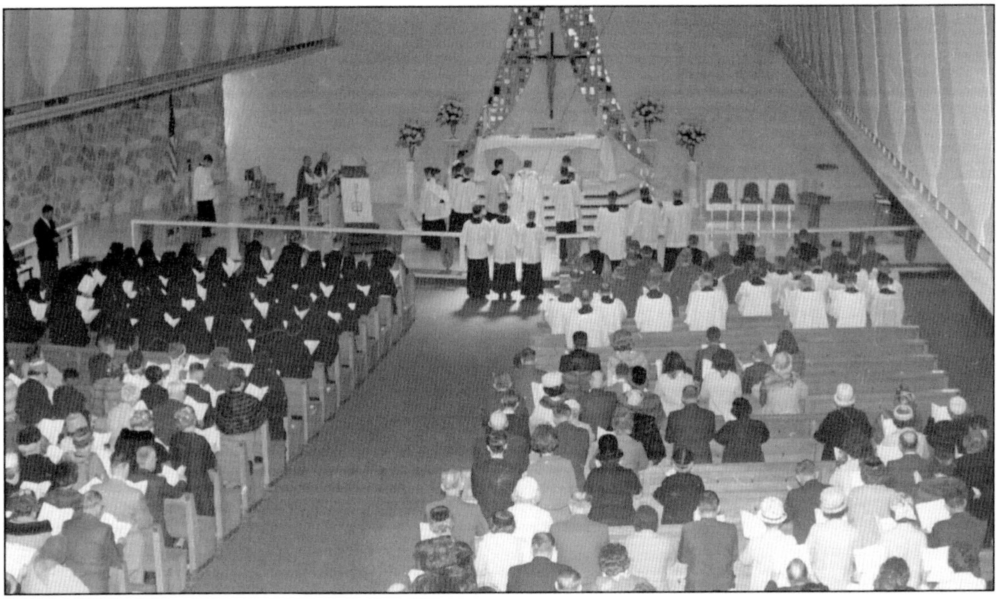

Immaculate Conception's new building was a big event for the Brighton Park neighborhood. In this image, parishioners gather for the inaugural mass in 1966. (LRSC.)

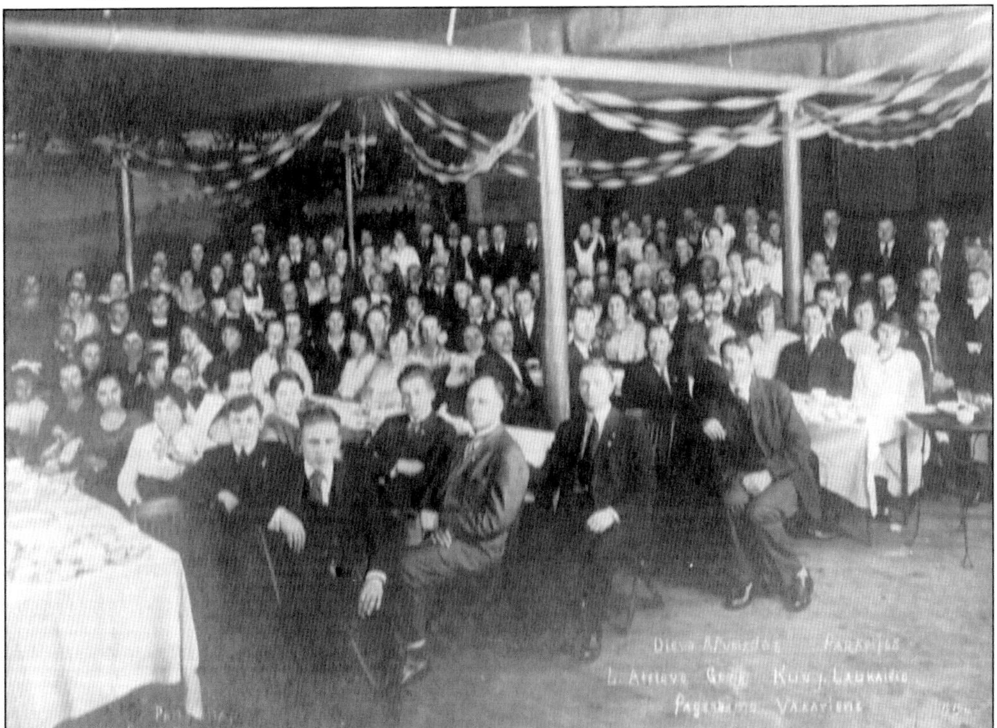

Lithuanian Roman Catholic parishes served as the center of social life for immigrant communities. Each church was often home to several different organizations. Immaculate Conception was no different. With more than 1,000 parishioners by 1916, the parish supported a Temperance Society, a choir, and a branch of the Knights of Lithuania. This large social gathering at Immaculate Conception Parish is for a dinner honoring Father Laukaitis. (LRSC.)

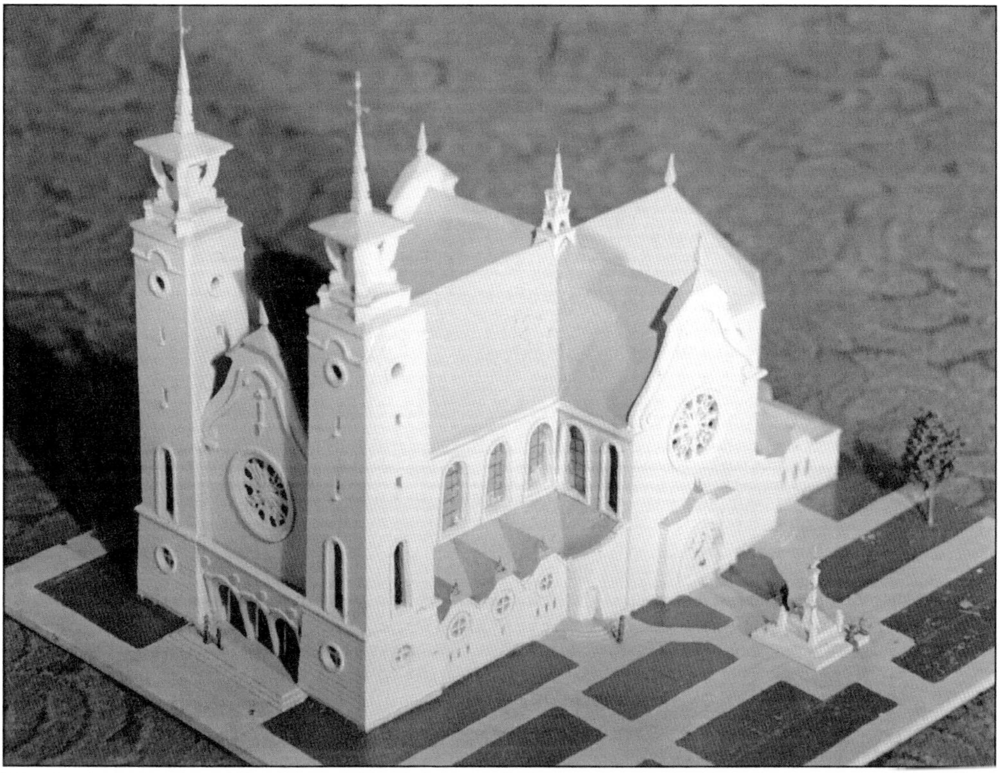

Not far from Immaculate Conception, another Lithuanian parish was quickly growing. Nativity Blessed Virgin Mother Parish in Marquette Park grew to become one of the most successful and longest lasting Lithuanian parishes in Chicago. The original church building, constructed in 1927, was later replaced by a magnificent structure built in a uniquely Lithuanian Baroque style designed by the architect Jonas Mulokas. Construction was completed by 1957 and cost over $1 million. Pictured above is the model used in designing the church. At right is a postcard of the actual structure, located next to Holy Cross Hospital at Sixty-ninth Street and Washtenaw Avenue. (Above, LRSC; right, Nijole Riskus-Gierstikas.)

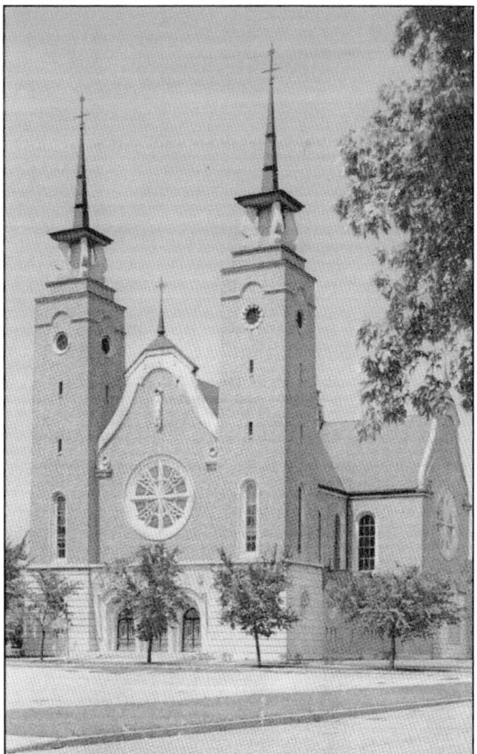

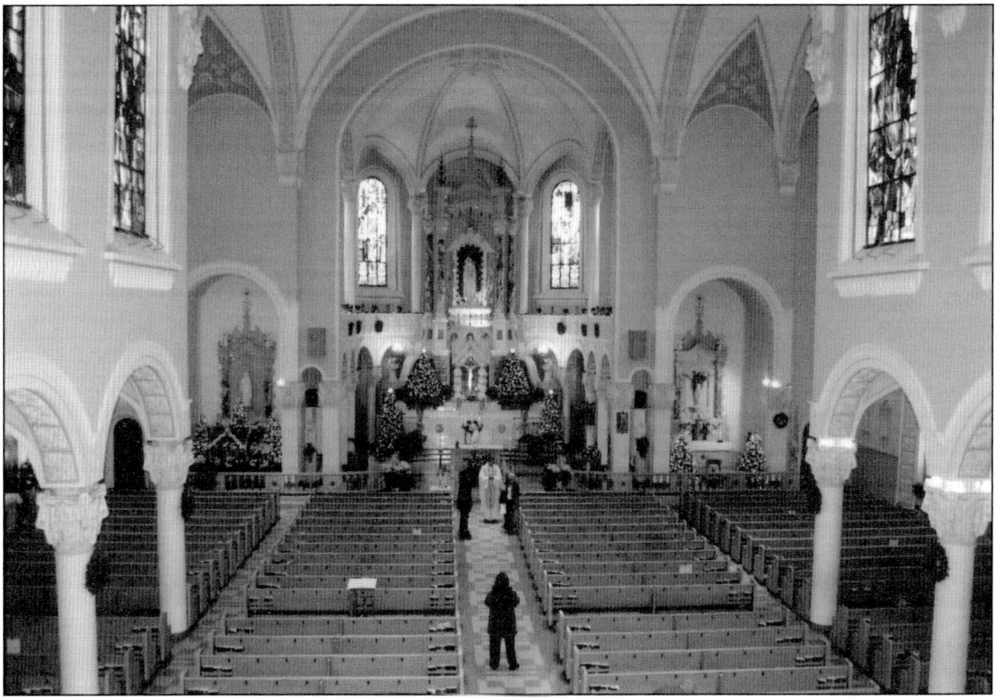

The interior of Nativity BVM Church, shown here at Christmastime, incorporates many Lithuanian themes in its design. (Nijole Riskus-Gierstikas.)

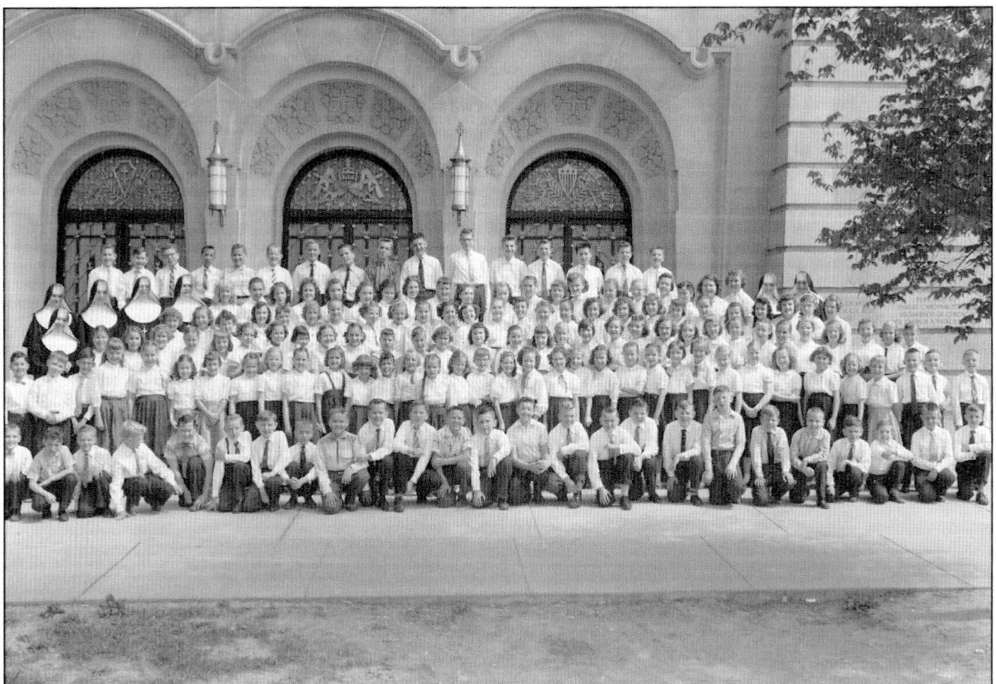

In addition to the church, the parish housed a successful school that catered to the Lithuanian community in the neighborhood, particularly after the arrival of refugees following World War II. For much of its history, Nativity BVM School offered daily classes in Lithuanian. (LRSC.)

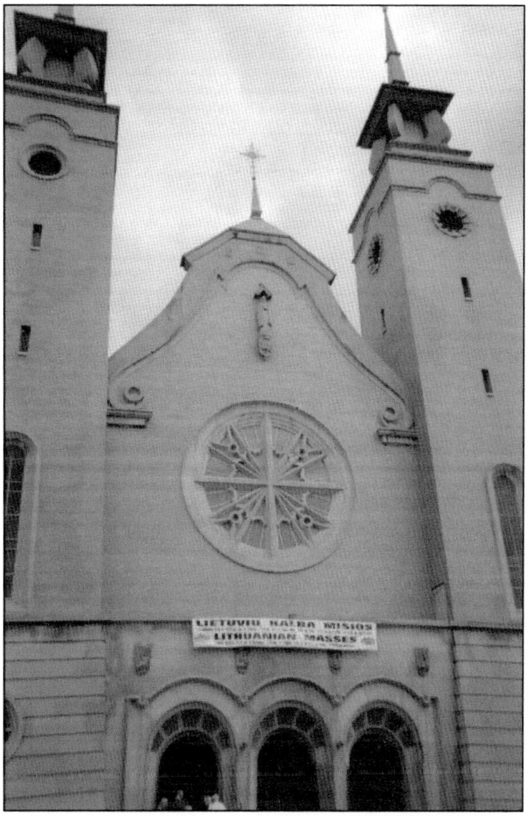

As indicated by the sign on the front of the church, Nativity continues to hold weekly mass in the Lithuanian language. (Nijole Riskus-Gierstikas.)

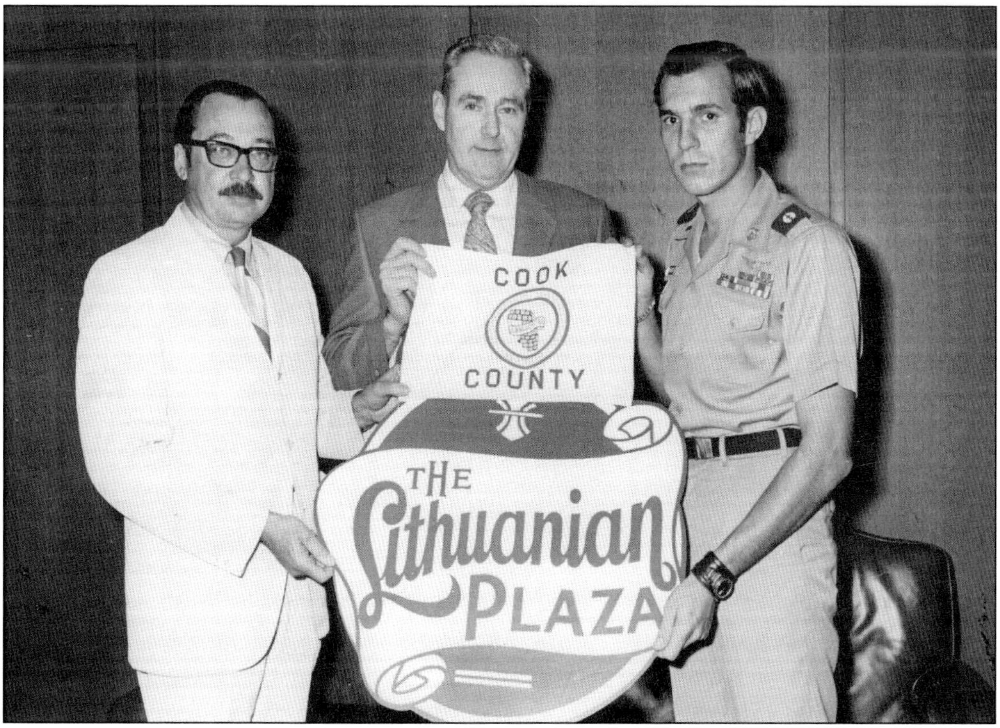

The presence of Lithuanians in Chicago Lawn, particularly near Marquette Park (many refer to the area simply as the "Marquette Park" neighborhood), led to the naming of Lithuanian Plaza, the strip of Sixty-ninth Street between Western and California Avenues. Lithuanian presence in the area is commemorated by this sign, held here by Stanley Balzekas Jr. (far left) with Cook County board president George Dunne and an unidentified individual. (LRSC.)

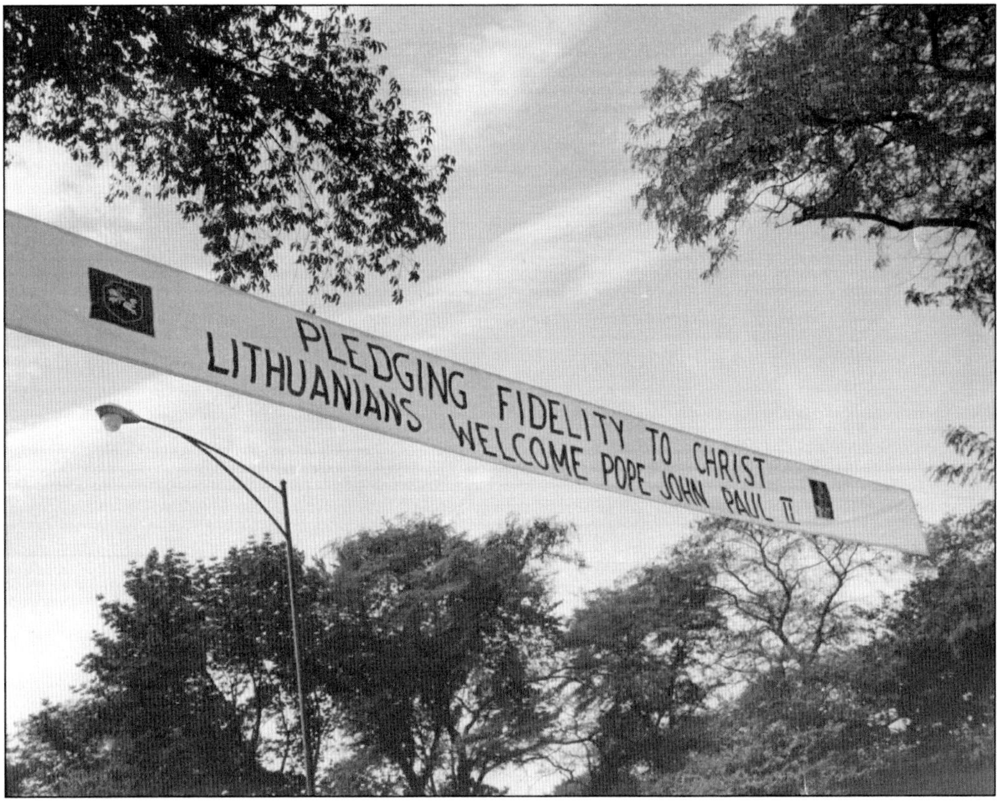

One of the biggest events for the Lithuanian community of Marquette Park was Pope John Paul II's visit on October 5, 1979. Seen above is a sign greeting Pope John Paul II on behalf of the Lithuanian community. Seen below is the pope driving down the streets of Marquette Park. The pope's charisma, anticommunist sentiment, and partial Lithuanian heritage on his mother's side made his visit particularly well received. (Both, LRSC.)

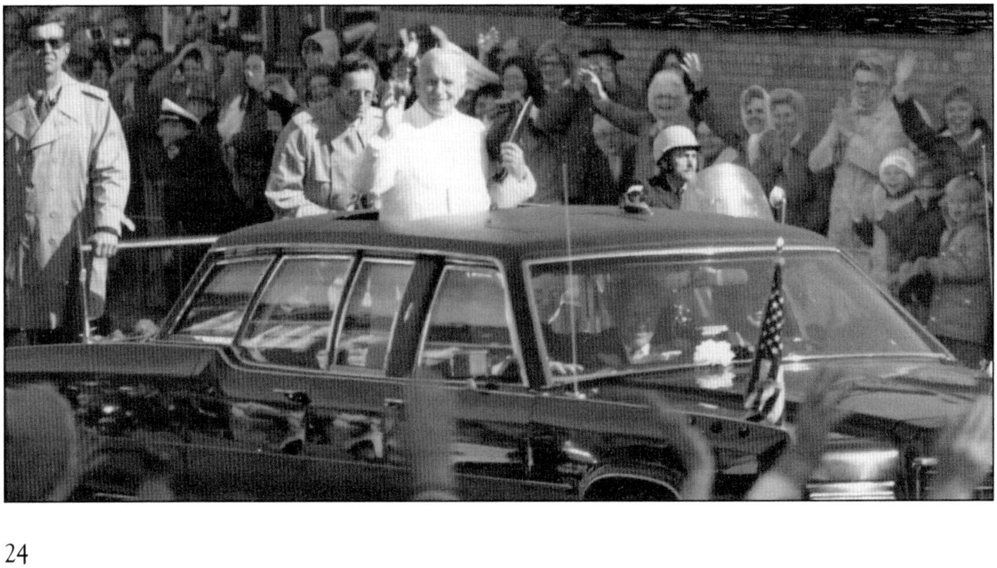

With so many Lithuanians in Chicago, efforts were made to establish a Lithuanian Catholic cemetery. The origins of St. Casimir Lithuanian Roman Catholic Cemetery began in 1903, when, under the direction of Father Kriauciunas, 40 acres of land were purchased on the outskirts of the city. By 1952, St. Casimir Lithuanian Cemetery spanned more than 523 acres of land. Shown here are the cemetery gates in the 1950s. (St. Casimir Cemetery.)

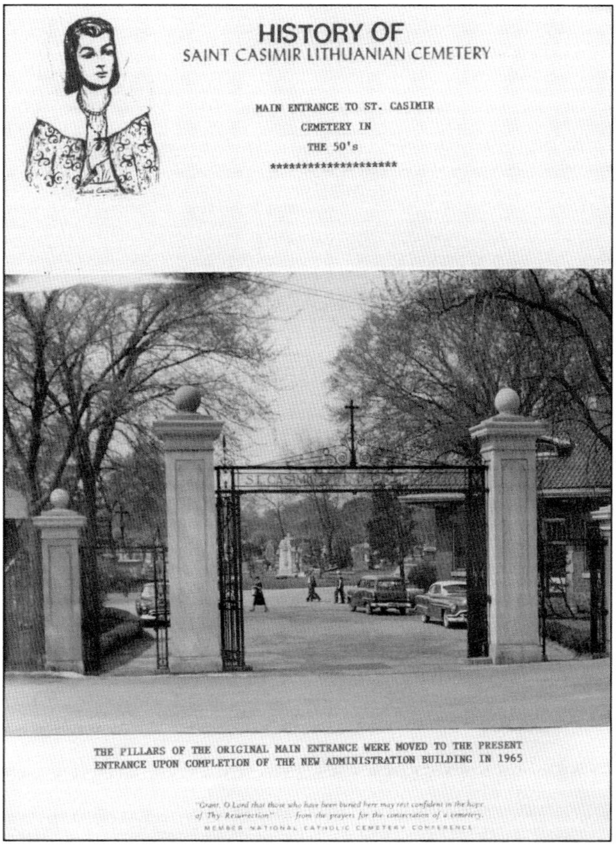

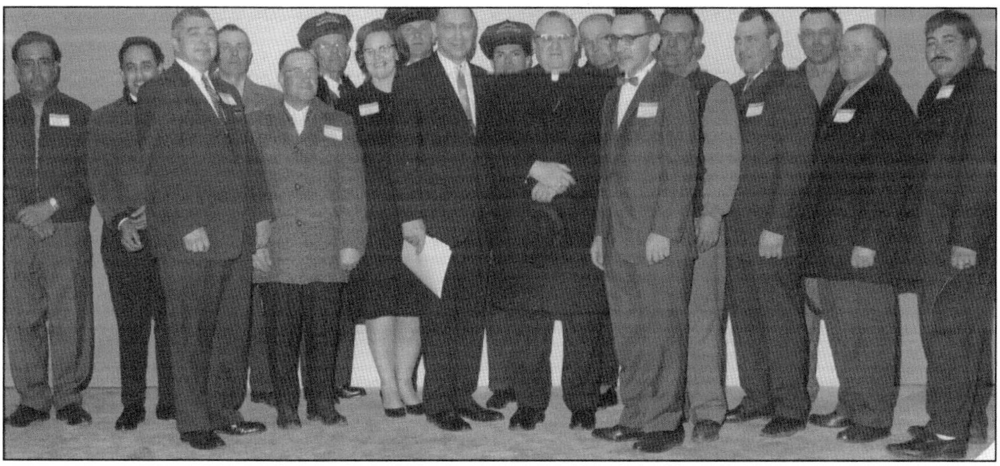

The success of St. Casimir Lithuanian Cemetery led to a series of efforts to renovate and expand its existing structures. In 1966, a new administrative building and chapel were constructed and inaugurated on March 4. Shown here are attendees and organizers of the inauguration ceremony, from left to right, Martin Ramos, Roberto Baeza, Bruno Beneckis, Domininkas Pocius, Anatanas Zilinskas, Mykolas Ramanauskas, Antoinette Elmer, Jonas Zaksas, Louis F. Kulp, Sexton Leonard Aquillar, Cardinal Cody of Chicago, Walter Rimkus, Casimir E. Petkonas, Leonido Fernandez, Andy Youngblood, Alexander Kikilas, Kristof Patiejun, and Domingo Medina. (St. Casimir Cemetery.)

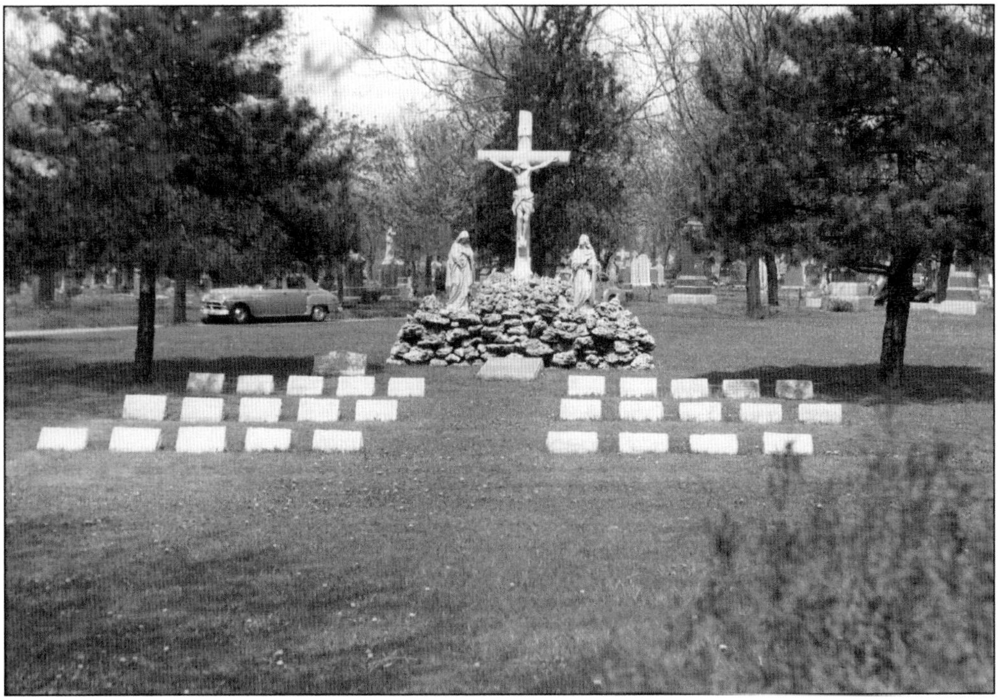

The beautifully landscaped and idyllic grounds of St. Casimir Lithuanian Cemetery made it a desirable place to bury loved ones.

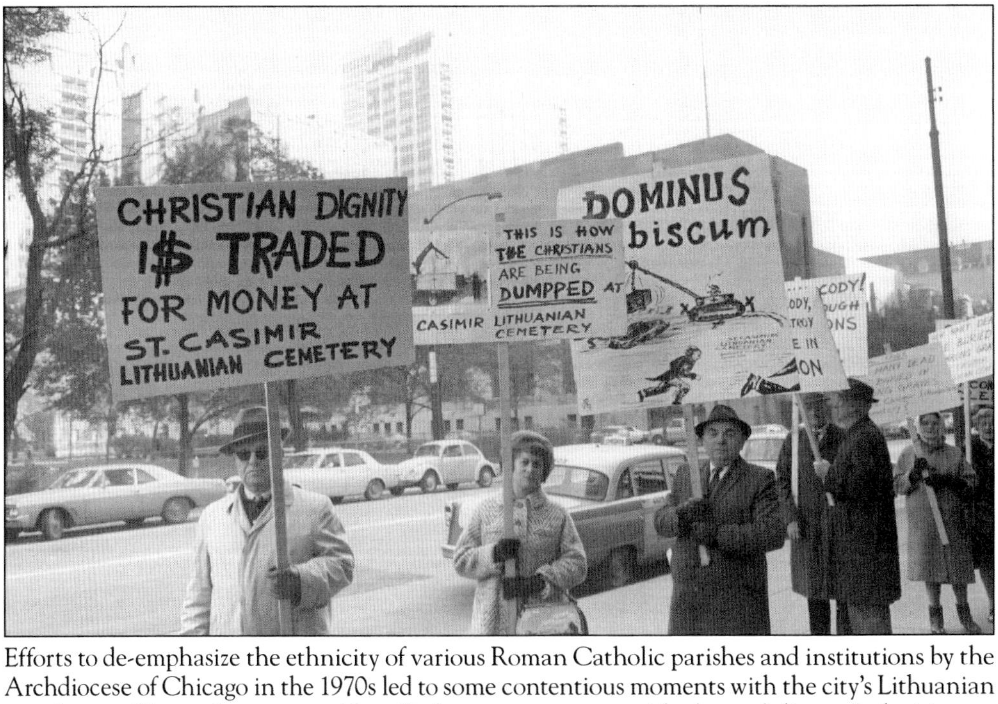

Efforts to de-emphasize the ethnicity of various Roman Catholic parishes and institutions by the Archdiocese of Chicago in the 1970s led to some contentious moments with the city's Lithuanian population. Shown here are unidentified protestors upset with the archdiocese's decision to decrease St. Casimir Cemetery's Lithuanian identity. Following the decision, the Lithuanian title was removed and the cemetery was opened to non-Lithuanians. (LRSC.)

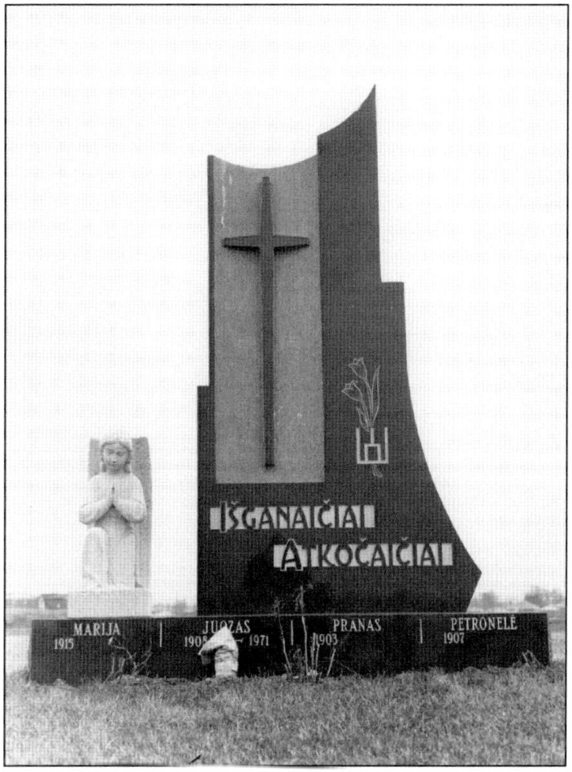

Although no longer called St. Casmir Lithuanian Cemetery, it has never lost its Lithuanian identity. The cemetery grounds are home to the remains of more than 50,000 Lithuanians. Many of the tombstones and monuments pictured here, right and below, contain uniquely Lithuanian features. (Both, LRSC.)

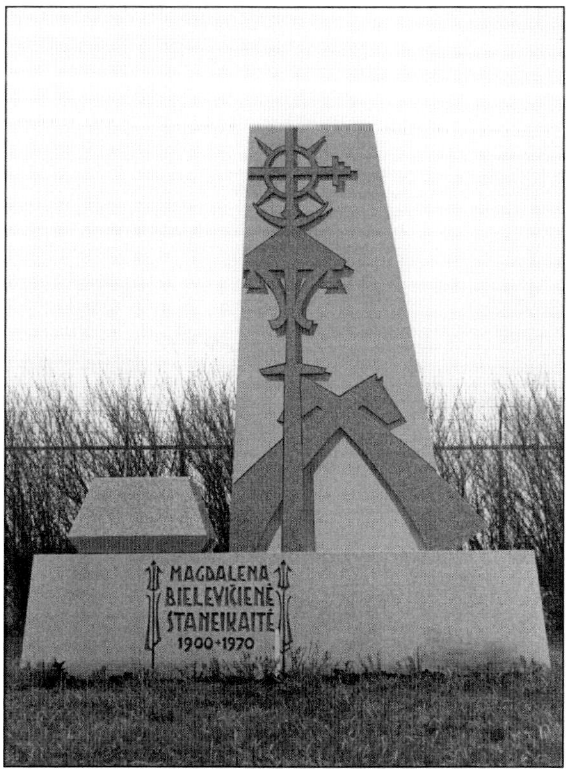

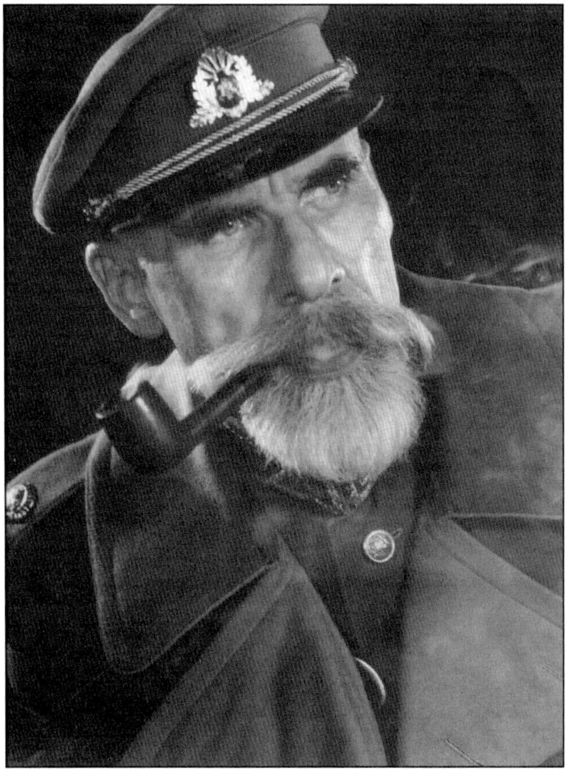

Numerous well-known Lithuanians are buried in St. Casimir Cemetery. One of them is Gen. Povilas Plechavicius, whose portrait is shown here. Under the German occupation of 1941–1944, Plechavicius attempted to create a Lithuanian national force to oppose the Soviet Union. Fearing Lithuanian nationalism, Nazi Germany disbanded the army. When Soviet forces retook Lithuania in 1944, Plechavicius fled west and ended up in the United States. (LRSC.)

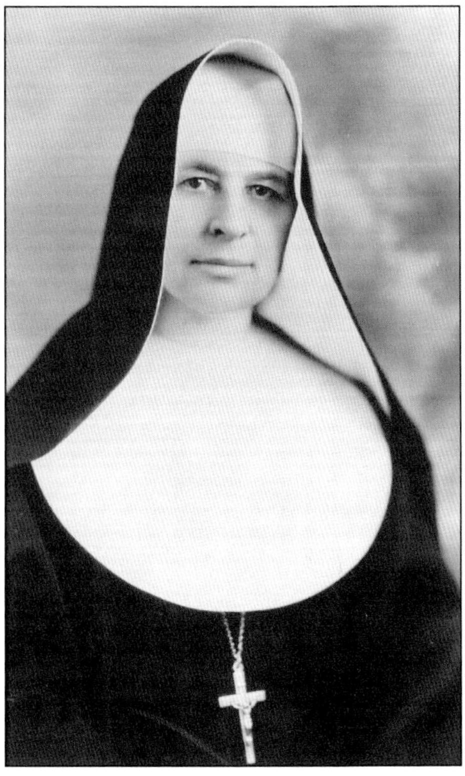

Prior to the transfer of her remains to the Sisters of St. Casimir motherhouse in 1999, another prominent Lithuanian buried at St. Casimir Cemetery was Mother Maria Kaupas. (SSC.)

Although the majority of Lithuanian parishes in Chicago were Roman Catholic, there exists a sizable minority of Lutherans. The history of Lutherans in Lithuania began with Germanic conquests near Lithuanian territory in the Middle Ages by the Teutonic and Livonian Orders. One of the most successful Lutheran churches was Zion Lithuanian Lutheran Evangelical Church, which flourished under the direction of its pastors. Shown here are Rev. Martin Keturokoitis and Rev. Dr. Valdas Ausra. Reverend Keturokoitis (right) was the first pastor. His leadership from 1903 to 1911 resulted in the church's formation and successful establishment. Pictured below is Rev. Dr. Valdas Ausra, who took over in 1998. Through his efforts, Zion Lithuanian has continued to flourish through numerous renovations and the addition of a Lithuanian Lutheran day care school, albeit at a newer location in the suburb of Oak Lawn. (Both, Zion Lithuanian Lutheran Church.)

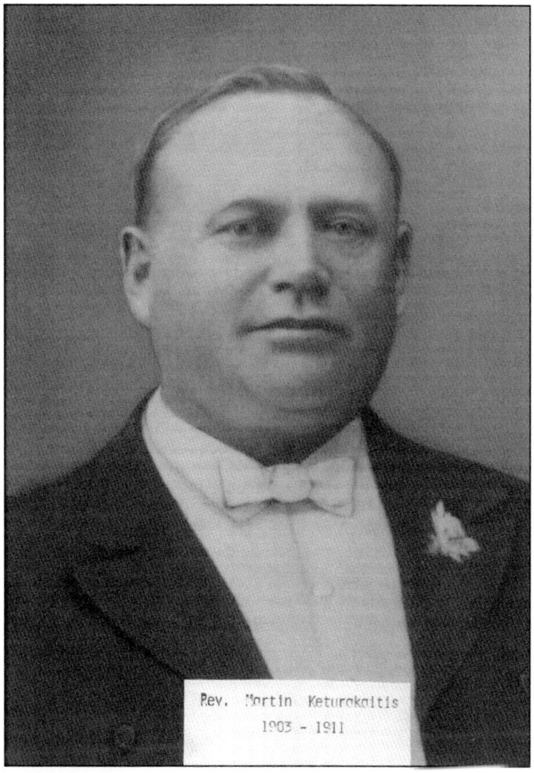

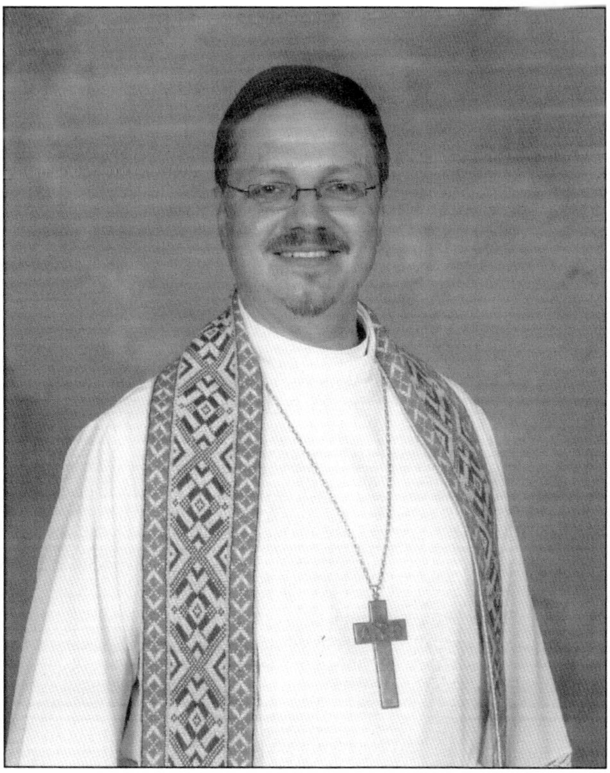

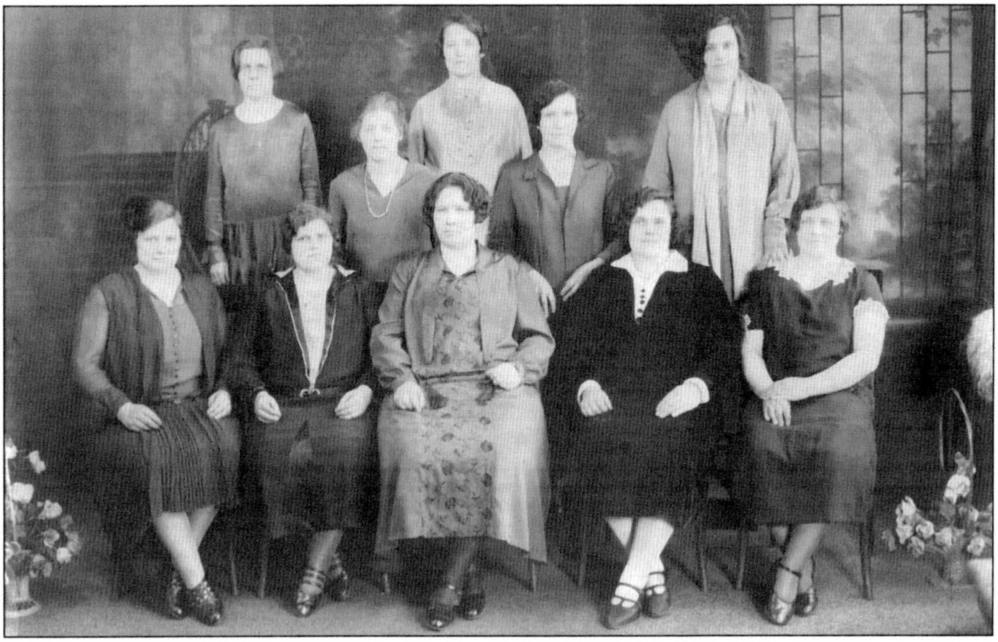

Like their Roman Catholic counterparts, Lithuanian Lutherans established numerous organizations and social groups. One example was the Dorcas Women's Fellowship of Zion Lithuanian Lutheran Evangelical Church. Shown here in a group portrait are some early unidentified members of the fellowship around 1936. (Zion Lithuanian Lutheran Church.)

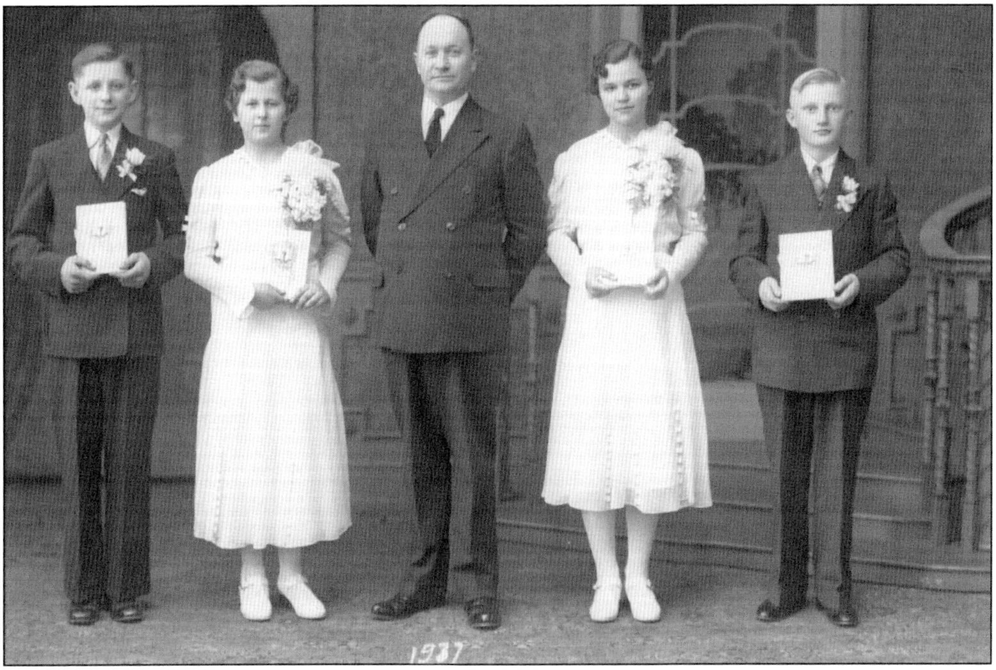

The formation of Zion Lithuanian Lutheran Evangelical Church allowed for Lithuanian immigrants to provide their children with an ethnic and religious upbringing similar to their own back home. Shown here in 1937 are unidentified teenagers confirmed within the church with its third pastor, Rev. Ewald Kories. (Zion Lithuanian Lutheran Church.)

Two

The Sisters of St. Casimir

Founded in Pennsylvania by Maria Kaupas on August 29, 1907, the Sisters of St. Casimir is a Lithuanian Roman Catholic order of religious women that has been instrumental to the formation and success of Chicago's Lithuanian community. The order built its motherhouse in Chicago in 1911, due to the city having the highest concentration of Lithuanian immigrants in the country. Far from home and struggling to adjust to a new life, Lithuanian immigrants benefited immensely from the charitable work of the order.

Mother Maria's success resulted in a significant expansion of the order. In addition to continuing to serve the needs of Lithuanian communities in Pennsylvania and Chicago, the order established a branch near Kaunas, Lithuania, in 1920. Like in the United States, the sisters established schools and other institutions, all sorely needed following the end of World War I and the restoration of Lithuanian independence in 1918. While the Soviet occupation of Lithuania in the later half of the 20th century curtailed the order's efforts, the sisters persevered and resumed their efforts in Lithuania in 1992, following its second independence.

The efforts of the Sisters of St. Casimir have resulted in an impressive legacy. Chicago's largest Lithuanian community, Marquette Park, formed around the Sisters of St. Casimir Motherhouse at 2601 West Marquette Road. Institutions in the area founded by the sisters, such as Holy Cross Hospital and Maria High School, provided needed services while promoting religious values and Lithuanian culture. Outside of Chicago, the sisters have branched out to more than 14 states as well as Lithuania and Argentina. For over 100 years, they have served the community around them with humility, devotion, and compassion.

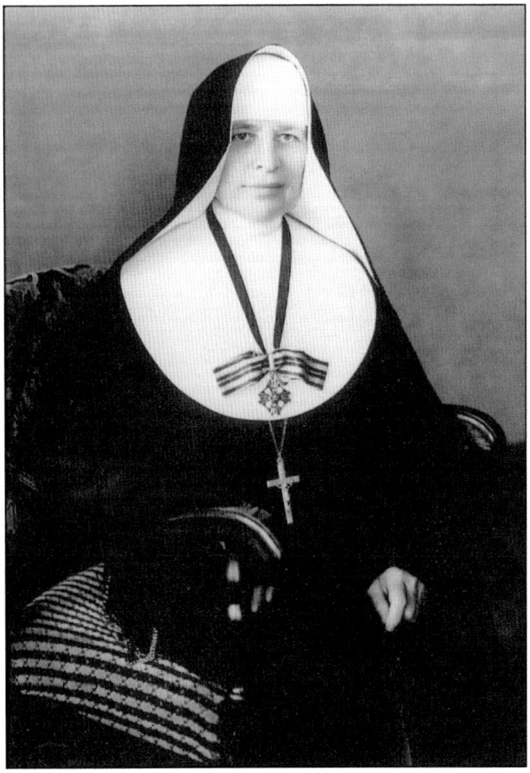

Casimira Maria Kaupas was born in Ramygala, Lithuania, on January 6, 1880, and can be considered one of the most significant members of the Lithuanian American community. She initially came to Scranton, Pennsylvania, in 1897 to serve as a housekeeper for her brother, a priest. Under her leadership, the religious order expanded its role in serving the Lithuanian community of Chicago, chiefly by establishing numerous schools and hospitals. This portrait, taken on June 14, 1933, is of Mother Maria wearing the Order of Grand Duke Gediminas medal, presented to her by the government of Lithuania for her contributions to that country and Lithuanian causes. Below is a postcard of the Sisters of St. Casimir convent in Pazaislis, Lithuania, established by Mother Maria in 1920. (Both, SSC.)

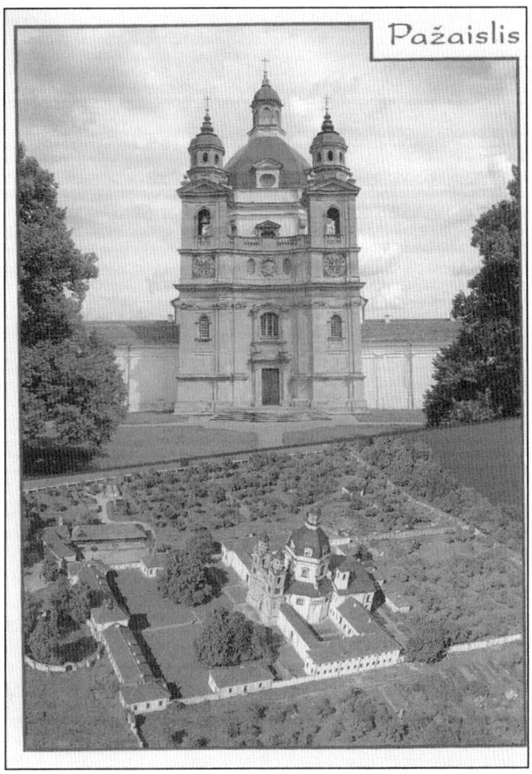

Ordained a priest in Lithuania in 1889, Rev. Dr. Anthony Staniukynas played an instrumental role in the formation of the Sisters of St. Casimir. His desire to promote Lithuanian nationalism and customs led him to the United States in 1904, where he served Holy Cross Lithuanian Parish in Mount Carmel, Pennsylvania. Seeing the great need among the Lithuanian community there, Staniukynas then worked with Maria Kaupas to form the first Lithuanian congregation of sisters in America. (SSC.)

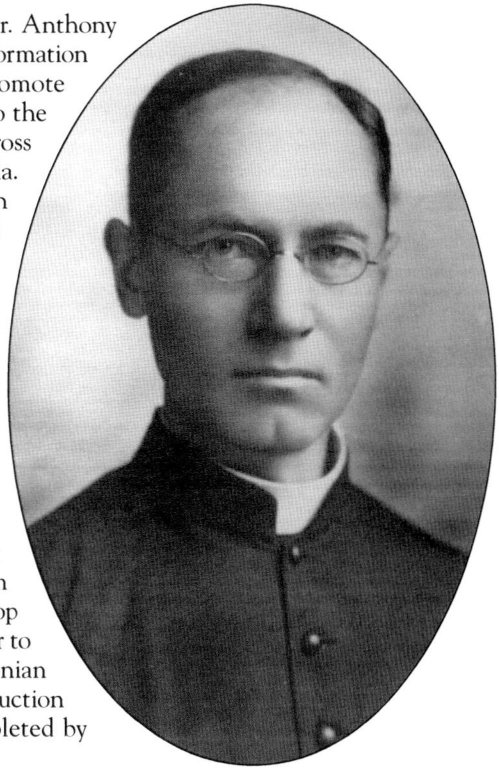

Pictured below are, from left to right, Rev. Francis Serafinas, Rev. Alexander Skripka, and Rev. Anthony Staniukynas standing on the site of the Sisters of St. Casimir Motherhouse prior to construction in 1908. The site, not far from Marquette Park, was chosen by Chicago archbishop James E. Quigley, who wanted the religious order to move to Chicago and administer to its large Lithuanian population. Despite the marshy location, construction began on September 23, 1908, and was completed by February 28, 1911. (SSC.)

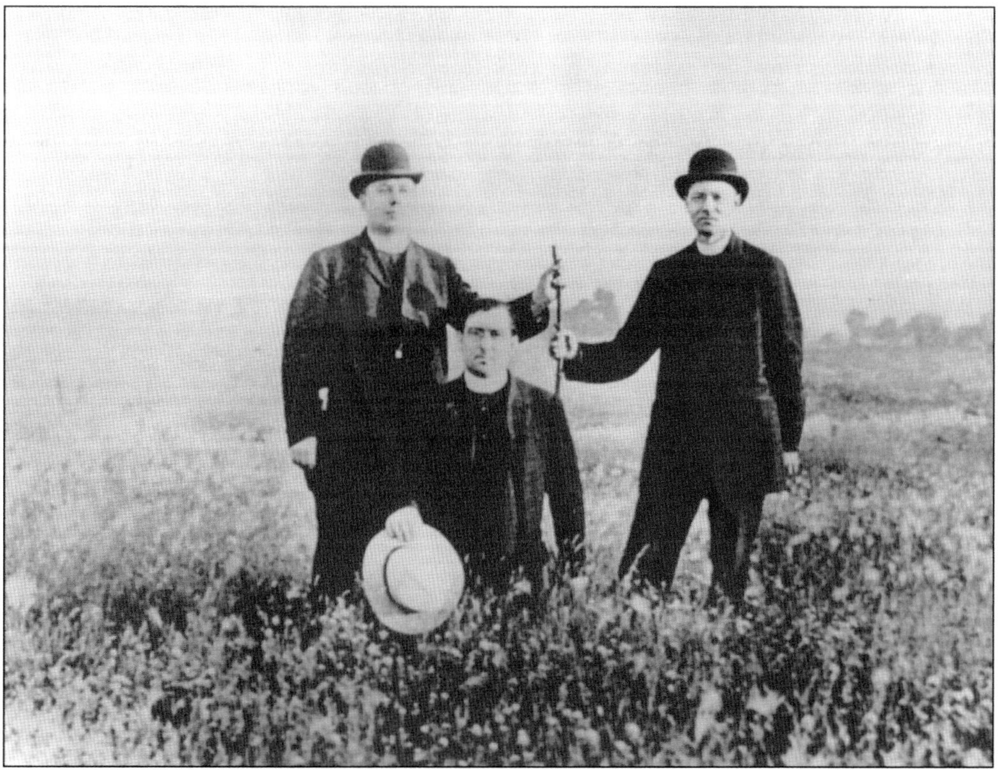

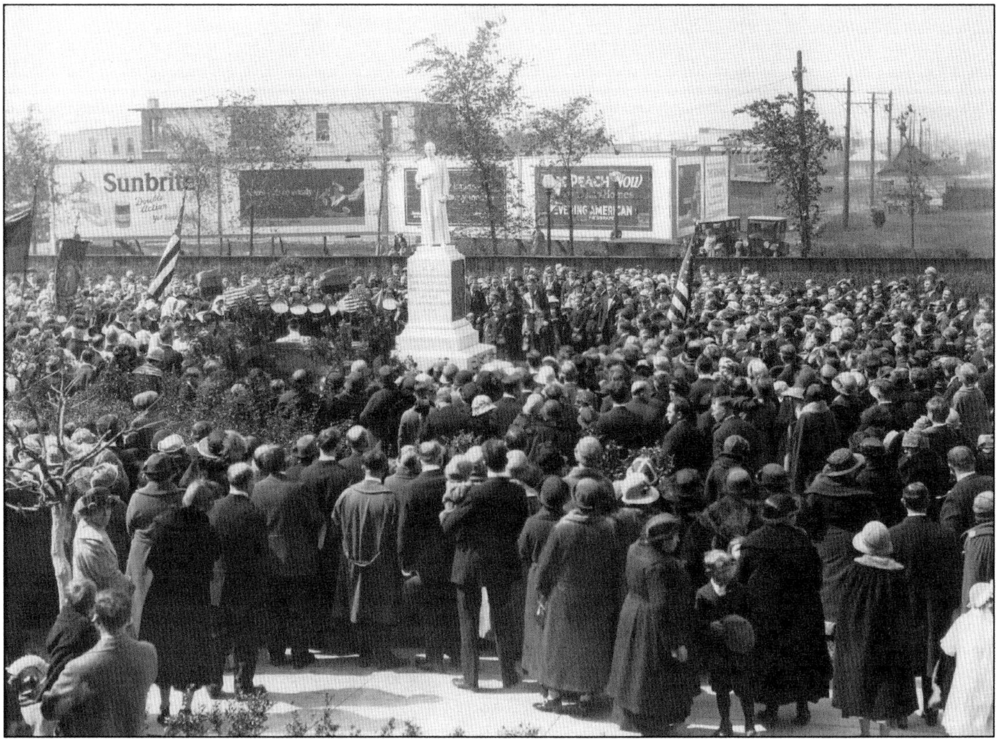

Rev. Dr. Anthony Staniukynas died in 1918 at the age of 53. His instrumental role in the formation of the Sisters of St. Casimir was honored by the construction of a monument bearing his likeness on the grounds of the motherhouse. Shown here is its widely attended dedication in 1921; the statue was paid for with pennies collected from schoolchildren. (LRSC.)

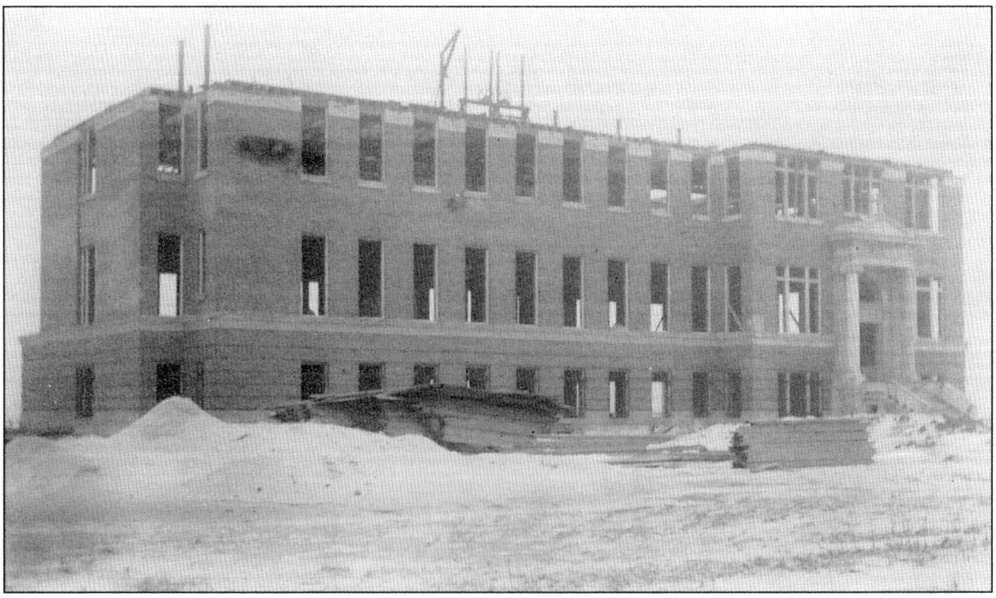

Shown here is the Sisters of St. Casimir Motherhouse in the early stages of construction. Located at 2601 West Marquette Road, the land for the structure was first bought in August 1909. Mother Maria and a handful of young sisters moved in following its completion in February 1911. (SSC.)

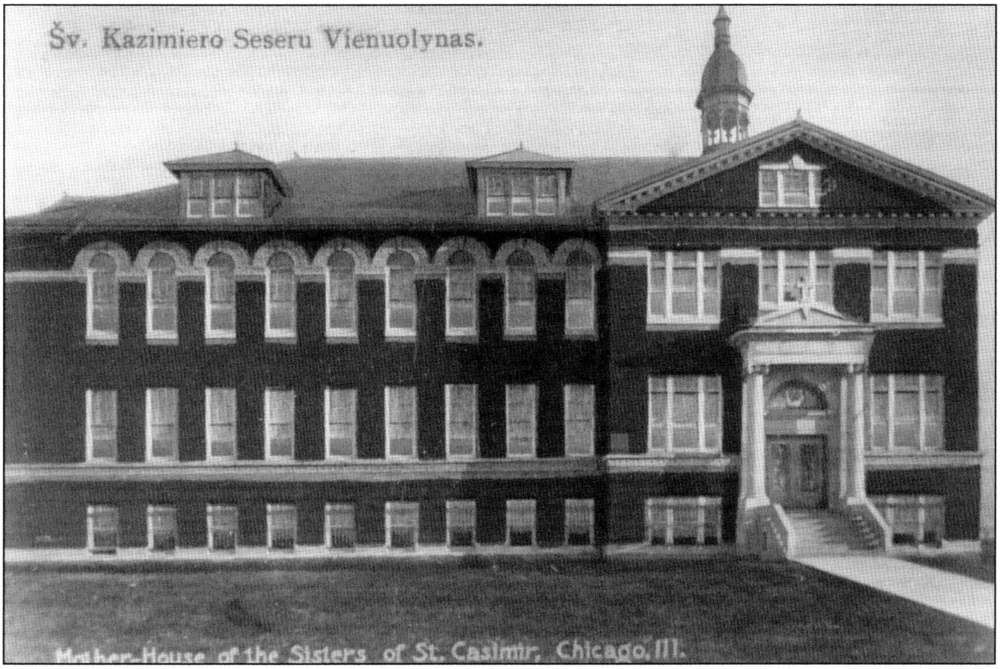

Located in Marquette Park, the motherhouse (shown above) has been the headquarters of the Sisters of St. Casimir for more than a century. The grounds have maintained their bucolic setting as the neighborhood continued to grow around it. From this structure, the Sisters of St. Casimir successfully administered to the needs of the city's Lithuanian community. The beautiful redbrick and stone building steadily expanded through numerous additions and renovations throughout the 20th century, including the one pictured below around 1925. By choosing Marquette Park as the site of their new headquarters, the order made the area a center for their activities, thus attracting greater Lithuanian settlement from other areas of Chicago. (Both, SSC.)

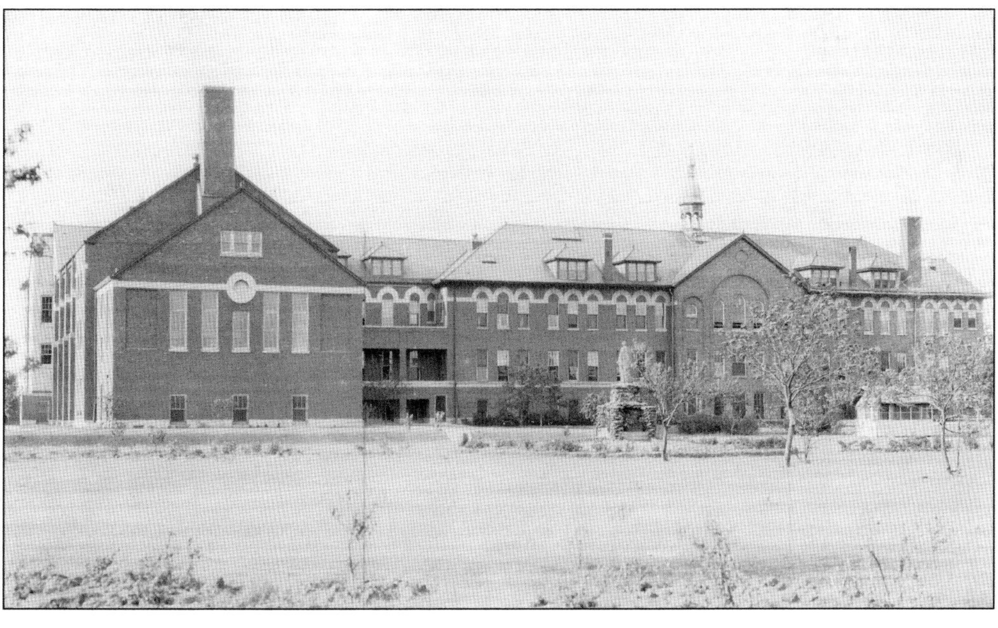

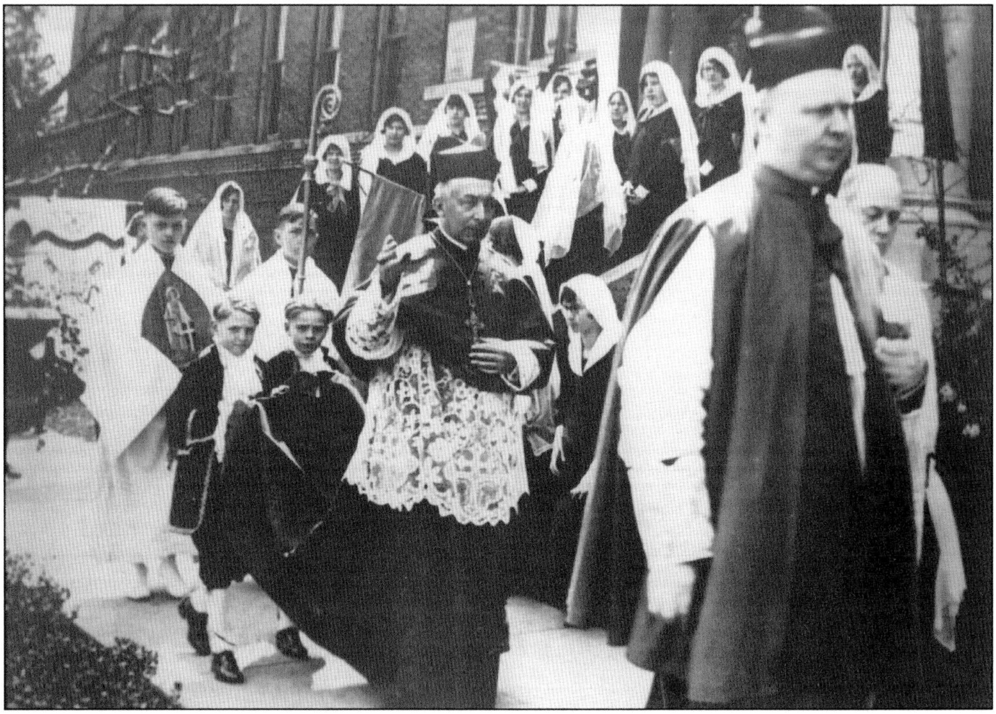

Throughout the 20th century, the headquarters of the Sisters of St. Casimir underwent numerous renovations to accommodate the expansion of the order. One beautiful feature among many, a new chapel, consecrated by Blessed Jurgis Matulaitis, MIC, was completed in 1925. Shown here are Msgr. P. Rempe and Cardinal Mundelein on the occasion of the chapel's blessing on May 17, 1925. (SSC.)

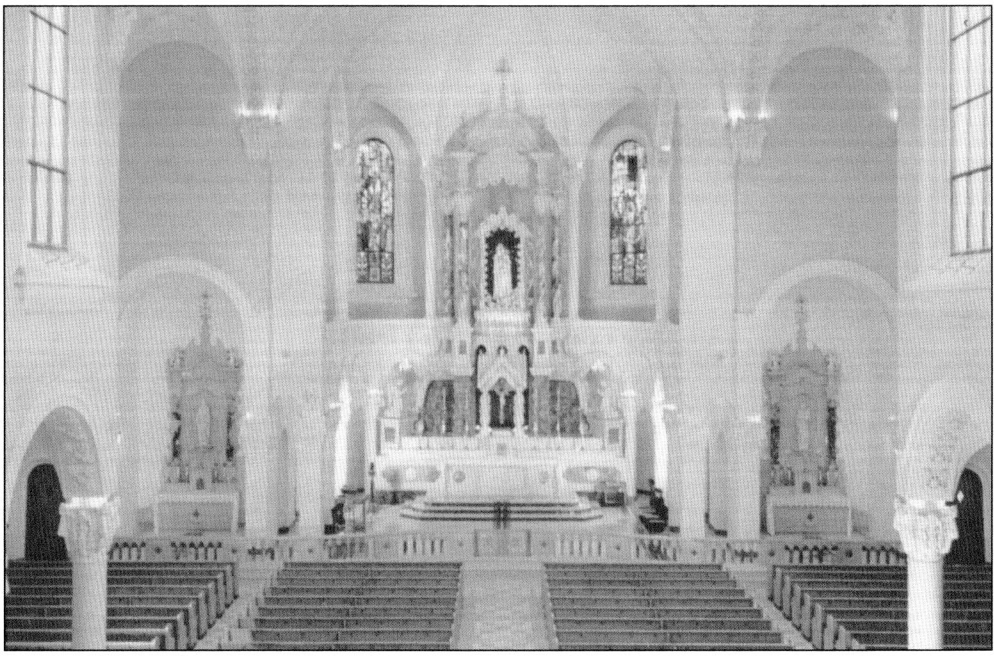

Pictured here is the interior of the motherhouse chapel. (SSC.)

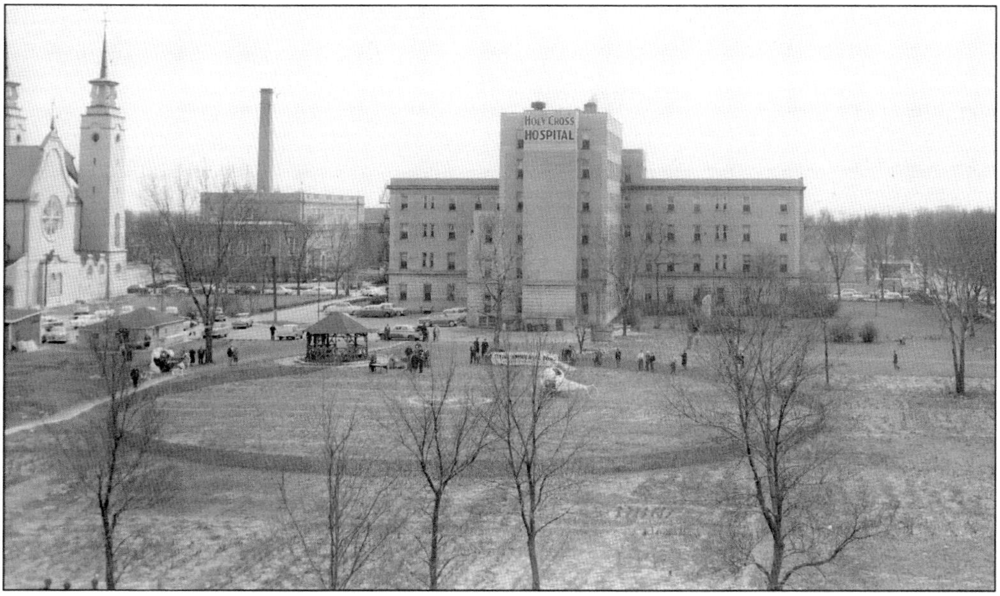

Initially, the primary focus of the order was providing a Roman Catholic education to the children of Lithuanian immigrants. Under the guidance of Rev. Dr. Anthony Staniukynas, the Sisters of St. Casimir expanded their efforts to the field of health care. What began in 1910 as a desire to care for orphans and the elderly transformed into the creation of Holy Cross Hospital. When Lithuanian Catholic Charities was unable to sustain its construction, Mother Maria took out a $250,000 mortgage and assumed management of the facility. Started in 1927, the hospital opened a year later to serve the needs of the surrounding community. For Lithuanians, it was a place for excellent health care staffed by many of their own. The hospital employed numerous Lithuanians in Chicago throughout the years. Pictured above is the hospital around 1958. Below is a more current image. (Both, SSC.)

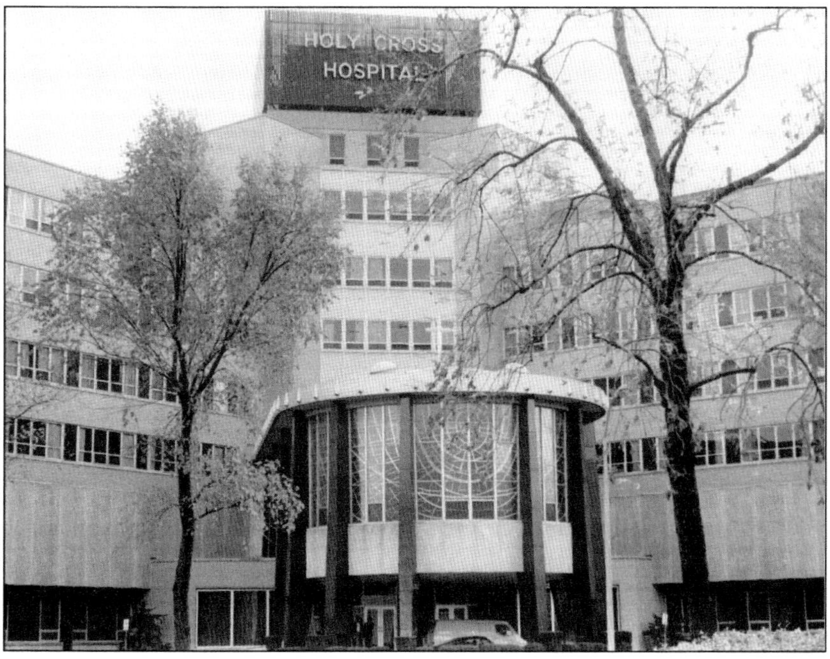

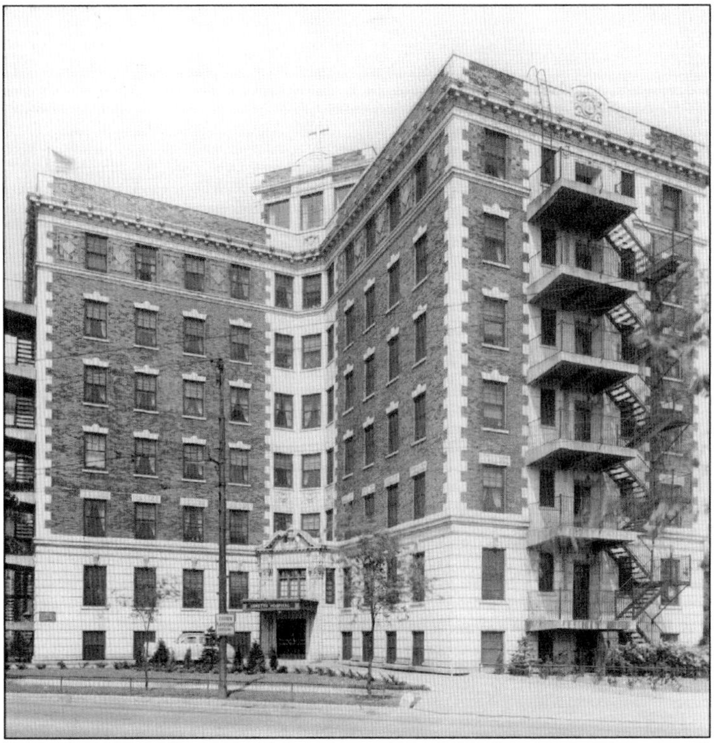

The order's dedication to compassion and healing is evident through the numerous health-related institutions that they created and staffed. Following the success of Holy Cross Hospital, the Sisters of St. Casimir purchased Loretto Hospital, located in the Austin neighborhood of Chicago, on December 10, 1938. (SSC.)

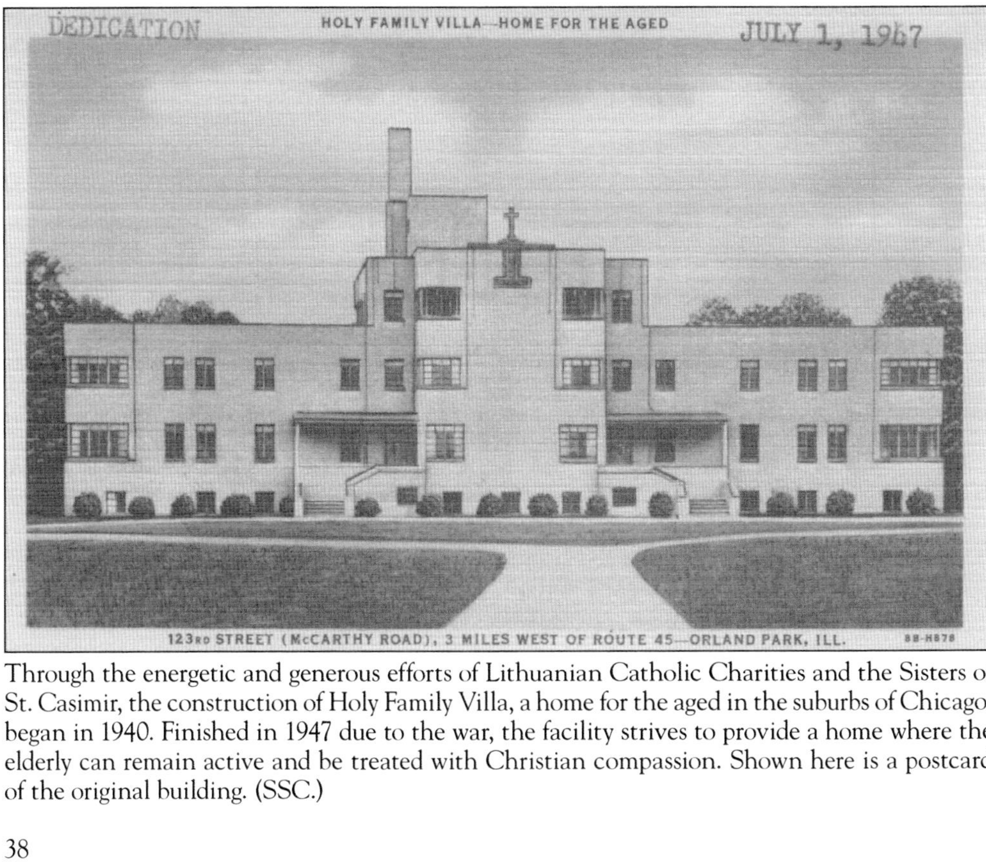

Through the energetic and generous efforts of Lithuanian Catholic Charities and the Sisters of St. Casimir, the construction of Holy Family Villa, a home for the aged in the suburbs of Chicago, began in 1940. Finished in 1947 due to the war, the facility strives to provide a home where the elderly can remain active and be treated with Christian compassion. Shown here is a postcard of the original building. (SSC.)

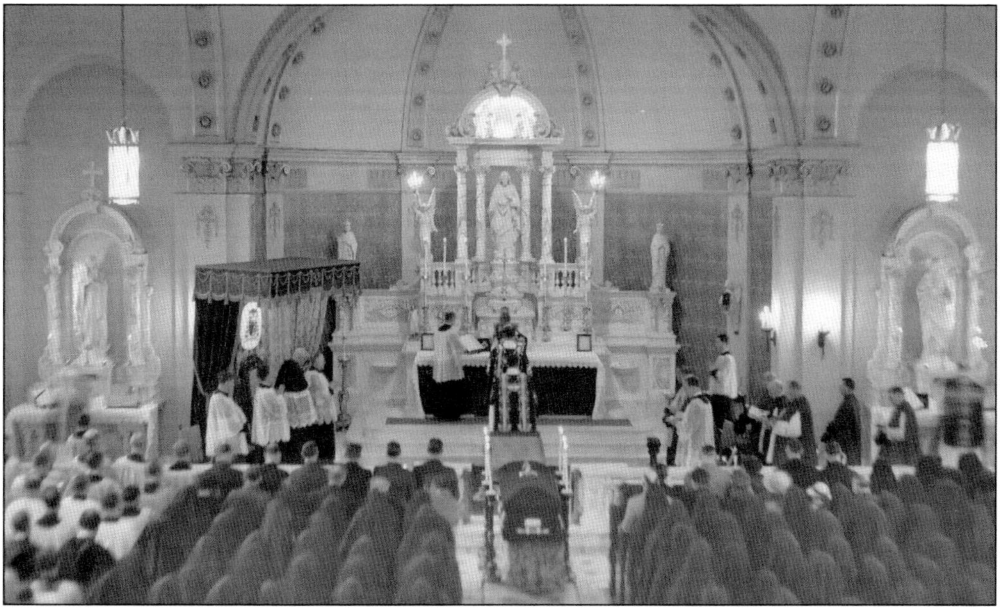

Mother Maria Kaupas passed away on April 17, 1940. During her 27-year term as general superior of the Sisters of St. Casimir, she had helped the order become an integral part of the Lithuanian community of Chicago. Shown here is her funeral mass, held in the motherhouse chapel. Initially buried at St. Casimir Lithuanian Cemetery, her remains were later brought to a vault in the motherhouse chapel on May 6, 1999. (SSC.)

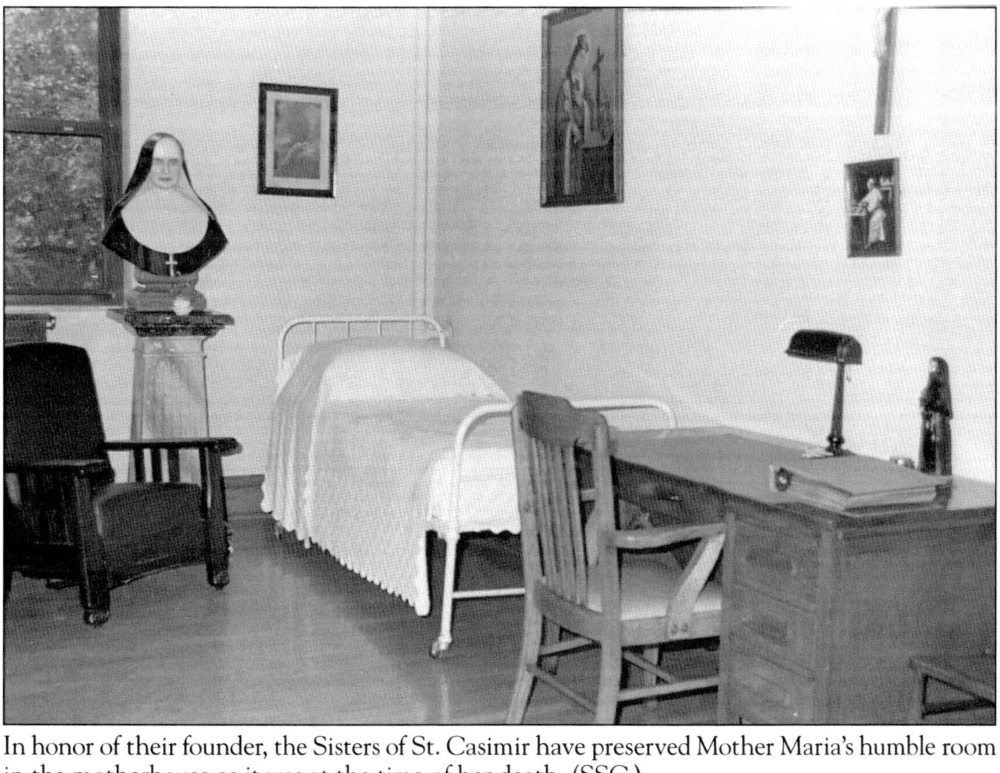

In honor of their founder, the Sisters of St. Casimir have preserved Mother Maria's humble room in the motherhouse as it was at the time of her death. (SSC.)

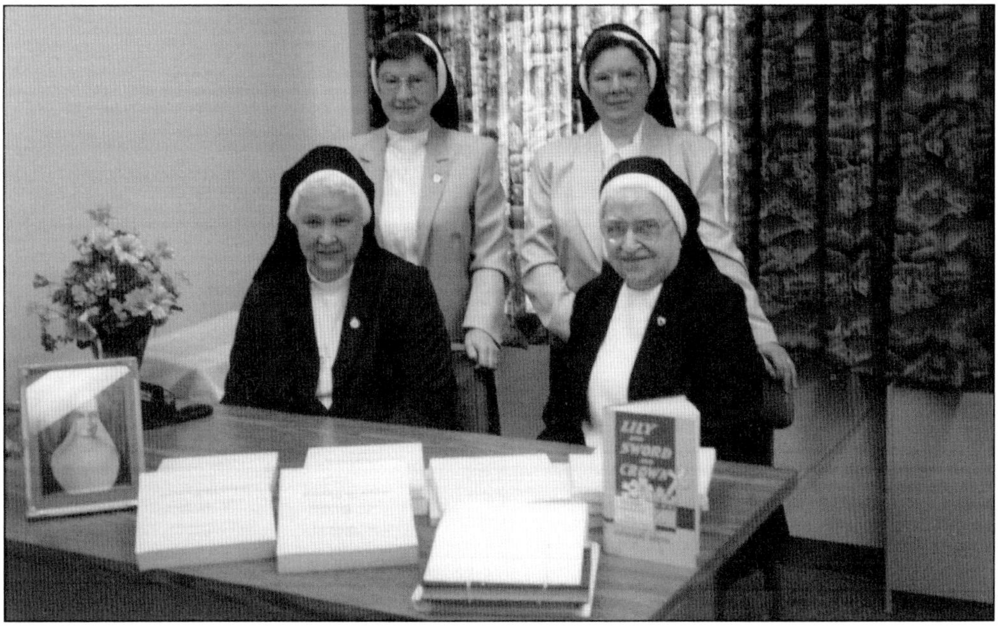

The process for the canonization of Mother Maria Kaupas started not long after her death, with prayers and later the assembling of the necessary documentation. Shown here with 972 pages of material documenting the life of Mother Maria are, from left to right, (seated) Sr. Christella Danish and Sr. Edwarda Burdulis; (standing) Sr. Margaret Petcavage and Sr. Grace Ann Kalafut. (SSC.)

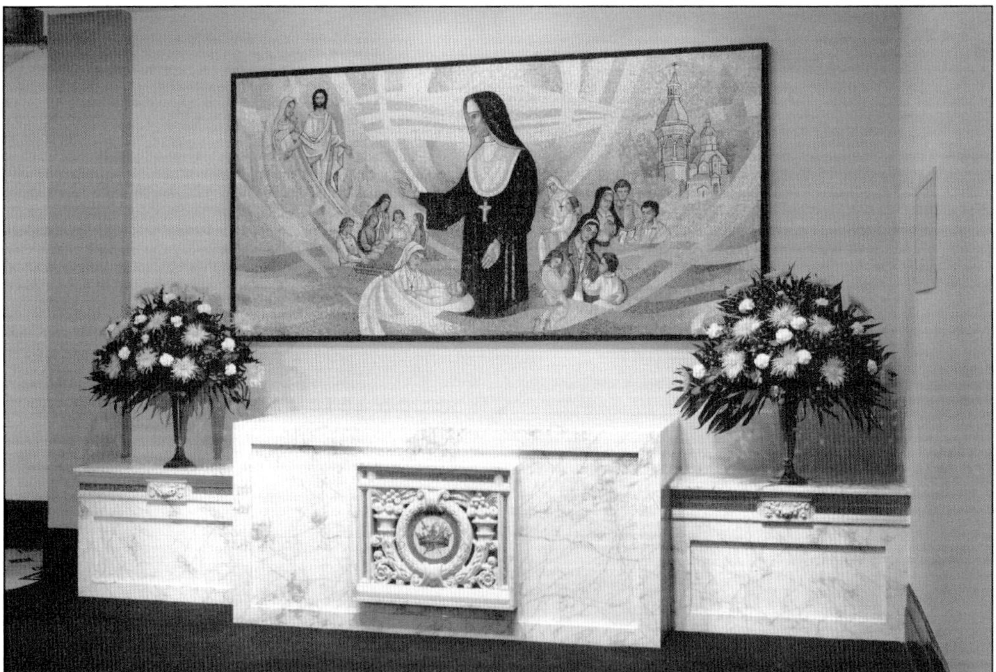

Made from elegant materials, including original components of the motherhouse chapel, the remains of Mother Maria Kaupas now rest inside this beautiful vault. (SSC.)

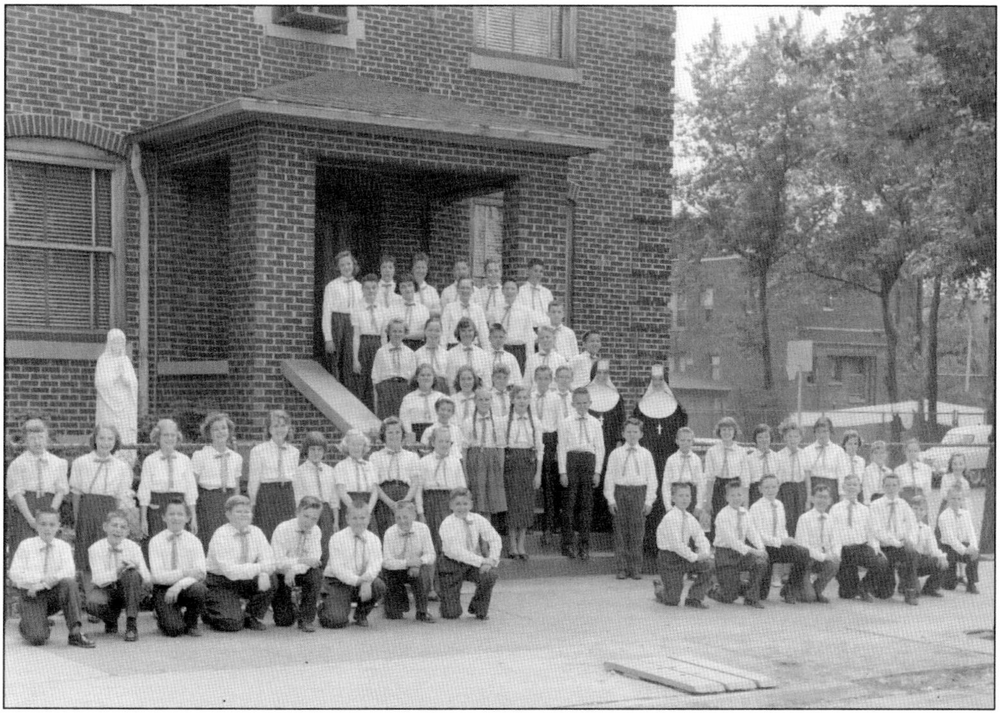

Education was vital to the success of Chicago's Lithuanian immigrants. The sisters were some of the first to educate the city's Lithuanian children through parochial schools, such as Our Lady of Vilna (shown above) on the West Side. In 1911, the order founded its own school, St. Casimir Academy, located within the structure of the motherhouse. This all girl's high school provided its students with a quality education and boasted an enrollment of 550 students by 1952. In the image below are SCA students from the 1920s. (Both, SSC.)

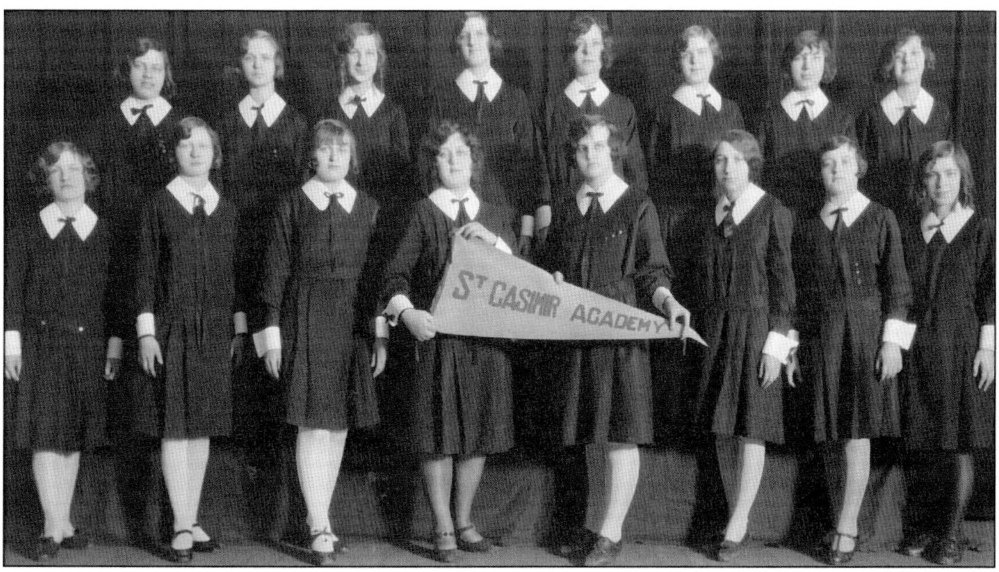

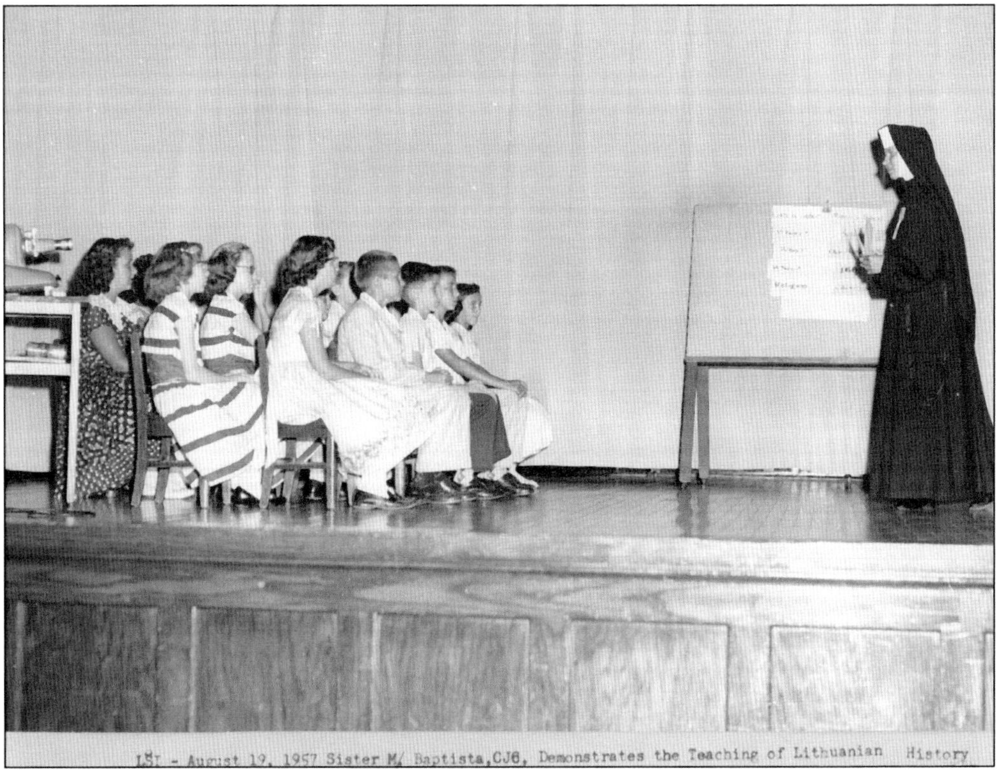

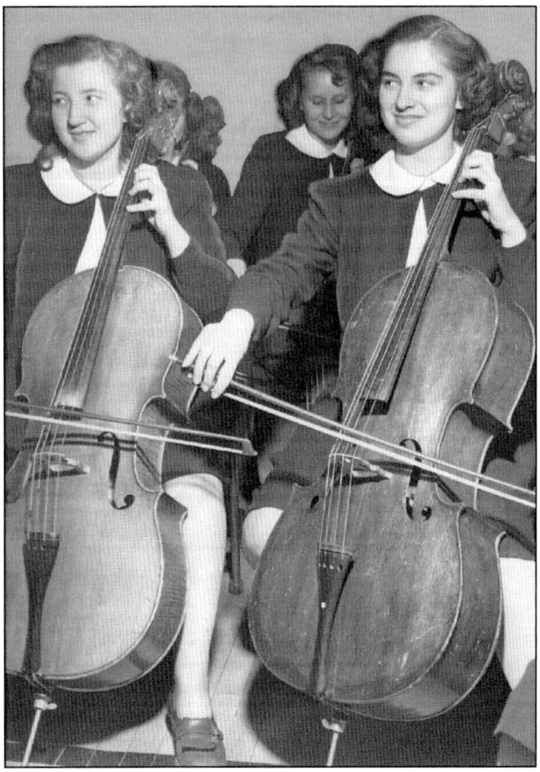

Through their efforts in education and other fields, the Sisters of St. Casimir played an instrumental role in preserving Lithuanian culture in Chicago and much of the United States. In the photograph above, taken at the Lithuanian Sisters Institute on August 19, 1957, the professionalism of the order is evident as Sr. M. Baptista, a Sister of Jesus Crucified in Pennsylvania, demonstrates the teaching of Lithuanian history to a group of students in front of an audience of sisters who taught in Lithuanian parish schools. (SSC.)

Along with providing an excellent education, St. Casimir Academy offered its students a well-rounded experience. Although the order was initially formed to deepen the faith life of Lithuanian children in the United States, it readily accepted all who sought their assistance. In the photograph at left, taken on December 14, 1947, Loretta Oleszkiewicz (left) and Zanaida Jankauskas (right) demonstrate their skills with the cello. (SSC.)

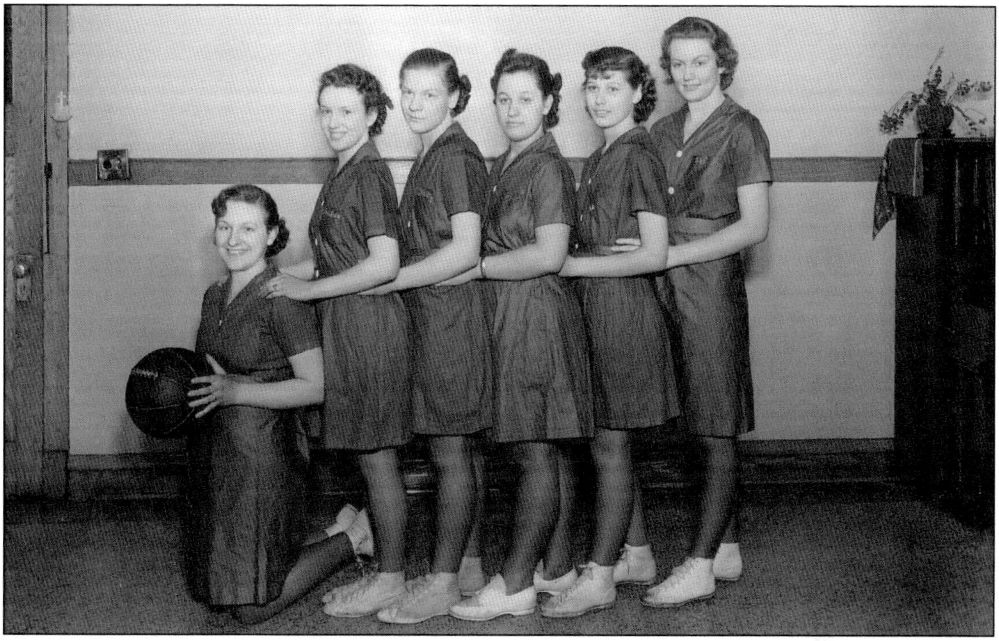

Pictured here is a St. Casimir Academy basketball team. (SSC.)

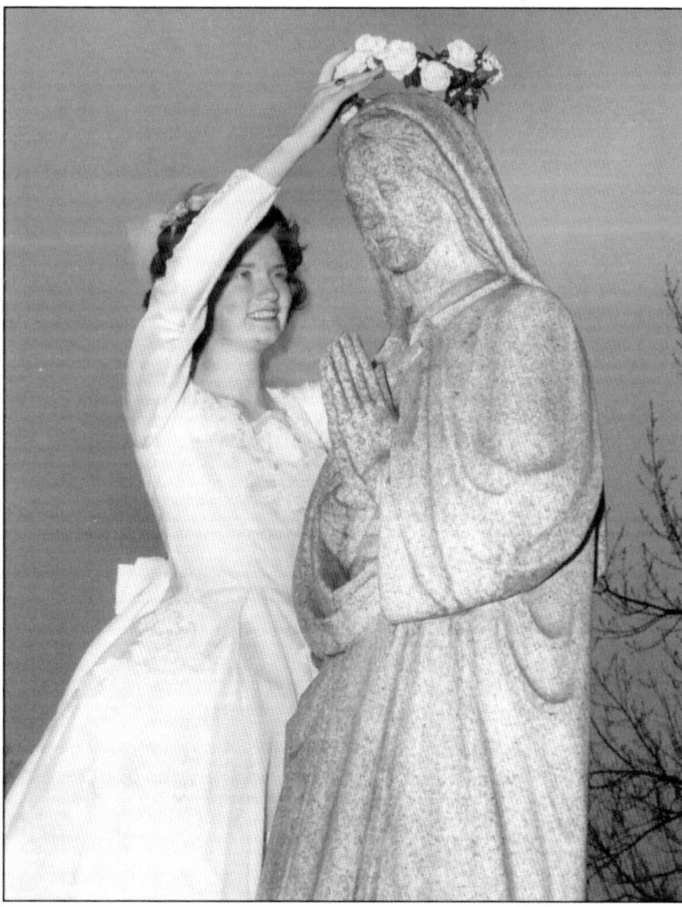

Although athletics and numerous other extracurricular activities were available to students of St. Casimir Academy, religion still played a prominent role. Shown here, an unidentified student takes part in a May Crowning ceremony on campus. The Statue of Our Lady, shown here being crowned, still graces the school grounds. (SSC.)

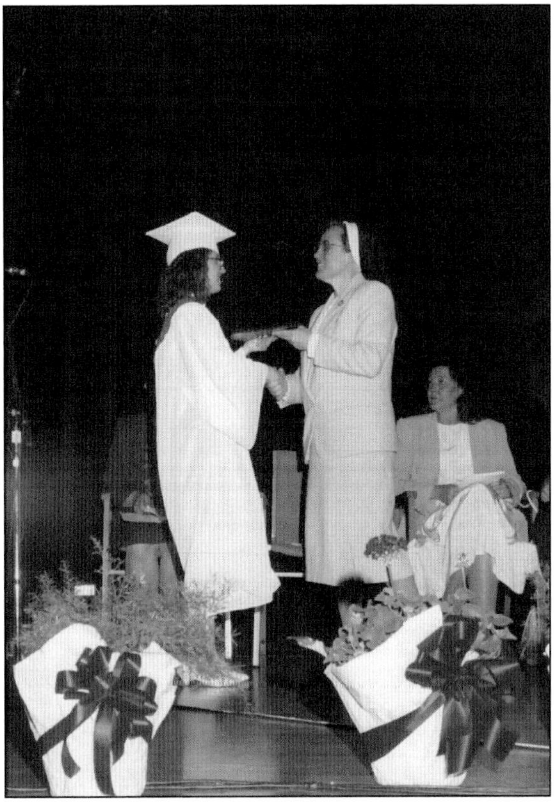

Enrollment at St. Casimir Academy steadily grew, and the need for space led to the construction of a new high school separate from the motherhouse. St. Casimir Academy became Maria High School, which opened its doors on September 8, 1952. Its enrollment was bolstered by the arrival of a new wave of Lithuanian immigrants to Chicago in the aftermath of World War II, reaching 1,400 students. The order provided a quality Catholic education to young women for more than a century. Pictured here is Sr. Margaret Zalot, principal of Maria High School, awarding a diploma on May 22, 1994. (SSC.)

Along with teaching their values to students, the Sisters of St. Casimir have always provided a high-quality education. This included updating the high school's technology with the addition of a third computer lab in 1998. (SSC.)

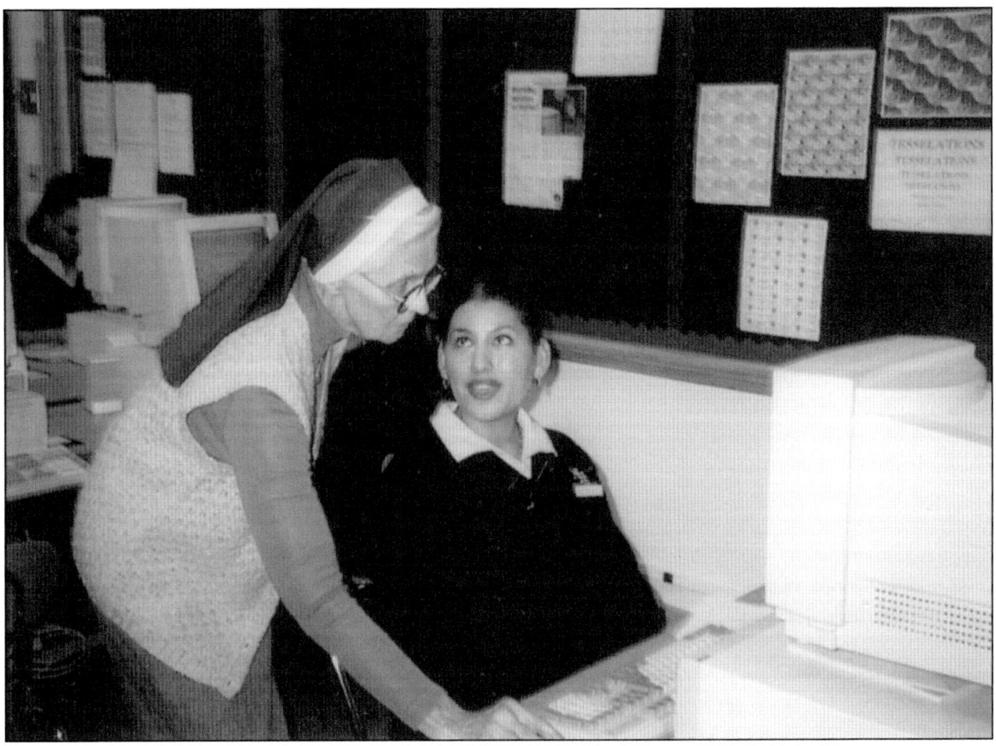

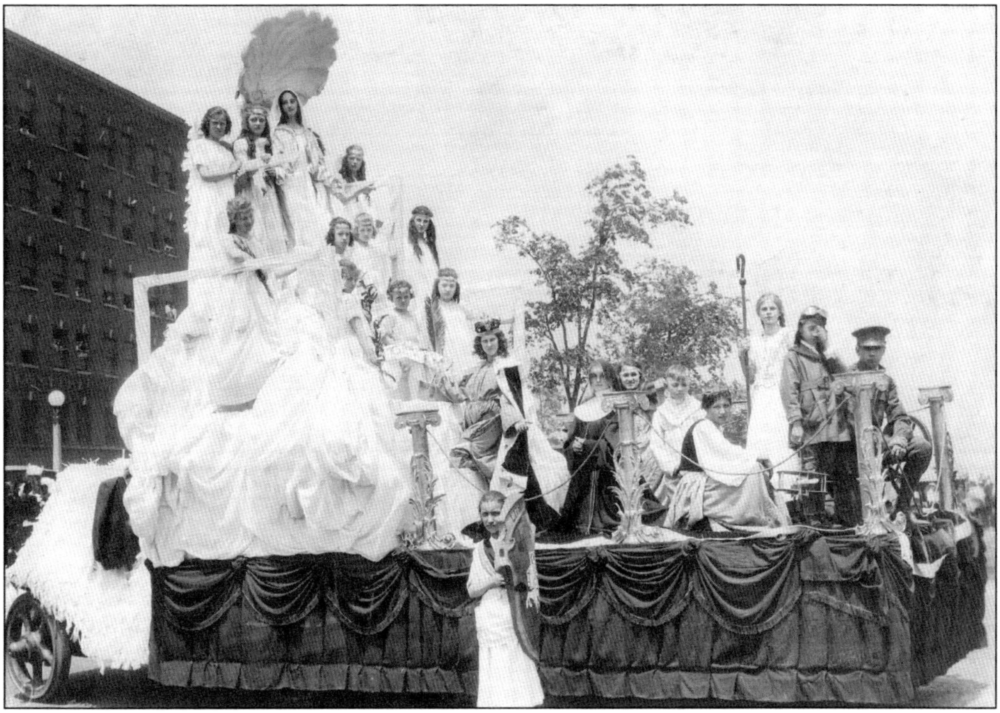

The students of St. Casimir Academy and later Maria High School are a walking legacy of the order's dedication to the community and its success. In public events, the students of these schools proudly represented the Sisters of St. Casimir. Shown above is the St. Casimir Academy float at the Chicago Archdiocesan Festival of Faith in 1920. Held at Navy Pier, the festival was likely attended by numerous Lithuanian Roman Catholic schools in Chicago. Pictured below are Maria High School students commemorating the life of Mother Maria Kaupas on May 2, 1993, declared "Mother Maria Kaupas Day" in Chicago. Although she passed away in 1940, her passion and dedication lives on through the members of the order she founded. (Both, SSC.)

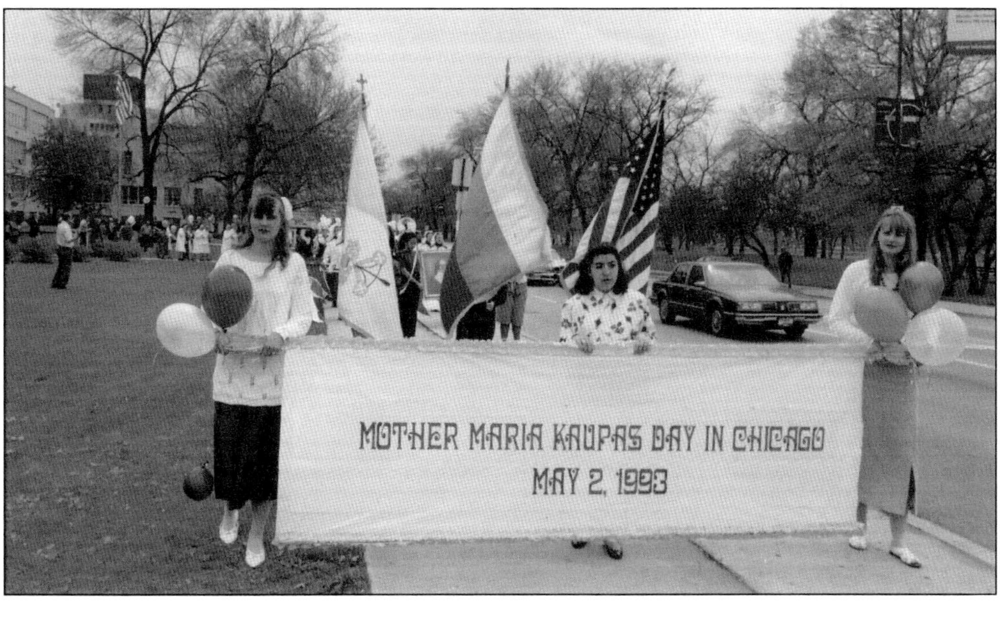

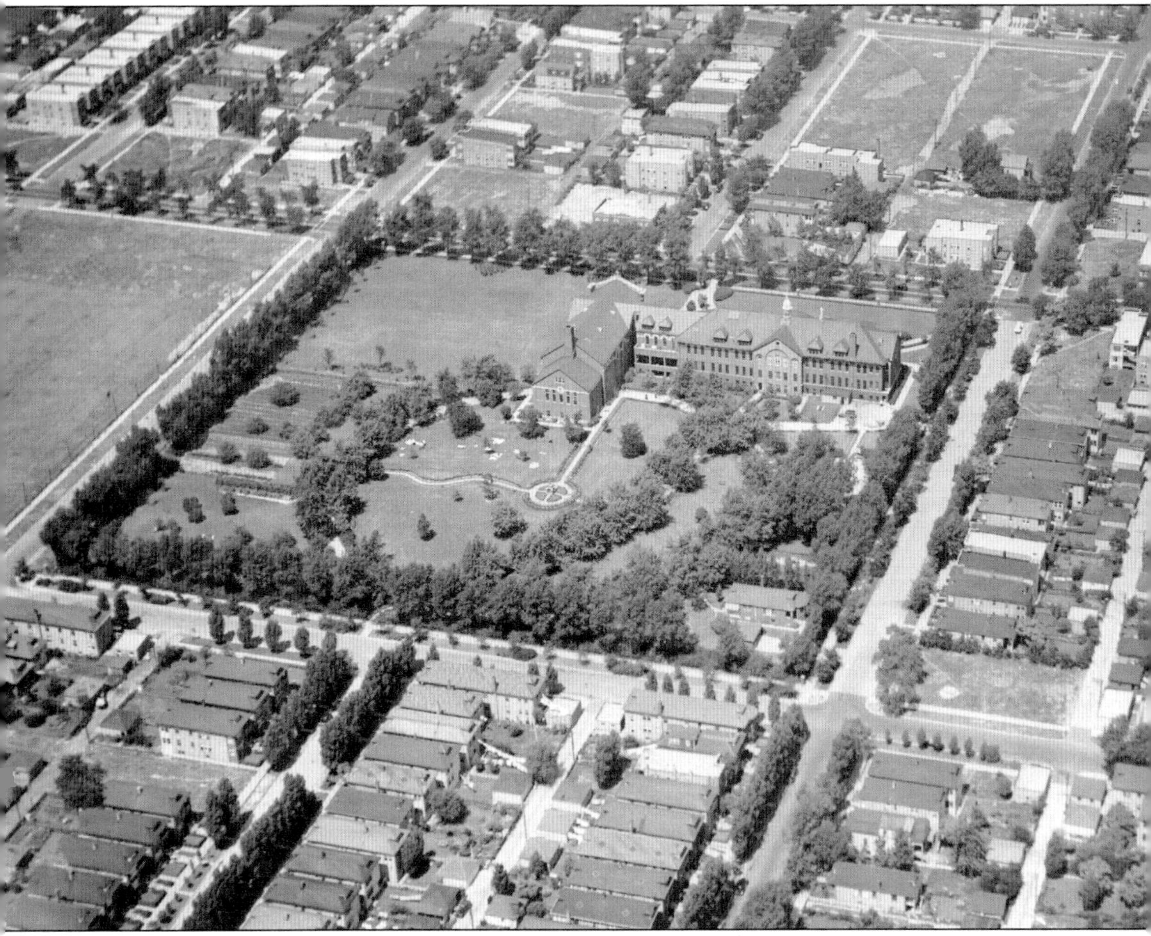

For over 100 years, the Sisters of St. Casimir have served the people of Chicago with humility and devotion. The city's Lithuanian community benefited immensely from the work of the sisters. From staffing parish schools to administering hospitals, the Sisters of St. Casimir have left an indelible impression on the history of Lithuanian Chicago. Shown here is an aerial view of the grounds of the motherhouse, the center of their activities in Chicago. (SSC.)

Three

BUSINESSES AND OCCUPATIONS

Although the three major waves of Lithuanian immigration to Chicago occurred under different circumstances, the individuals involved all underwent the challenge of transitioning to life in America. Chicago's size and variety of industries meant that employment was often readily found. The earliest Lithuanians were often unskilled laborers who were used to farm life in their rural homeland. Many of these immigrants found work in manufacturing, especially the steel and meatpacking industry. Following World War II, a new wave of more specialized and educated workers sought employment related to their previous occupations in Lithuania and included architects, doctors, and engineers. The third wave, arriving after the fall of the Soviet Union, has often found work in fields such as construction, domestic service, and trucking and transportation. Common to Lithuanians in Chicago throughout history has been the challenge of adjusting to life in a foreign country. This transition has always been made easier through the existence of numerous Lithuanian-owned businesses.

Lithuanian-owned businesses were an important component of the community and fulfilled a variety of needs as time went on. Owning a business provided opportunities for immigrants that likely would have been much more difficult to attain in their native Lithuania. In *Lithuanians in Multiethnic Chicago until World War II*, David Fainhauz reveals numerous statistics related to Lithuanian businesses in the city. By 1910, more than 500 Lithuanian businesses existed. A stroll down Halsted Avenue in Bridgeport in 1925 would have revealed some 90 Lithuanian-owned businesses within a four-block radius.

From the beginning to present day, Lithuanian-owned businesses have catered to the multiple needs of the community. Stores, restaurants, and taverns provided a place where immigrants could purchase familiar groceries, eat familiar food, and socialize with each other. Chicago was home to a thriving Lithuanian press and media, where immigrants could read and listen to material that they were most comfortable with. As time went on, Lithuanians opened financial institutions, car dealerships, and funeral homes. Lithuanian business owners were a visible symbol of Chicago's Lithuanian presence and at times served as ambassadors of Lithuanian culture.

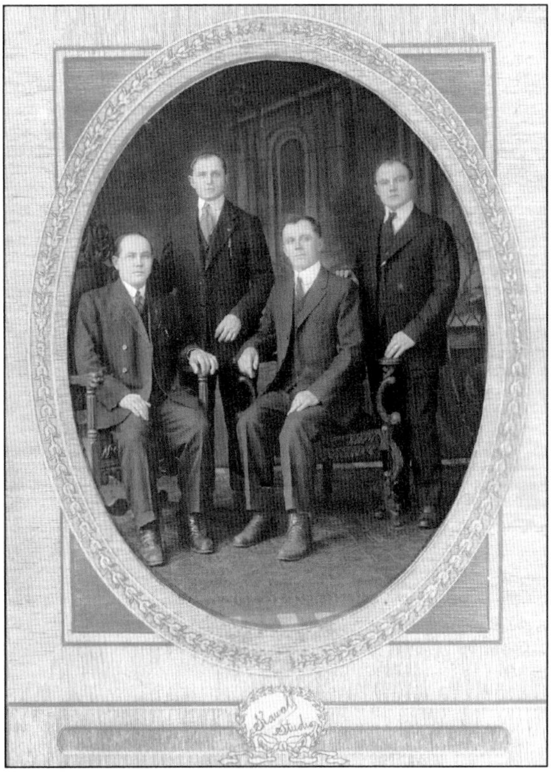

The first wave of Lithuanian immigrants to arrive in the United States were often male and sought economic opportunities or were avoiding conscription into the Russian army. The Ezerski brothers from Varnios, Lithuania, are a good example. Shown here in 1915 are, from left to right, Andrew, Michael, Stanley, and Joseph. Michael and Joseph found employment in the steel mills of the Chicago area before finding success in other ventures. (Michael and Loretta Ezerski.)

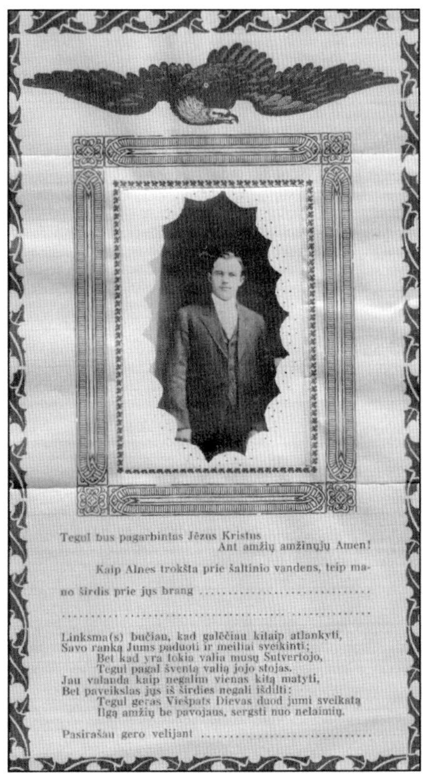

Tegul bus pagarbintas Jėzus Kristus
Ant amžių amžinųjų Amen!

Kaip Alnes trokšta prie šaltinio vandens, teip mano širdis prie jųs brang ....

....

Linksma(s) bučiau, kad galėčiau kitaip atlankyti,
Savo ranką Jums paduoti ir meiliai sveikinti;
Bet kad yra tokia valia musų Sutvertojo,
Tegul pagal šventą valią jojo stojas.
Jau valanda kaip negalim vienas kitą matyti,
Bet paveikslas jųs iš širdies negali išdilti:
Tegul geras Viešpats Dievas duod jumi sveikatą
Ilgą amžių be pavojaus, sergsti nuo nelaimių.

Pasirašau gero velijant ....

Born in 1890, Joseph Ezerski was the youngest of four brothers who came to the United States to avoid conscription. This letter, likely sent not many years after his arrival, includes his portrait and is preprinted. Such form letters were common and quite popular among Lithuanian immigrants in Chicago. Briefly translated, this letter regrets not being able to greet its recipient in person and wishes them the best of health. (Michael and Loretta Ezerski.)

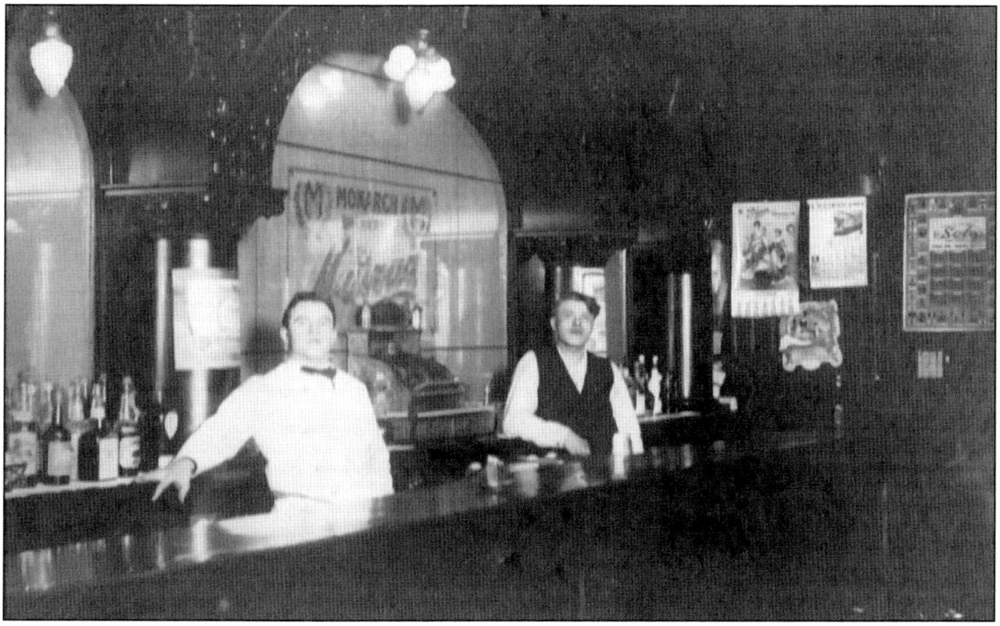

In Chicago's numerous Lithuanian neighborhoods, an enterprising immigrant always stood a decent chance of success in starting a business. Some of the most common Lithuanian-owned businesses were shops and taverns. J.J. Tavern, located at 4600 South Paulina, was right down the street from Holy Cross Parish and amidst a thriving Lithuanian community. Tending bar in the white shirt is Joseph Ezerski, the owner. (Michael and Loretta Ezerski.)

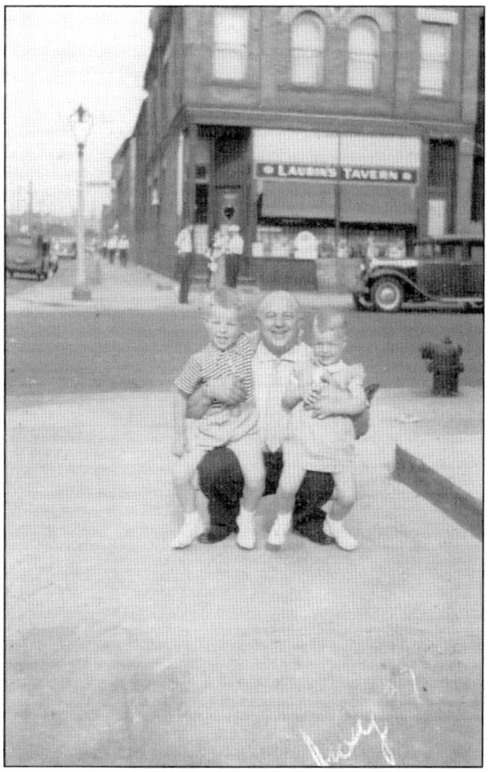

According to statistics cited in David Fainhauz's *Lithuanians in Multiethnic Chicago Until World War II*, of the 500 Lithuanian businesses in the city in 1910, a total of 180 of them were saloons or taverns. Started in 1933, the Lithuanian Tavern Owners Alliance consisted of 2,000 Lithuanian owners in Cook County. In this 1937 photograph, Joseph Ezerski poses with two of his children, Joey (left) and Loretta, on the corner of 4600 South Paulina in front of J.J. Tavern. In the background is Laurin's Tavern, also Lithuanian. Taverns were commonly segregated along ethnic lines and fulfilled multiple needs for immigrants. In addition to socializing, Lithuanians could find out the latest news, collect their mail, and even attend to business. (Michael and Loretta Ezerski.)

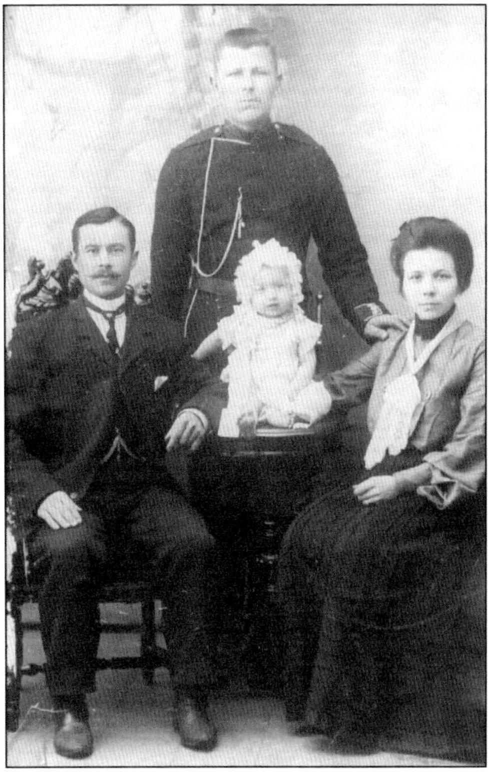

The Pavilionis family came to Chicago from Lithuania seeking better conditions at the turn of the 20th century. Anton Pavilionis, who served as a Cossack in the Russian Imperial Army, found work as a machinist for a crane company and then later at Swift & Company near the Union Stockyards. Pictured around 1898 are, from left to right, Joseph Bukauskas, Vincent Pavilionis, an unidentified woman, and Anton Pavilionis (standing). (Rodney Pavilionis.)

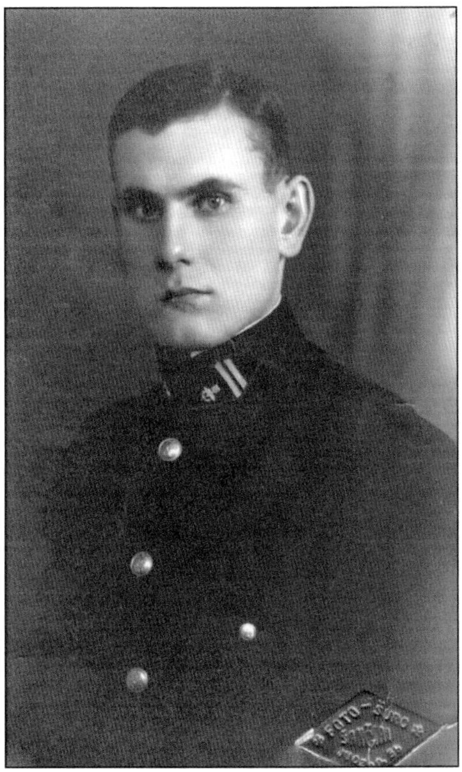

Most Lithuanians who came at the turn of the 20th century were unskilled laborers with a rural background. Those who came to Chicago after World War II, however, often were skilled and educated. Their motivations for leaving were political in nature. Fearing Soviet persecution, tens of thousands fled west, many to relatives in the United States. Kazimieras Riskus, shown here in his railroad uniform in Lithuania sometime in the 1930s, was no different. His skills transferred easily to Chicago, and he found employment with the Chicago, Burlington & Quincy Railroad. (Aldona Riskus.)

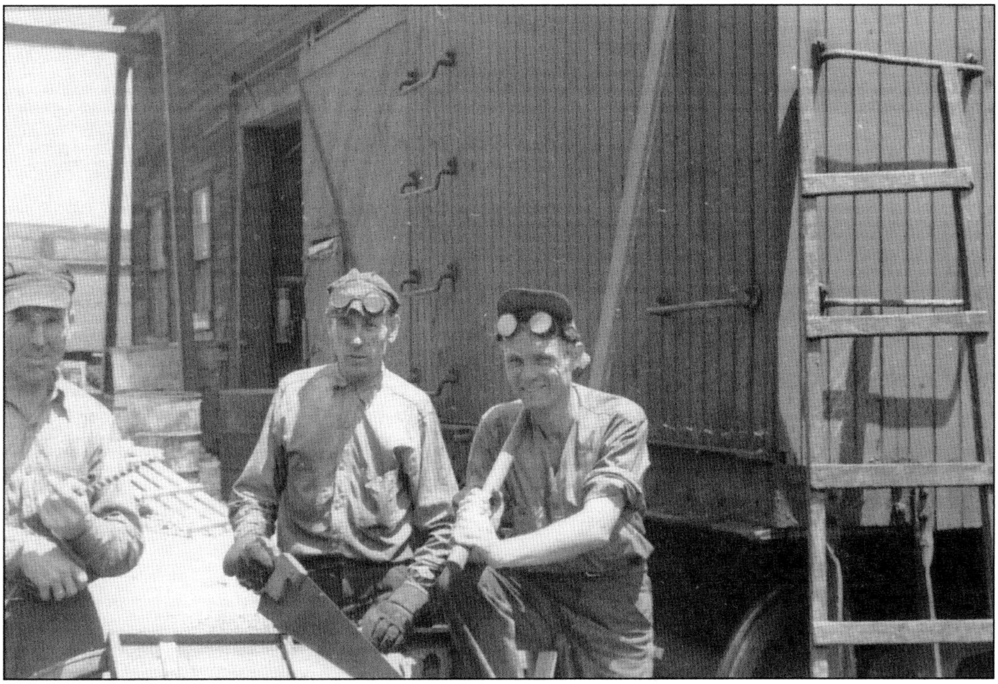

Like his brother Kazimieras, Stepas Riskus also found work in the railroad industry. Shown here in the 1950s are S. Buivydas (left), Stepas Riskus (center), and Alfonsas Brinka. (Nijole Riskus-Gierstikas.)

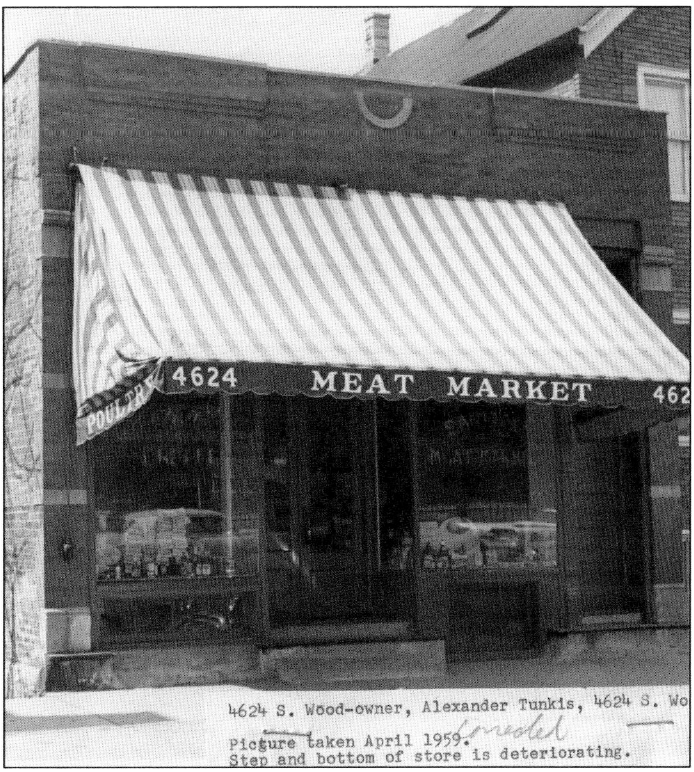

The Back of the Yards was home to numerous Lithuanian-owned businesses, such as this butcher shop at 4626 South Wood Street owned by Alexander Tunkis. This photograph was taken in April 1959 when there was still a significant Lithuanian presence in the Back of the Yards. (Back of the Yards Neighborhood Council.)

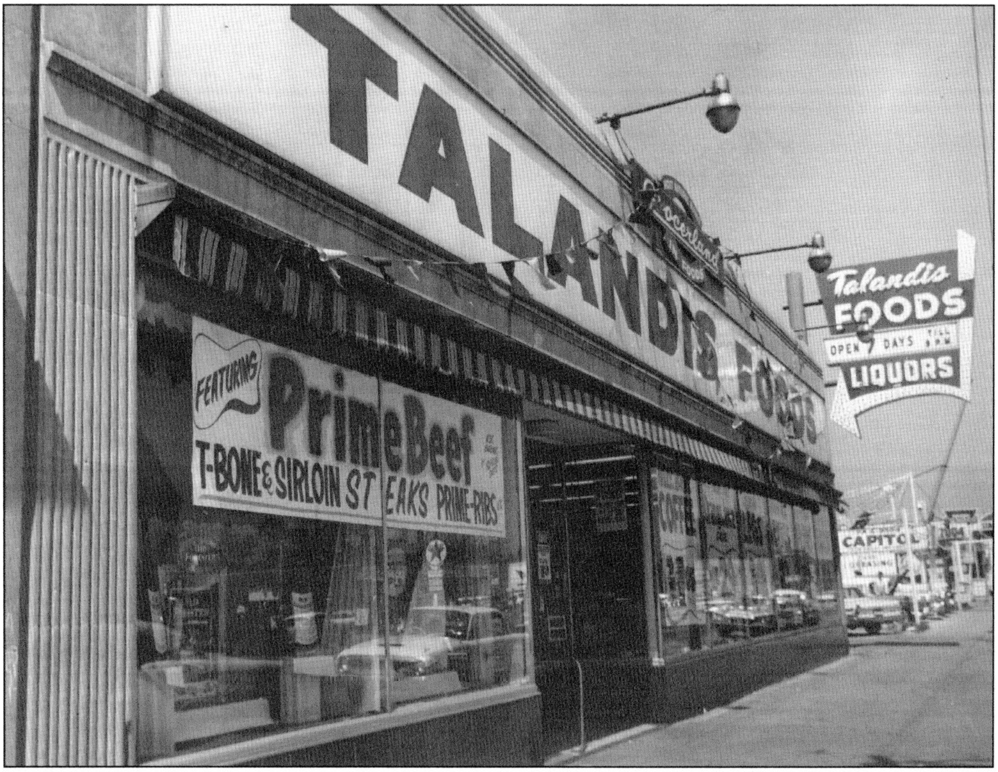

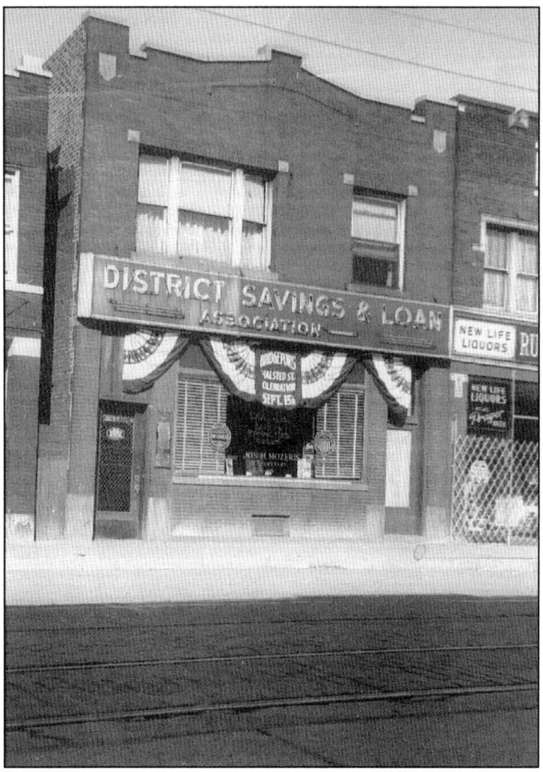

Grocery stores like Talandis Foods were important to Lithuanian immigrants. They were often the few places where one could go to buy foodstuffs that they were familiar with, such as black bread. (LRSC.)

Shown here is the District Savings and Loan Association building in Bridgeport, its Lithuanian connection made clear by the name of its secretary on the window, Joseph Mozeris. After 1938, the building at 3236 South Halsted Street became Healthy Foods Lithuanian Restaurant. Note the streetcar tracks in the foreground. (Grazina Biciunas-Santoski.)

In 1938, Healthy Foods Lithuanian Restaurant was founded by two Lithuanian women. It was purchased by Pranas and Julija Biciunas in 1960, Lithuanian immigrants who came to Chicago after World War II. Pranas worked for Draugas Publishing while Julija tended to eight children. A friend of the family, Msgr. Mykolas Krupavicius, convinced Julija to open a restaurant telling her, "If you can cook for 10, you can cook for 100." (Grazina Biciunas-Santoski.)

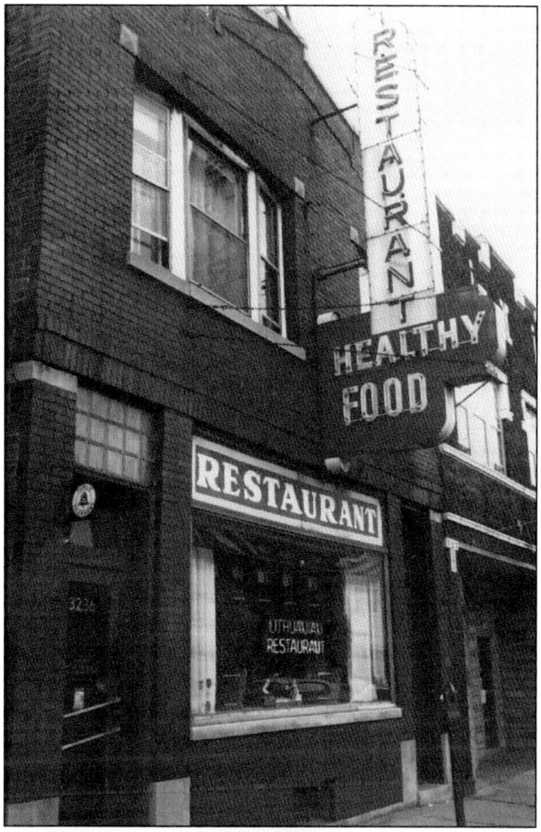

Shown here are two longtime employees of Healthy Foods Lithuanian Restaurant in the early 1960s, Jadviga Balskus and Judy Ratas. (Grazina Biciunas-Santoski.)

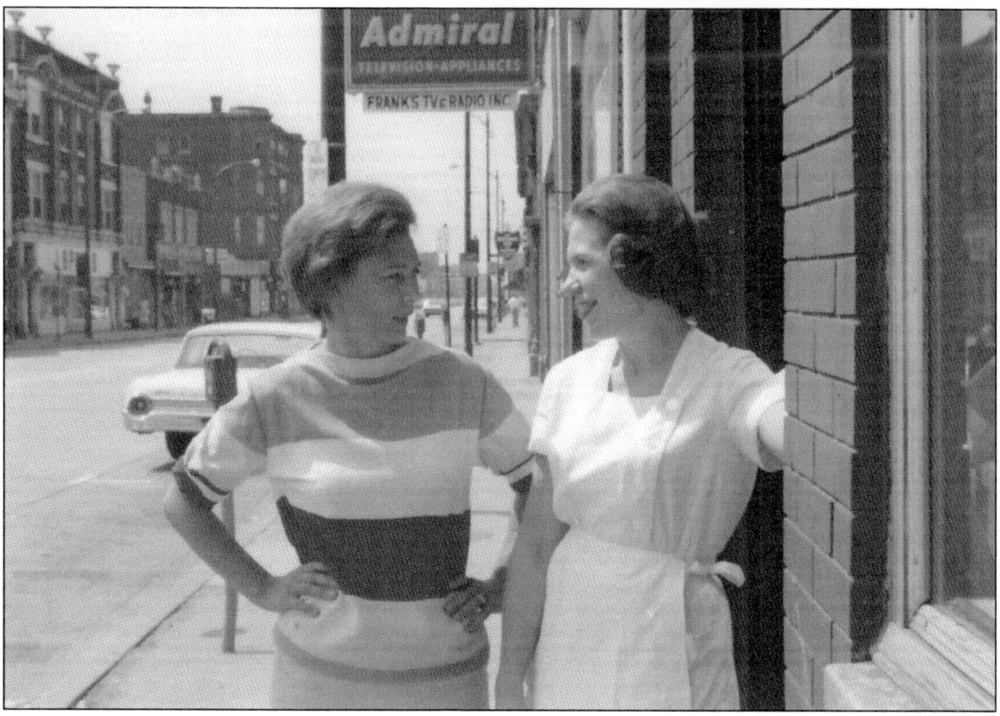

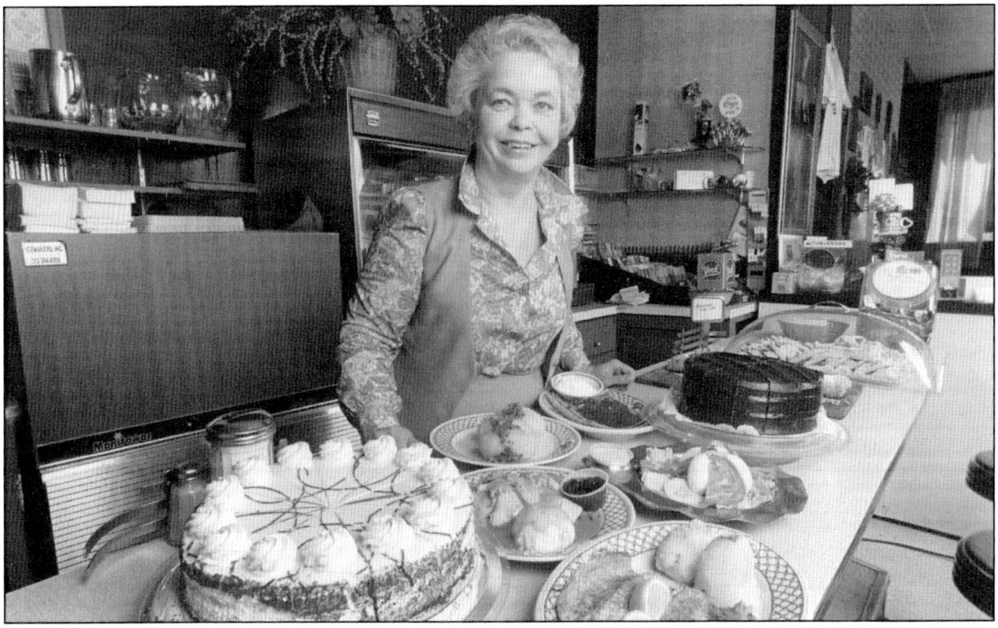

When her mother, Julija, passed away in 1979, Grazina Biciunas-Santoski took over Healthy Foods, anticipating it would only be for a few years. A few years turned into 30, as Grazina successfully ran the restaurant, providing her customers with good wholesome food like one would eat at home, until her retirement in 2009. She is shown here in the early 1980s with a variety of entrees and desserts, all made from scratch. (Grazina Biciunas-Santoski.)

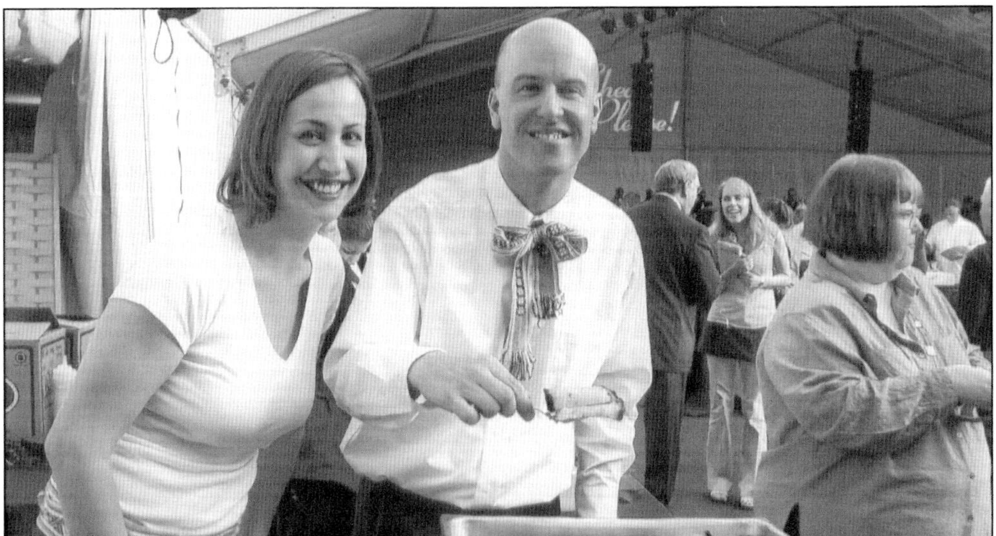

Believing that the best way to introduce people to Lithuanian culture is through the stomach, Grazina could always be counted on to serve up customer favorites such as kugelis, koldunai, or blintzes. Patrons of Healthy Foods also received a crash course in Lithuanian culture by visiting the restaurant, home to Lithuanian folk art and a collection of amber. Healthy Foods frequently was in the public eye. In this image, Corey Stankowicz and Leonardo Biciunas serve up some koldunai and kugelis at a reception for restaurants featured on the popular dining show *Check Please!* (Grazina Biciunas-Santoski.)

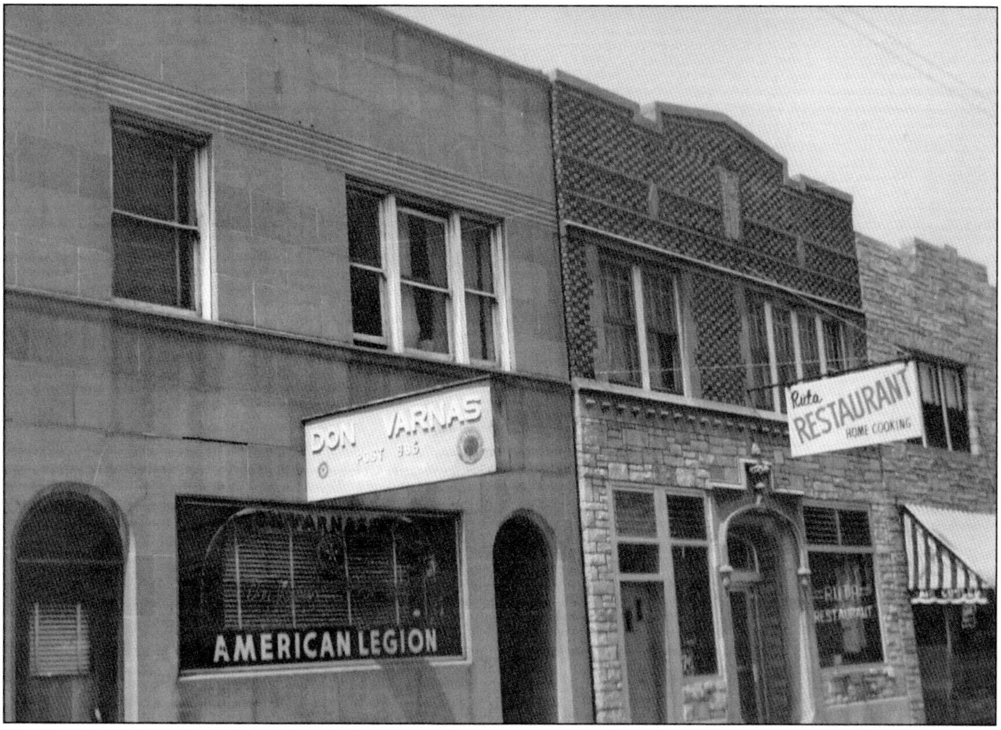

Healthy Foods was one of many Lithuanian restaurants that existed in Chicago. Shown here are the restaurants Ruta (above) and Palanga (below). Such restaurants provided Lithuanian immigrants and their descendants with a taste of their native land. Many Lithuanians in Chicago will likely recall weekly trips to restaurants such as Seklycia in Marquette Park following mass at churches like Nativity BVM. (Both, LRSC.)

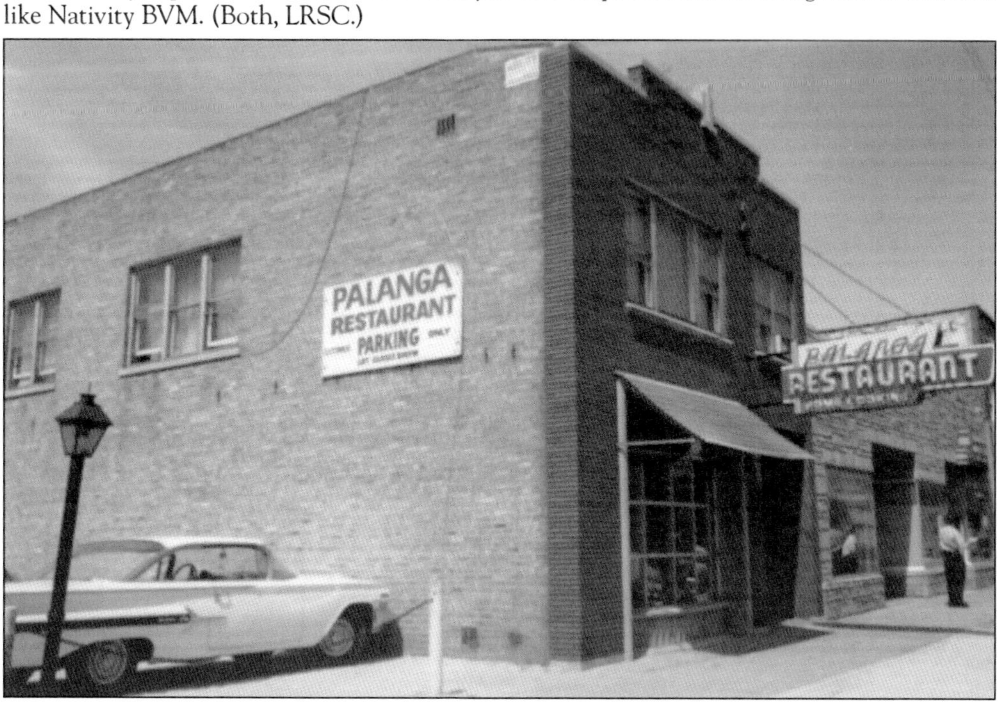

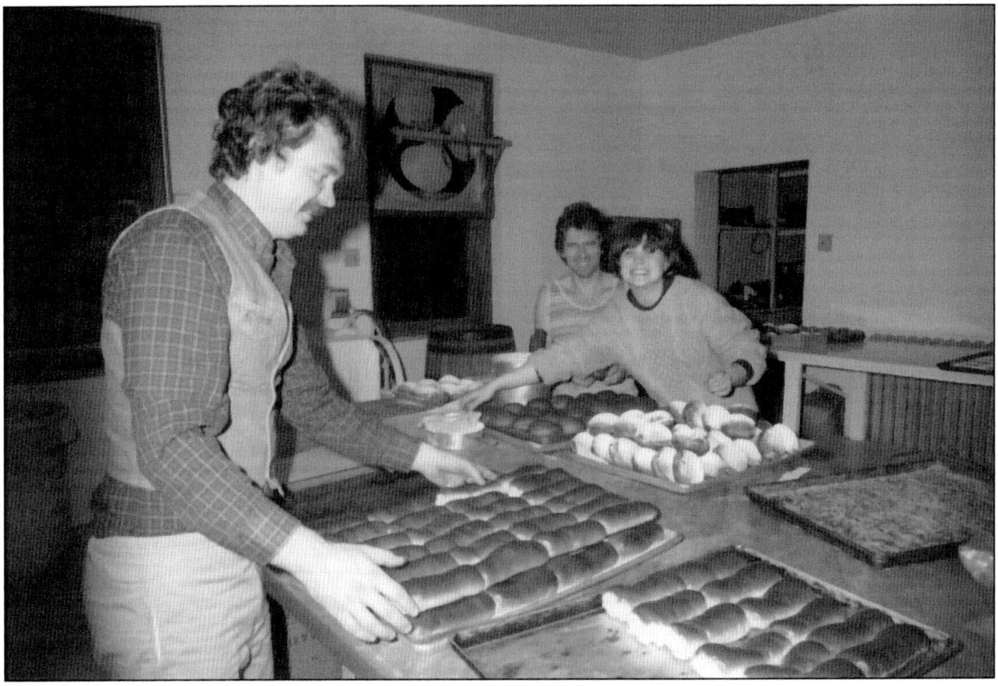

Food is important to Lithuanian culture, and within the community, there has always been a demand for traditional products, particularly staples like bread. One of the most successful Lithuanian-owned bakeries in Chicago has been Racine Bakery. In December 1984, the Kapacinskas and Juodwalis families purchased Racine Bakery, then located at Fifty-third Street and Damen Avenue in Chicago. Shown above are Gediminas Juodwalis (left), an unidentified bakery employee, and Dana Kapacinskas (right) preparing goods in the back. (Racine Bakery.)

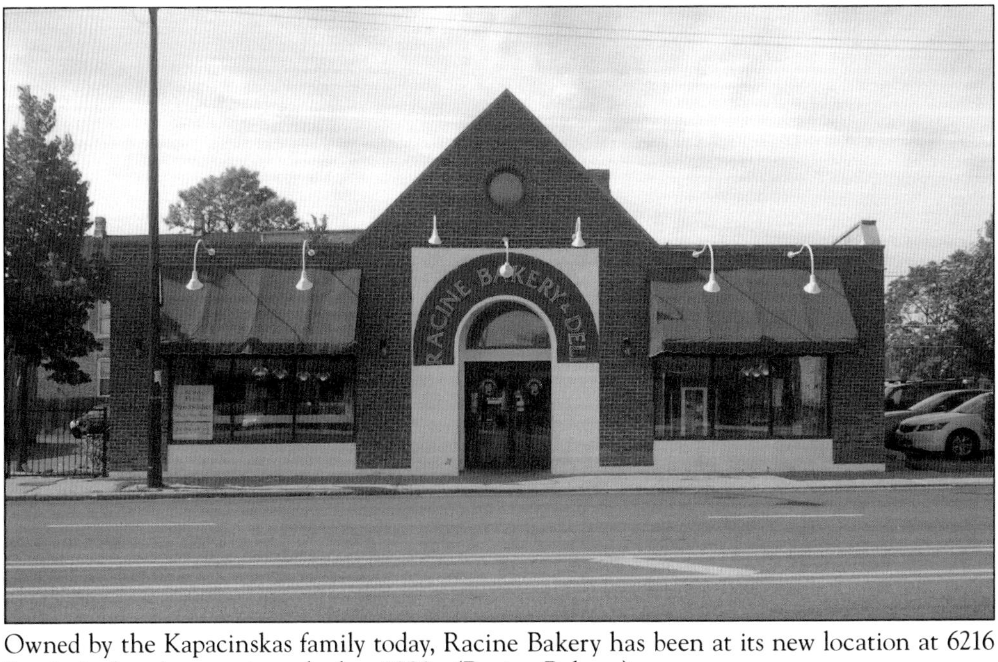

Owned by the Kapacinskas family today, Racine Bakery has been at its new location at 6216 South Archer Avenue since the late 1980s. (Racine Bakery.)

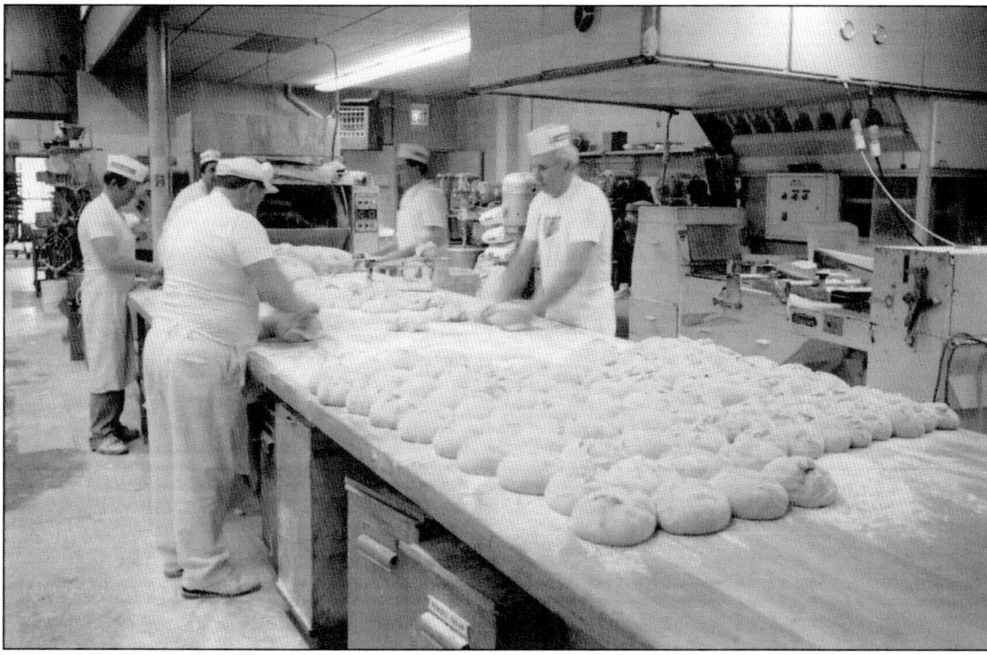

Racine Bakery employs over 50 people and distributes its products to over 100 retail outlets in the Chicagoland area. Shown here are employees baking bread in the back of the Archer Avenue store. It is not uncommon for them to bake 3,600 loaves on a busy night. No Lithuanian holiday would be complete without a loaf of Racine Bakery's Lithuanian rye on the table. (Racine Bakery.)

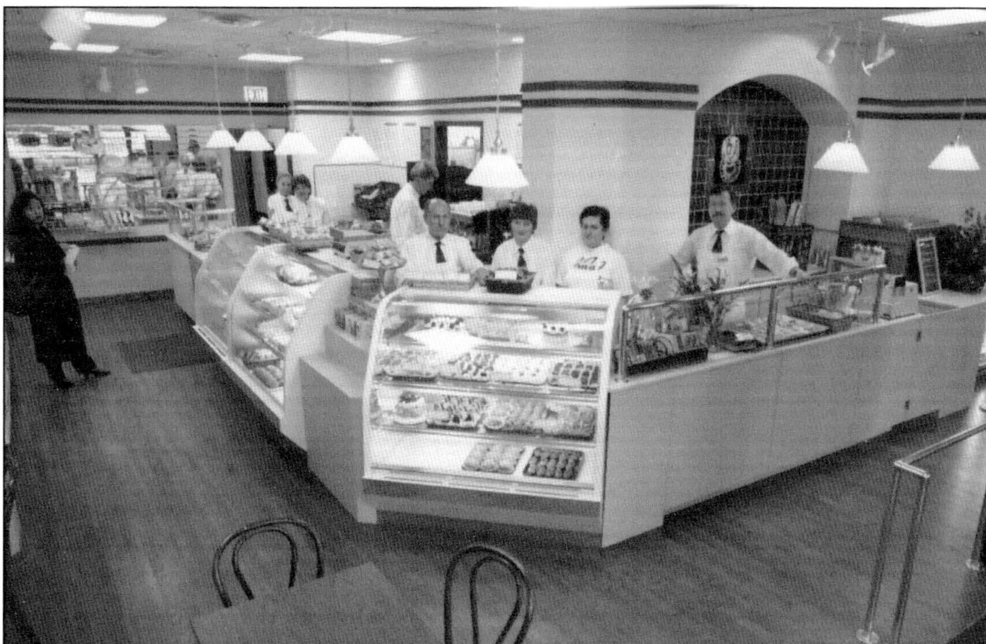

The success of Racine Bakery has led to its expansion under the Bake for Me name. Pictured here is one of the Bake for Me locations on North Clark Street in Chicago in 1991. Juozas Kapacinskas is standing at far right behind the counter. (LRSC.)

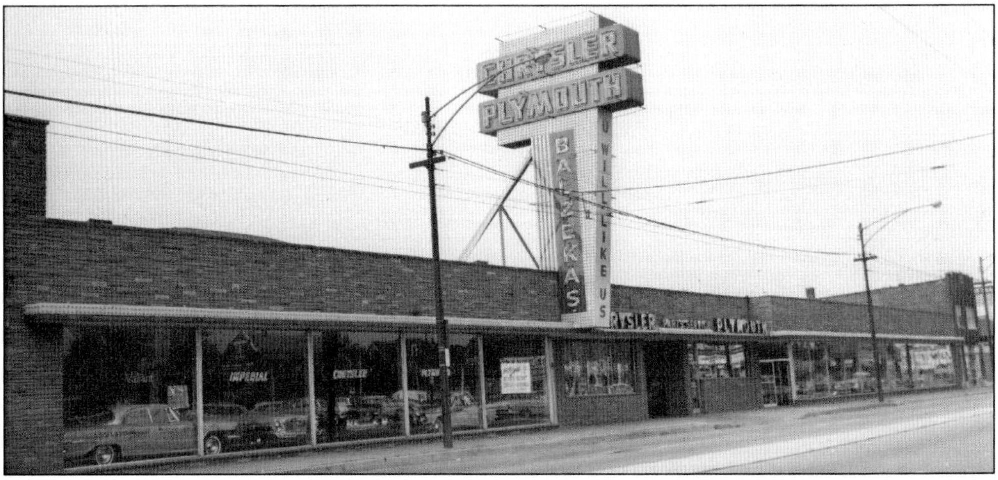

Initially, taverns and small shops were the most common Lithuanian-owned businesses in Chicago. Eventually, however, Lithuanians began to branch out into other areas of business. Stanley Balzekas Sr. came to the United States in 1912, graduated from Valparaiso University, and later opened a Chrysler Plymouth dealership at 4030 South Archer Avenue. The Balzekas family has been selling new and used cars in Chicago since 1919. (LRSC.)

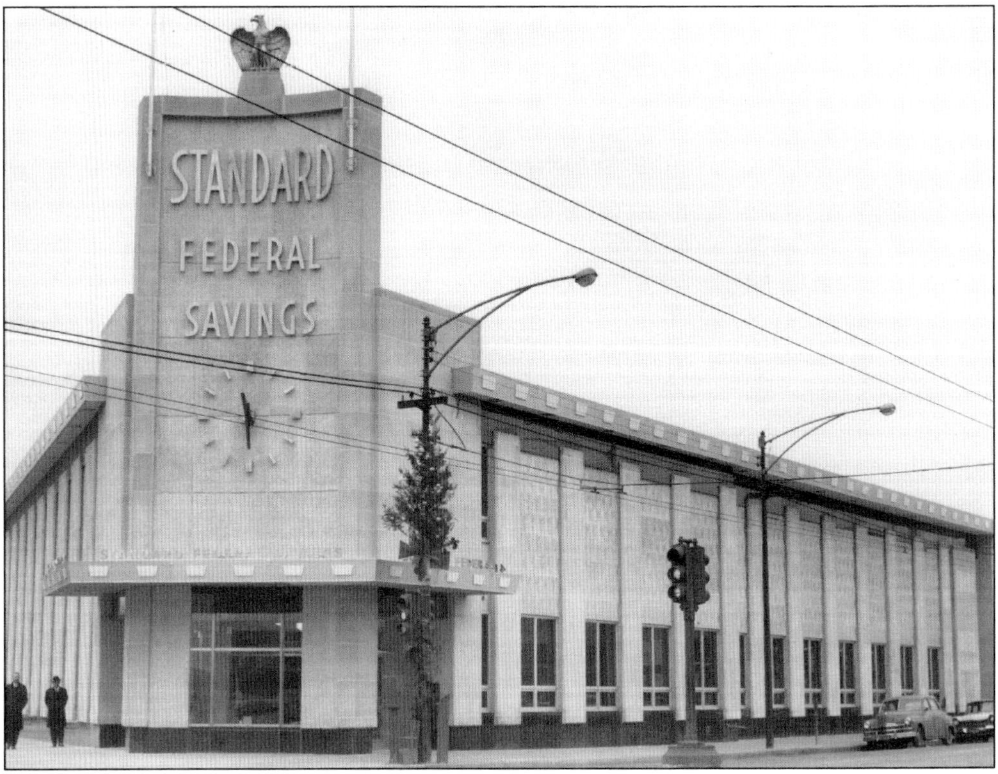

For Lithuanian immigrants, home ownership was a key part of the American Dream. Attaining this goal was made possible by Lithuanian-owned institutions like Standard Federal Savings and Loan. Founded in 1909 by Justin Machiewich, Standard Federal Savings and Loan was one of the oldest and most well-known banks to Lithuanians of Chicago. In 1997, it was purchased by TCF Bank. Pictured here is the bank's main location along Archer and Sacramento Avenues. (LRSC.)

Many Lithuanians found success in construction, such as George Juraitis, a general contractor who built this dream home in the Back of the Yards. The poster on the window boasts "Nowhere can you buy a house like this for $25,300." (Back of the Yards Neighborhood Council.)

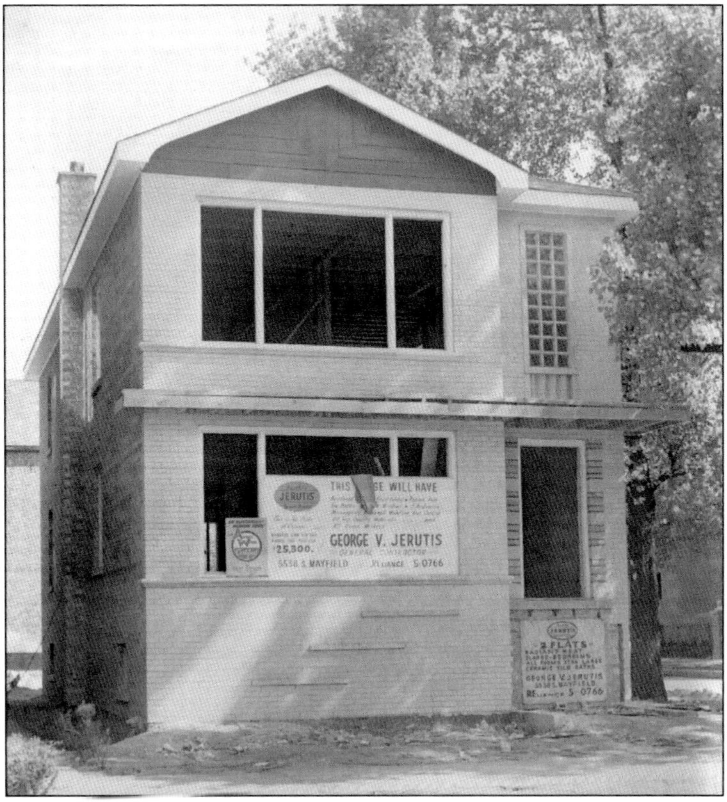

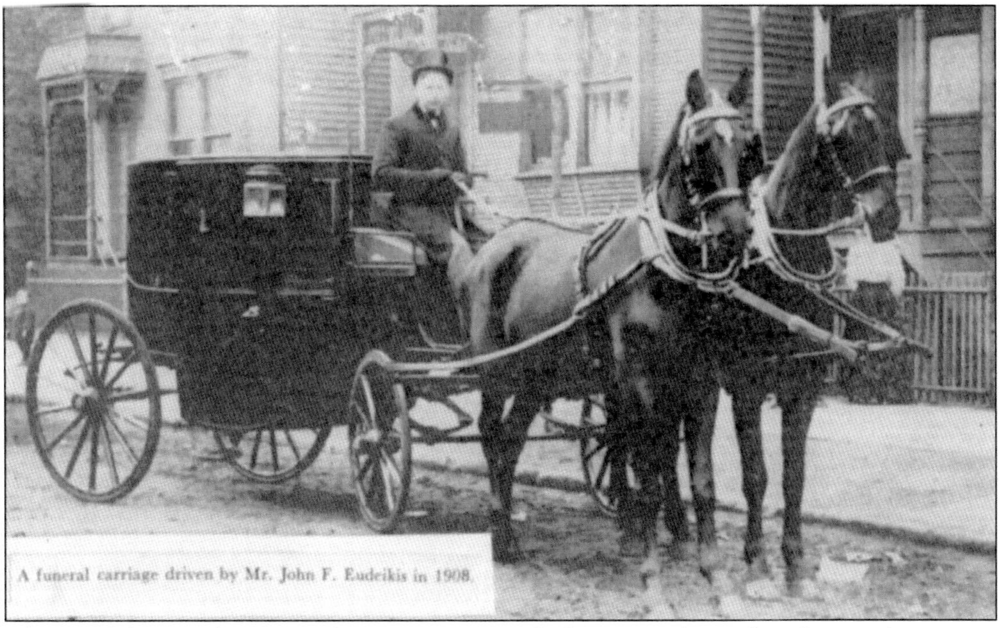

Along with having their own religious institutions, Lithuanians also preferred to use the services of Lithuanian undertakers. There have been a number of successful Lithuanian-owned funeral homes in Chicago. One of the oldest was started by John F. Eudeikis, pictured above driving a funeral carriage in 1908. (David Gaidas.)

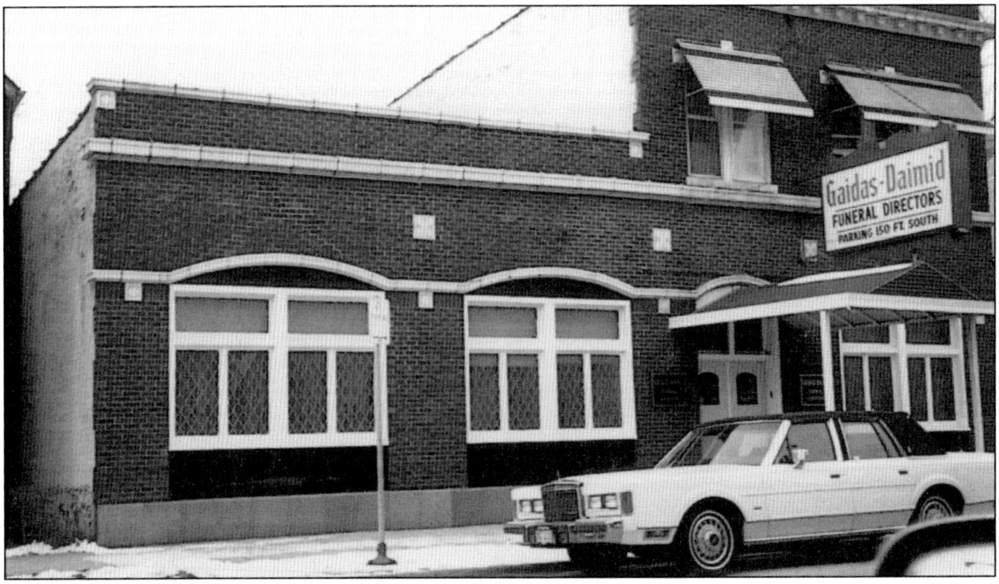

Initially working for John Eudeikis, David Gaidas Sr. purchased the business in 1969. Shown here is the Brighton Park location at Forty-third Street and California Avenue. His son David Gaidas Jr. stayed in the family business and now operates Palos Gaidas Funeral Home in the suburb of Palos Hills, Illinois. (David Gaidas.)

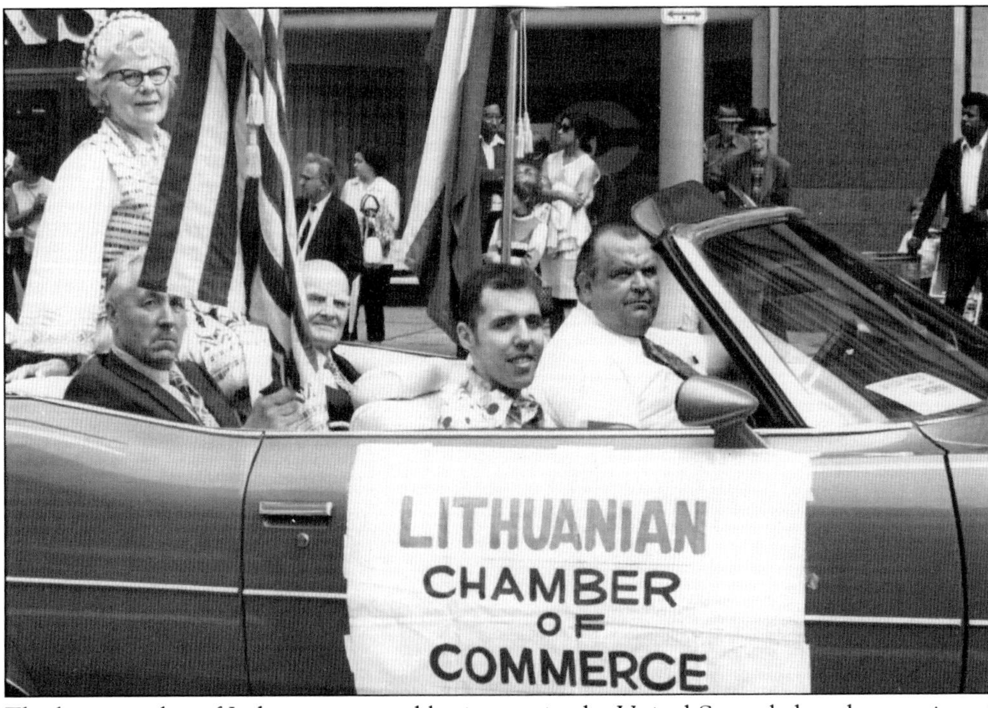

The large number of Lithuanian-owned businesses in the United States led to the creation of the Lithuanian American Chamber of Commerce in 1922, with its headquarters in Chicago. In addition to strengthening ties between Lithuanian American business owners, the group also forged partnerships with Lithuanian industry and business. In this image, members of the Illinois chapter represent the organization in a parade. (LRSC.)

A thriving press kept the numerous Lithuanian neighborhoods throughout the city connected and well informed. As stated by David Fainhauz in *Lithuanians in Multiethnic Chicago Until World War II*, Chicago was home to 90 newspapers and other publications by 1941. One of the oldest was the newspaper *Lietuva*, founded in 1892 and published daily by successful Lithuanian businessman Antanas Olsauskas. The headline of this front page, dated September 18, 1914, describes the beginning stages of World War I. (LRSC.)

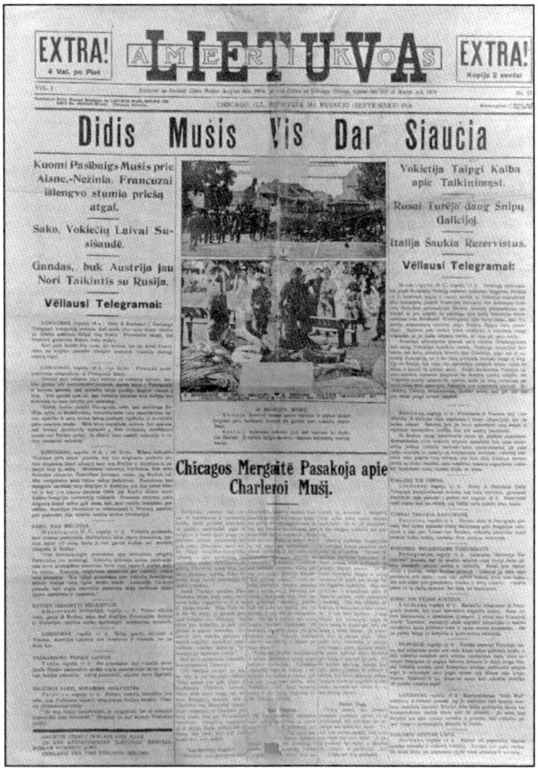

EXTRA! 4 Val. po Piet

AMERIKOS LIETUVA

EXTRA! Kopija 2 centai

Didis Musis Vis Dar Siaucia

Kuomi Pasibaigs Musis prie Aisne,-Nezinia. Francuzai islengvo stumia priesą atgal.

Sako, Vokiecių Laivai Susisaudė.

Gandas, buk Austrija jau Nori Taikintis su Rusija.

Vėliausi Telegramai:

Vokietija Taipgi Kalba apie Taikinimąsi.

Rusai Turėjo daug Snipų Galicijoj.

Italija Saukia Rezervistus.

Vėliausi Telegramai:

Chicagos Mergaitė Pasakoja apie Charleroi Musį.

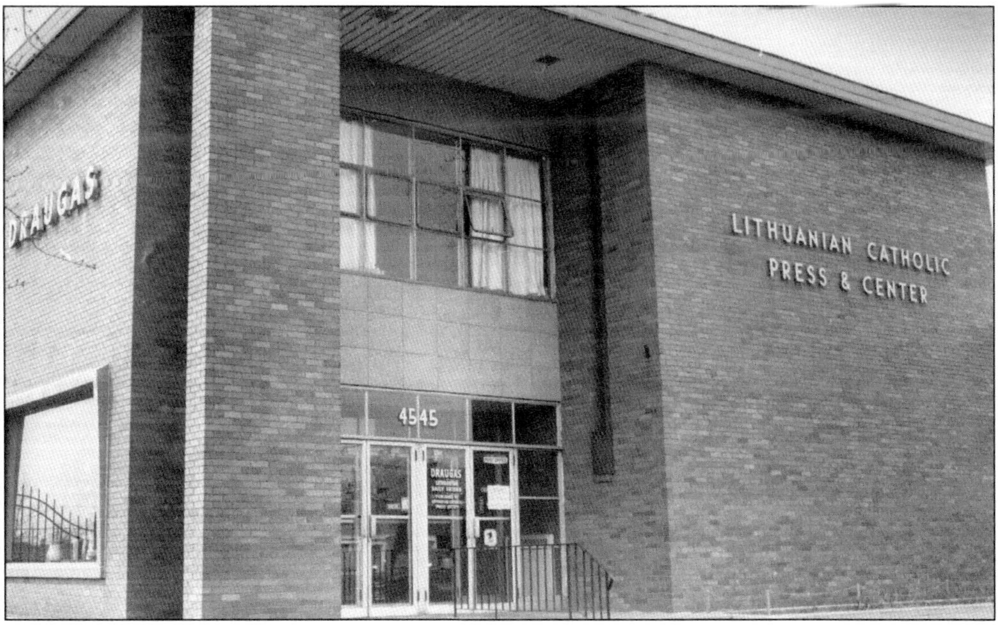

The best-known and longest lasting Lithuanian newspaper has been *Draugas*, founded in Pennsylvania in 1909 by the Lithuanian Roman Catholic Priests Association of America. Owned by the Marian Fathers, a religious order, the newspaper has historically been a Lithuanian language, Roman Catholic newspaper. It moved to Chicago in 1916. Shown here is the headquarters of *Draugas* at 4545 West Sixty-third Street not far from Midway Airport. (LRSC.)

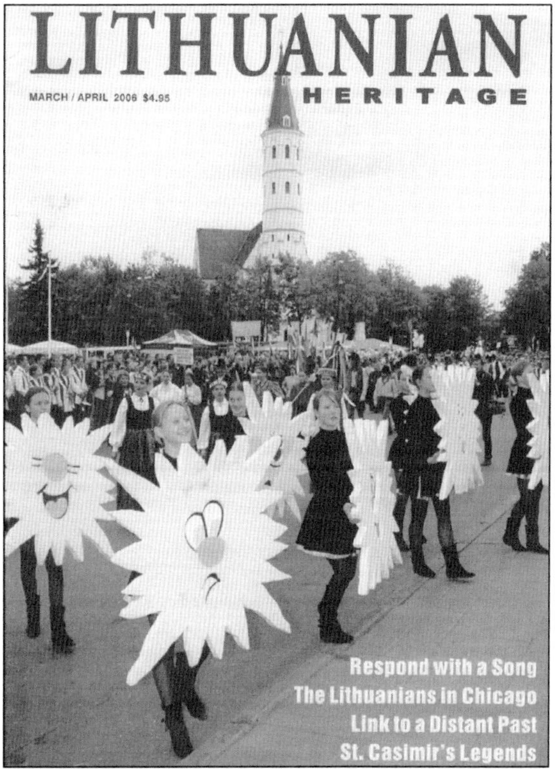

Lithuanian Heritage is an English-language magazine catered to those who wish to learn more about Lithuanian history, culture, ancestry, and more. Published bimonthly since 1994, it has a significant following around the world and is one of the most popular Lithuanian-related magazines outside of Lithuania itself. (Val Ramonis.)

In addition to newspapers, the Lithuanian community of Chicago also was home to the *Margutis Radio Hour*. Beginning in 1932, it was organized by Juozas Bachunas, Antanas Olis, and Antanas Vanagaitis. Shown here is one of the program's early radio stations. (LRSC.)

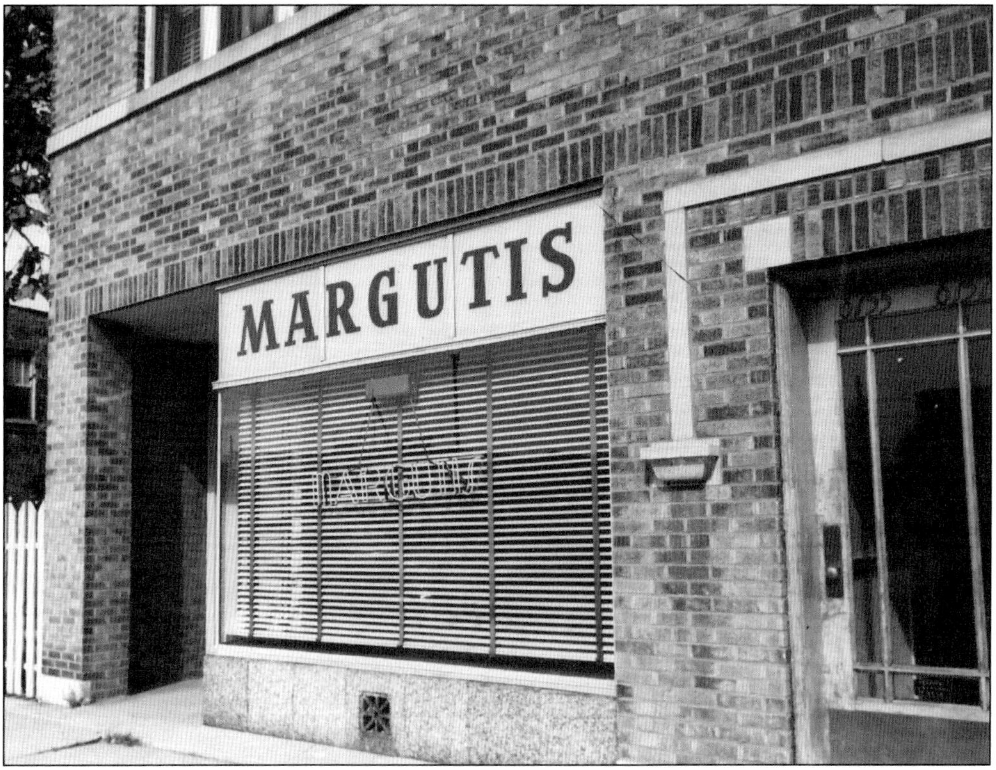

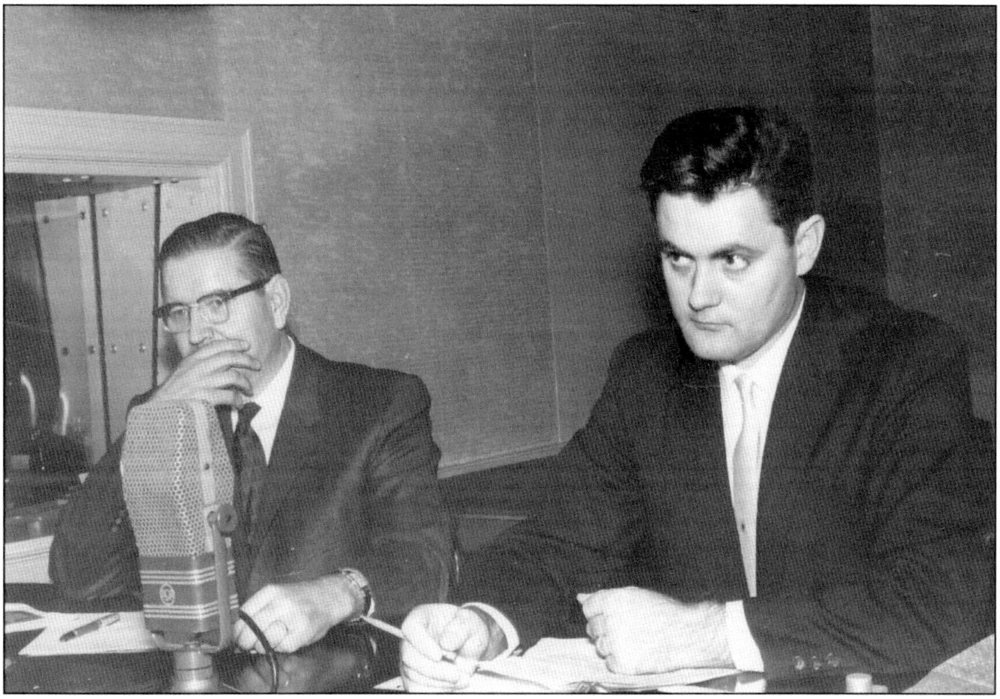

Politics was often a subject of tense debate among Chicago's Lithuanians. Shown here are Adolfas Baliunas (left) and Valdas Adamkus discussing the presidential election of 1960 on the *Margutis Radio Hour*. Adamkus was in favor of Nixon while Baliunas was for Kennedy. (LRSC.)

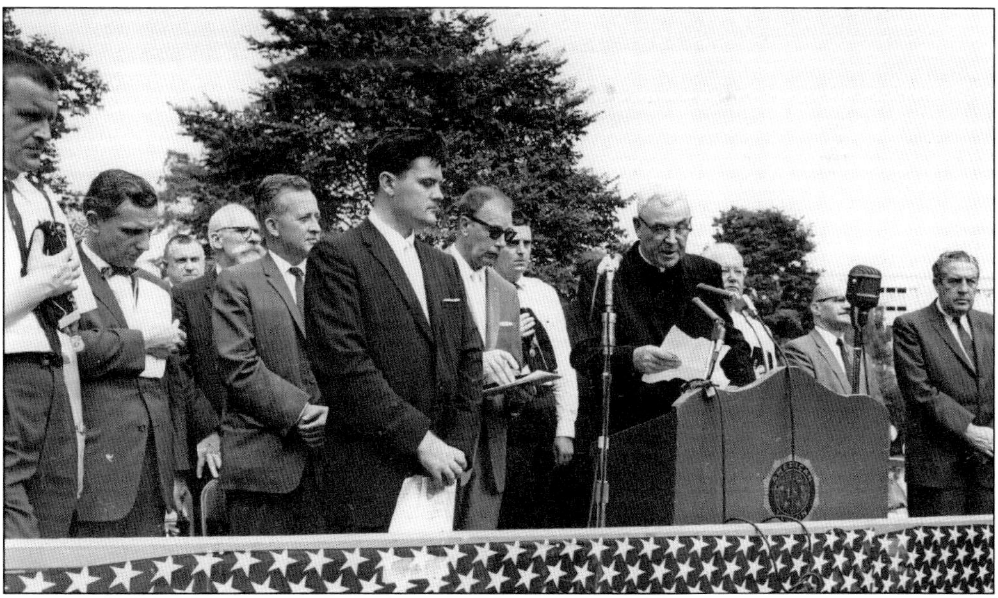

Public speaking was often a skill that many Lithuanians mastered at social events and gatherings among the community. One could expect a significant number of speeches at any commemoration. Shown here is Valdas Adamkus (front, in the dark suit) preparing to speak at a ceremony honoring the Lithuanian king, Vytautas the Great. (LRSC.)

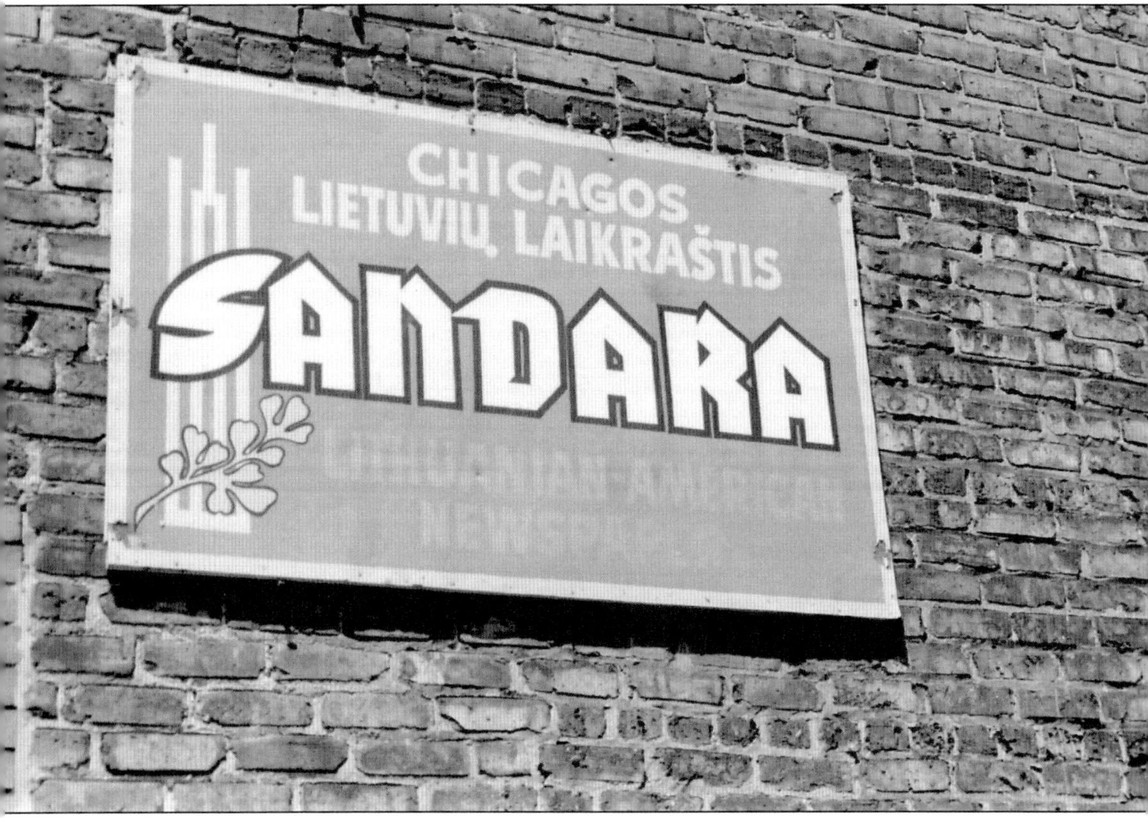

Lithuanian newspapers, as mentioned before, played an important role informing the community. In addition, reading in Lithuanian was much easier for many residents of Chicago, particularly those who came after World War II. Pictured here is a sign for another Chicago Lithuanian newspaper *Sandara*. (Eugenijus Butenas.)

Four

Social Activities and Organizations

The numerous Lithuanian neighborhoods of Chicago were the result of the immigrant's desire to be close to those he was familiar with. By clustering together and forming tightly knit communities, Lithuanians were increasing their chances of success in a new country. In addition, Lithuanian communities ensured that the children of immigrants would grow up associating with other Lithuanians, thus preserving the culture of their parents for future generations. Lithuanians desired to socialize with those they could identify with, and the result was the creation of a thriving Lithuanian social scene in Chicago.

For early Lithuanians, the center of their social lives was the local church. In addition to serving a religious purpose, parishes were home to a myriad of social organizations ranging from groups focused on charity to athletics. Upon arrival, the second wave of immigrants to Chicago either joined existing social groups or created new ones. The diversity and scope of Lithuanian social activities and organizations is a clear indicator of the community's success.

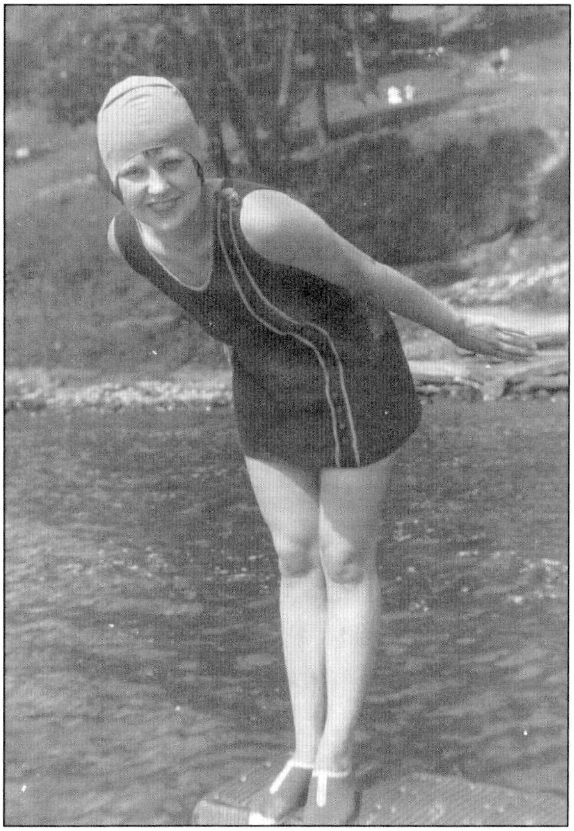

Pictured here in 1924, Antoinette Simonis-Ezerski escapes the crowded confines of the Back of the Yards by diving into Lake Geneva in Wisconsin. Lithuanians have long frequented vacation spots in nearby Wisconsin, Indiana, and Michigan. (Michael and Loretta Ezerski.)

One of the most popular Lithuanian vacation spots was the stretch of beaches along Lake Michigan in northwest Indiana and southwest Michigan. Many Lithuanians purchased summer homes in areas such as Beverly Shores, Michiana, and Union Pier. Here, the Kursius family and friends enjoy a trip to the beaches of Beverly Shores in the early 1960s. (Nijole Riskus-Gierstikas.)

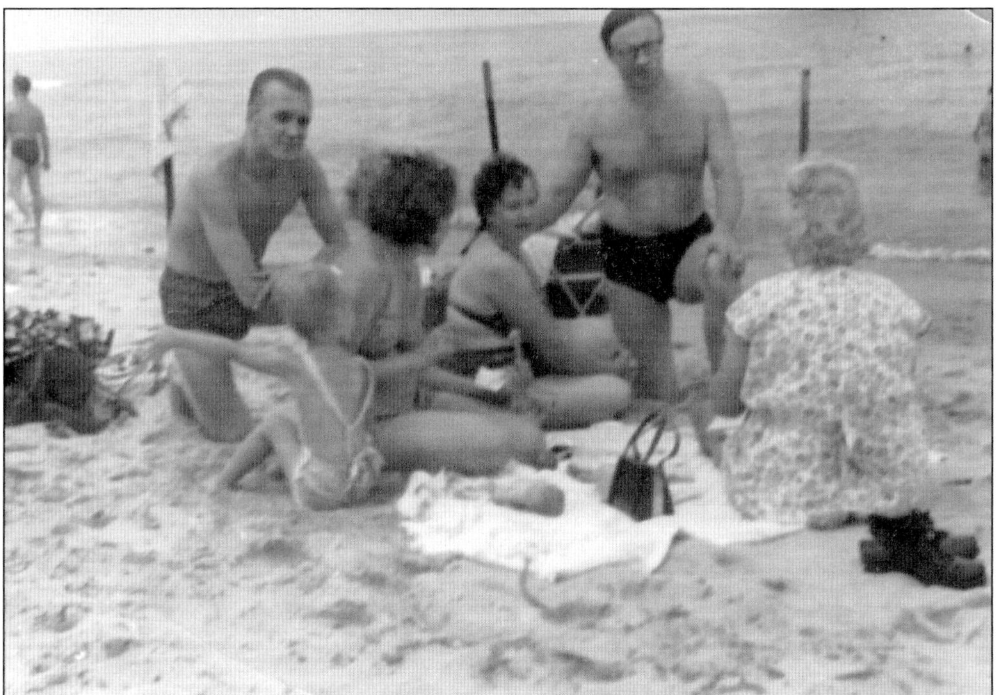

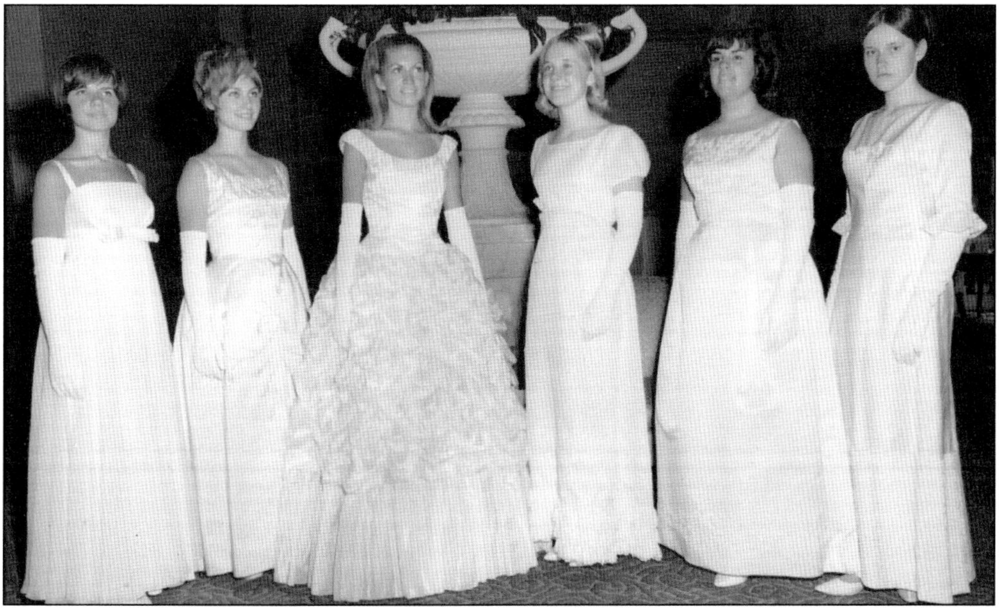

Shown here are debutantes taking part in a longtime tradition hosted by the Chicago Lithuanian Women's Club called the Amber Ball. Held for many years at the Beverly Country Club at Eighty-seventh Street and Western Avenue, the Amber Ball combined social and cultural traditions and symbolized the entrance into adulthood. Shown here in 1966 are, from left to right, Carol Ann Misevich, Cynthia Stahl, Christine Austin, Roberta Staskon, Patrice Yanas, and Alice Lapsatyte. (LRSC.)

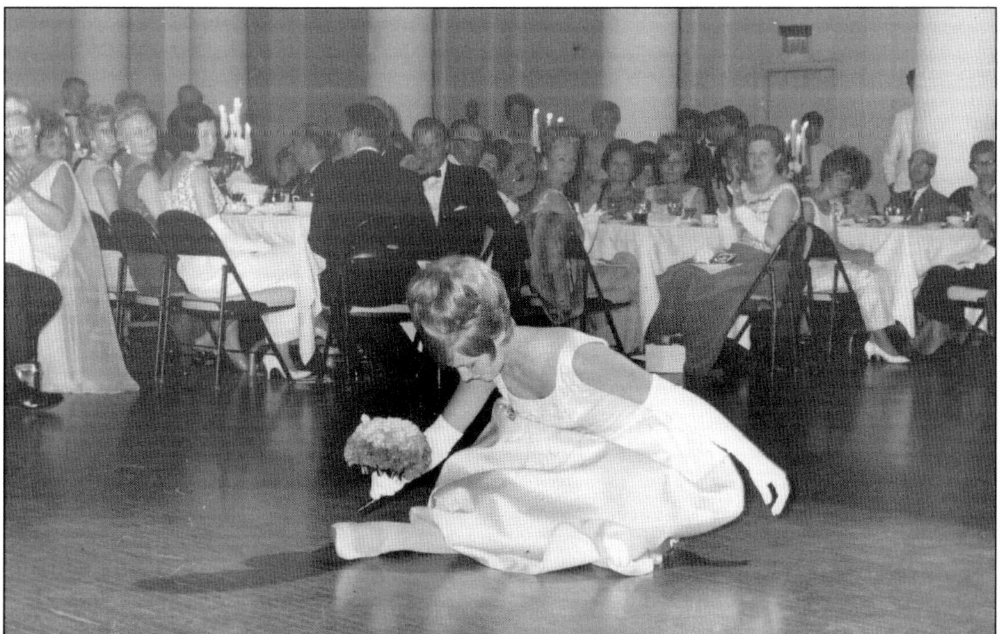

Part of the Amber Ball included a traditional dance known as the *vainikelis*, being performed in this image by Cynthia Stahl in 1966. The Chicago Lithuanian Women's Club was founded in 1923 and engages in numerous Lithuanian-related philanthropic and social activities. (LRSC.)

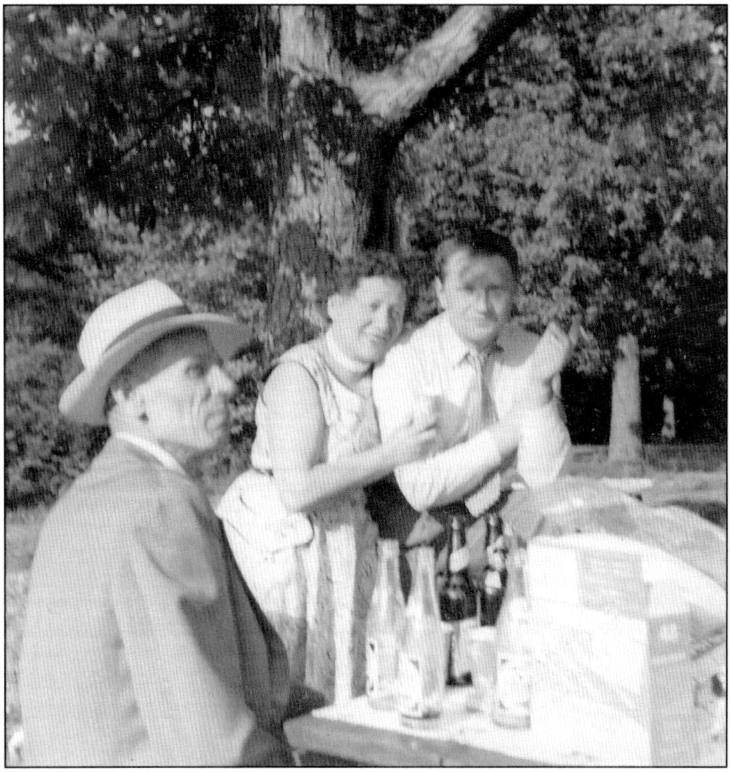

Chicago's Lithuanians did not have to leave the city to enjoy the outdoors. Pictured are, from left to right, Stepas Riskus, Anastasia Riskus, and a Mr. Shimaitis enjoying themselves at a picnic in June 1956. Summer picnics were popular among Lithuanians in Chicago and were often held on the grounds of Lithuanian institutions. (Nijole Riskus-Gierstikas.)

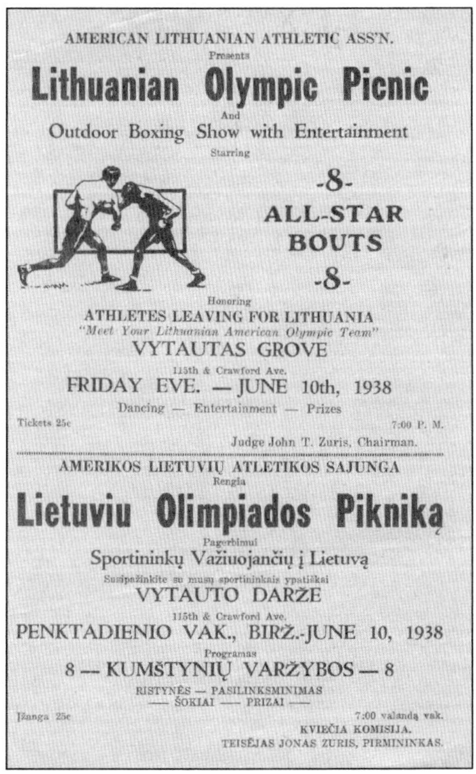

The grounds of St. Casimir Cemetery, far from the cramped quarters of the city, provided an idyllic setting for gatherings. In 1929, ten acres of the cemetery were set aside for social purposes and named Vytautas Grove in honor of Lithuania's greatest ruler. The park's inauguration on May 24, 1931, occurred in the year commemorating the 500th year since the monarch's death. For many years, Vytautas Grove was host to picnics, parish events, sports, and a host of other activities, such as this picnic held in honor of a delegation of Lithuanian American athletes leaving to compete in Lithuania in 1938. The end of the park came when the Archdiocese of Chicago used the land to build Marist High School in the early 1960s. (LRSC.)

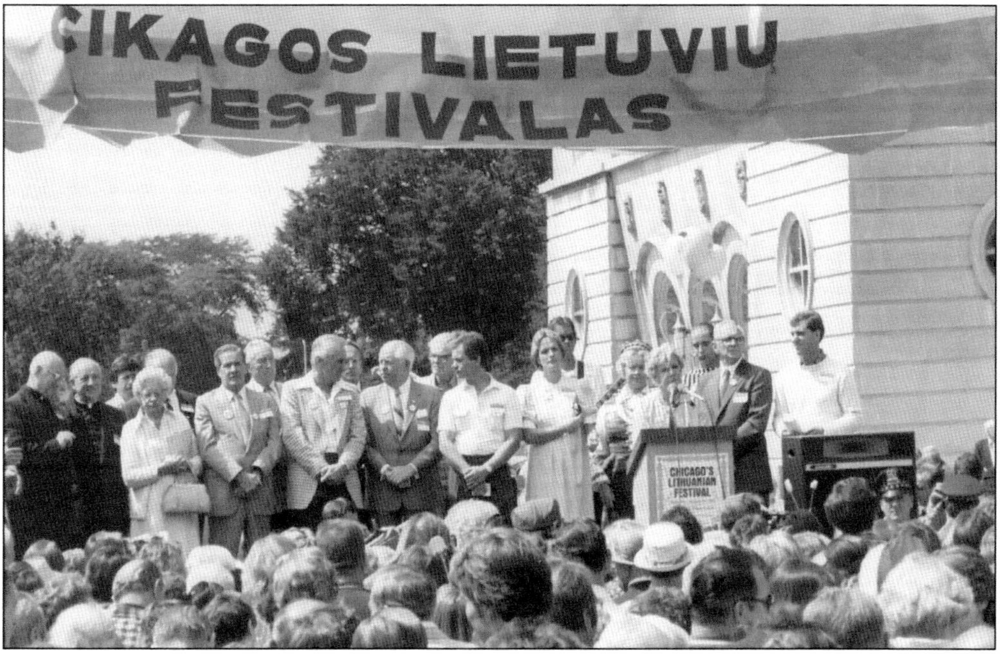

Summer always was a time for festivals for Lithuanians in Chicago. The Sixty-ninth Street Lithuanian Festival began in 1980 in Marquette Park and was an opportunity to socialize, buy Lithuanian goods, and enjoy Lithuanian food. This gathering near Nativity BVM Church is likely the opening ceremony of the 1982 festival. (LRSC.)

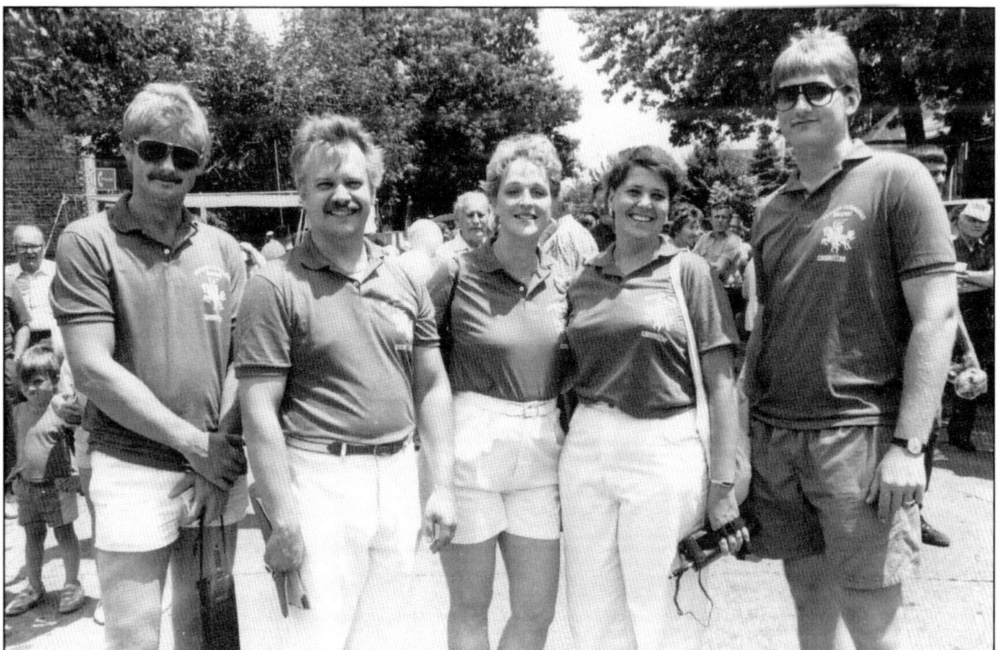

Shown here are members of the Chicago Lithuanian Festival committee. From left to right are Arvydas Vaitkevicius, Zigmas Mikuzis, Dana Mikuzis, and two unidentified friends in the 1980s. (LRSC.)

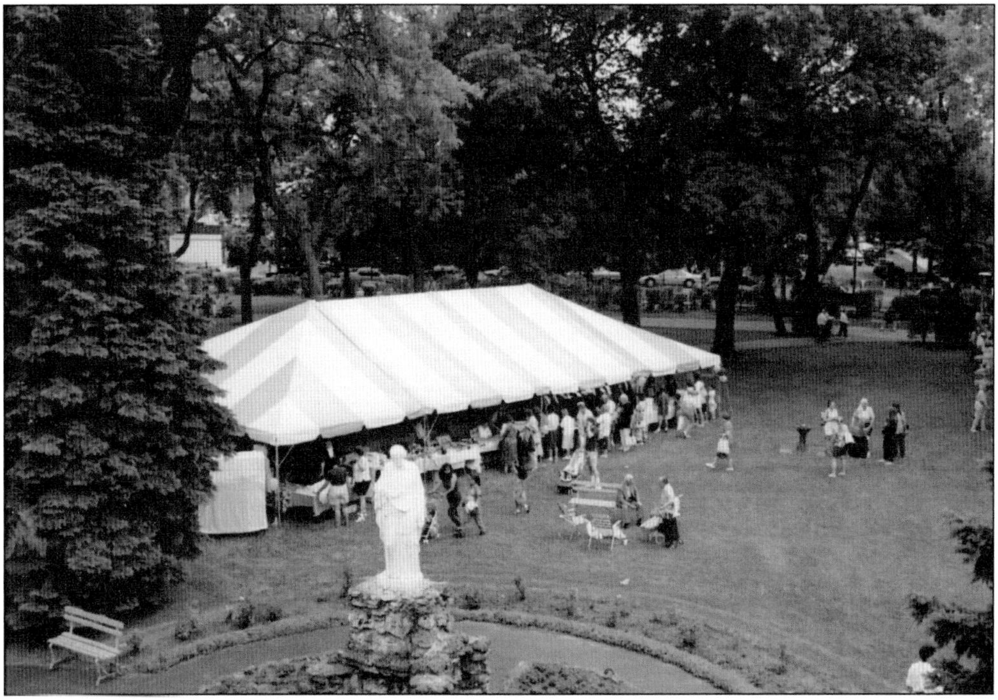

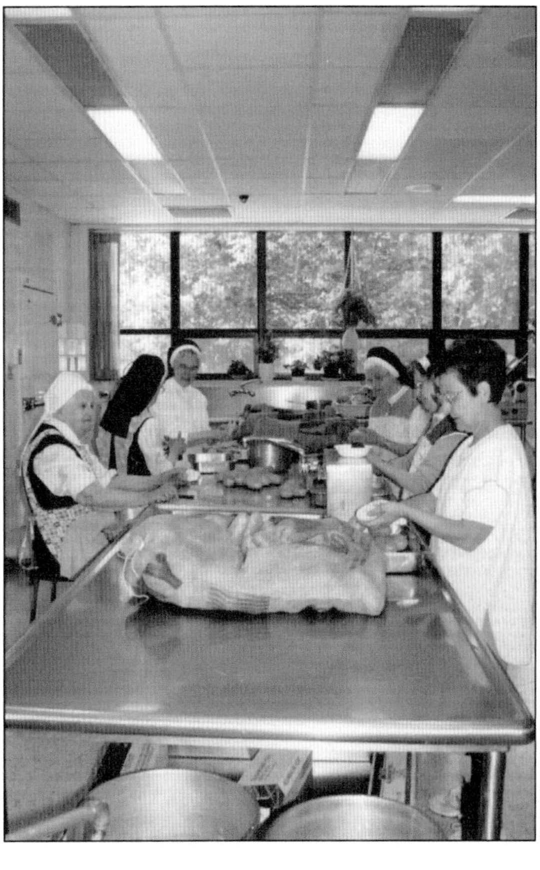

Another popular festival was the Sisters of St. Casimir Summerfest, held on the shaded grounds of the SSC Motherhouse every second Sunday in July. Each summer, the fest was filled with large diverse crowds of people enjoying music, games, and large slices of kugelis. (SSC.)

Kugelis is a staple of Lithuanian cuisine. A mix consisting mainly of potatoes, eggs, bacon, and onion baked in a pan, kugelis is a labor-intensive dish. In this photograph, the Sisters of St. Casimir peel hundreds of pounds of potatoes in anticipation of a high volume of kugelis sales at Summerfest 1996. (SSC.)

St. Casimir, who was a grandson of the Lithuanian king of Poland, Jogaila, is the patron saint of Lithuania. Every year around his feast day of March 4, it is common for Lithuanian communities to stage a festival. For many years, it was held at the Lithuanian Youth Center at 5620 South Claremont Avenue in the Gage Park neighborhood. Shown here sometime in the 1970s is a ribbon-cutting opening ceremony. Holding the scissors is the honorary consul general of Lithuania in Chicago, Josephine Dauzvardis. (LRSC.)

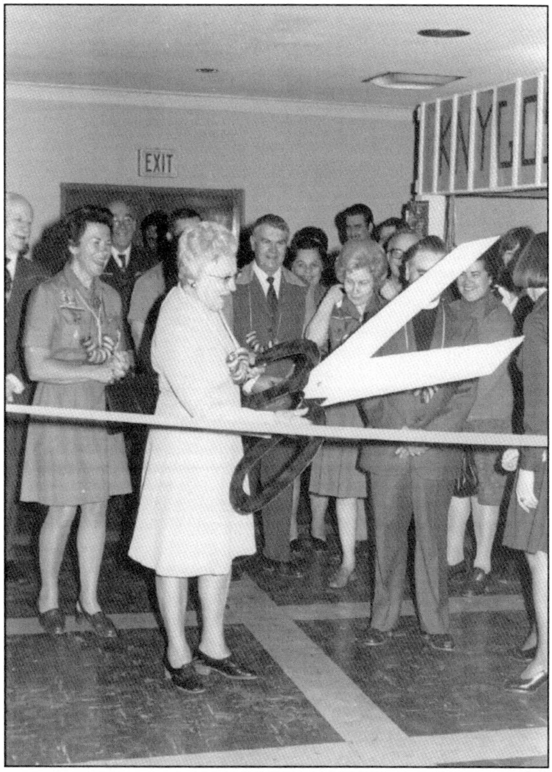

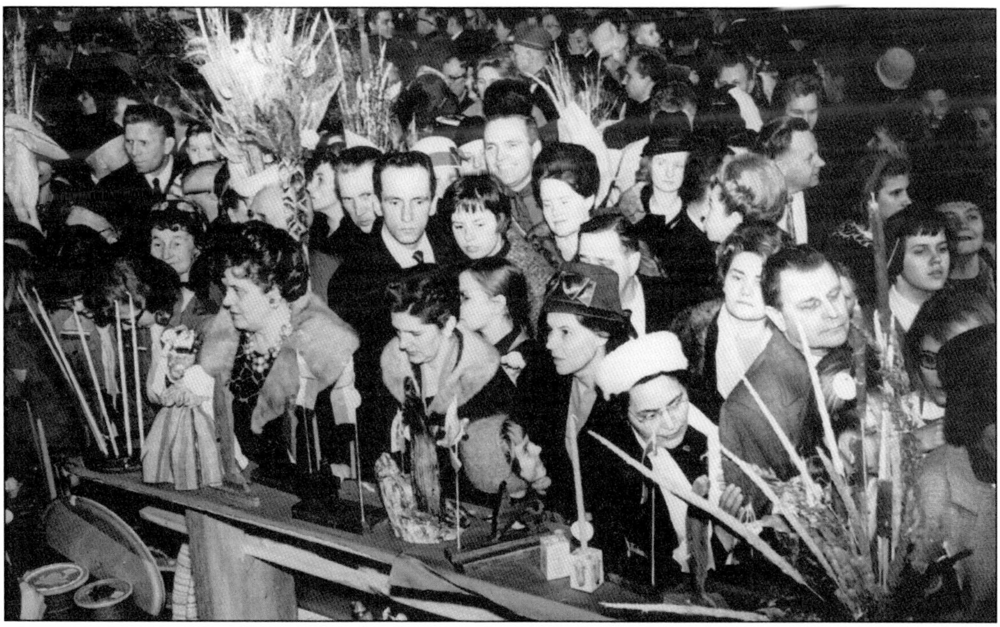

The annual Feast of St. Casimir, in Lithuanian known as Kaziuko Muge, always drew large crowds. Such occasions often involved the efforts of numerous organizations, particularly Lithuanian scouting groups. In every Kaziuko Muge, the numerous corridors, classrooms, and dance halls of the Lithuanian Youth Center would be filled with vendors, games, and other activities. Pictured here is a large crowd examining various traditional goods and enjoying the festivities. (LRSC.)

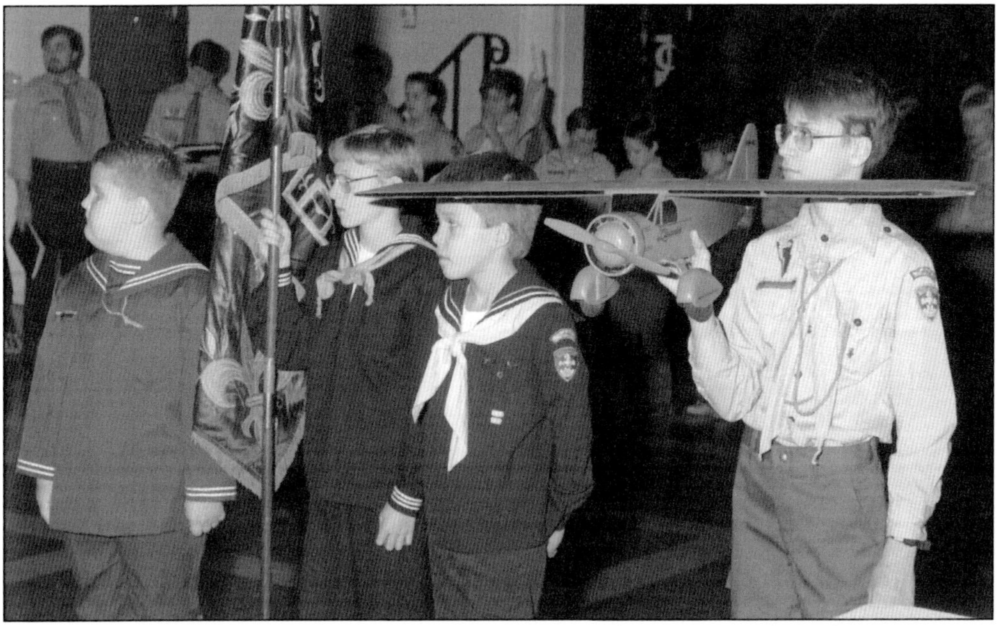

In Chicago, one of the most active groups in organizing Kaziuko Muge were the Lithuanian Scouts. Many Lithuanian Chicagoans fondly recall their scouting days. Organized along Lithuanian lines, these groups were not just social in nature and were often involved in political causes such as Lithuanian independence. In this formal gathering at the Lithuanian Youth Center, young Scouts stand at attention while displaying a flag and a replica of the plane *Lituanica*. (LRSC.)

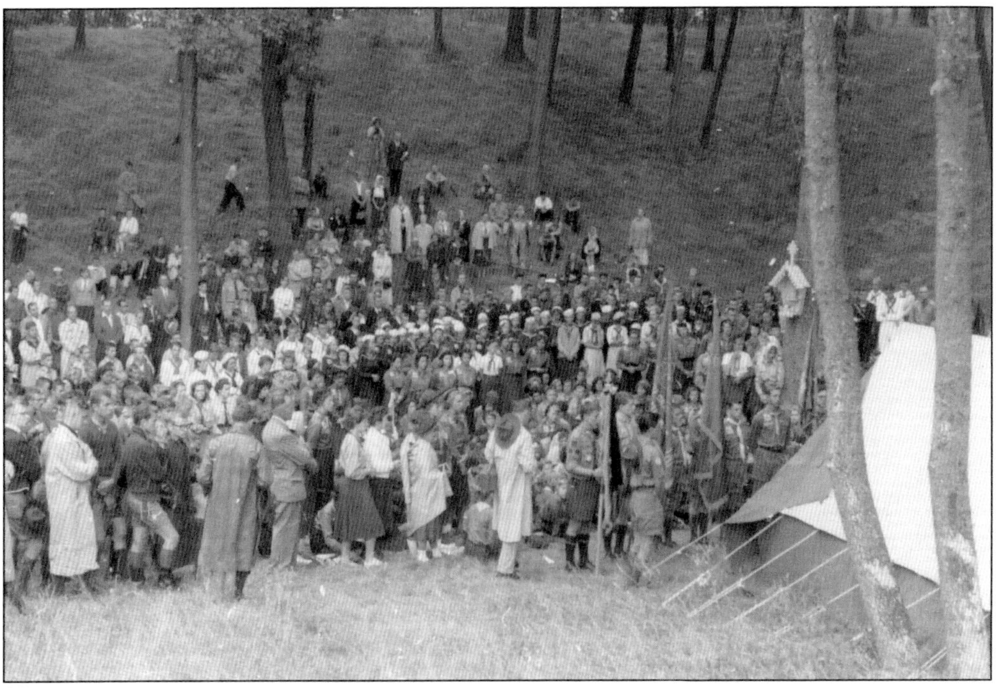

Lithuanian Scouts from Chicago often attended Rakas, a camp located in Custer, Michigan. It was common for Scouts to spend a few weeks outdoors in tents learning valuable skills and traditions. This large group has likely gathered for a mass or opening ceremony. (LRSC.)

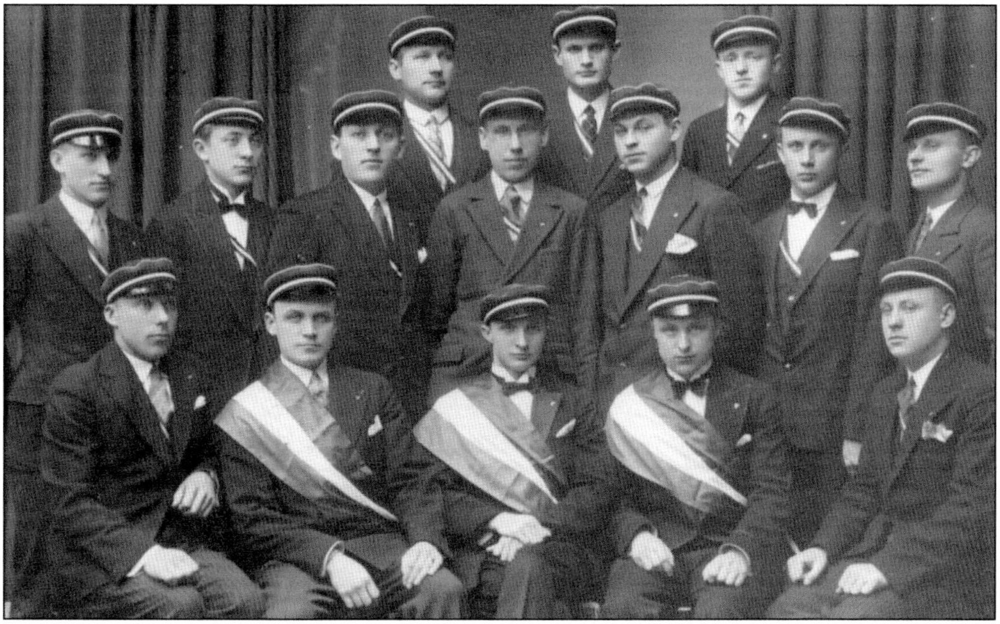

Neo-Lithuania began as a student organization in 1922 at the University of Kaunas. Modeled along the lines of a fraternity, hence the caps and colored sashes, the purpose of Neo-Lithuania was to support Lithuanian nationalism. Following the Soviet occupation of Lithuania during World War II, members established groups in the United States, one of the most active being in Chicago. Above is a group photograph of Neo-Lithuania members sometime in the 1930s. (LRSC.)

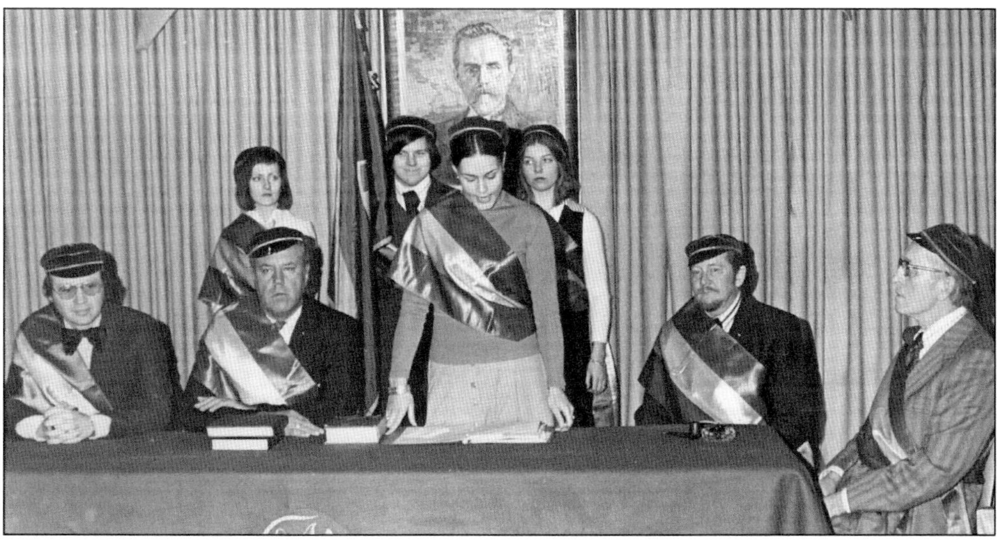

In Chicago, Neo-Lithuania fulfilled an important social purpose as well. Especially in the years following the arrival of the second wave of Lithuanian immigrants to the city, families were often quite selective on which organizations they would join. Unlike the Ateitis Federation, a Roman Catholic organization, Neo-Lithuania members did not emphasize religion and were more aligned with the views of nationalist Lithuanian president Antanas Smetona, whose portrait hangs above Audra Gulbinas as she speaks at a Neo-Lithuania meeting. (LRSC.)

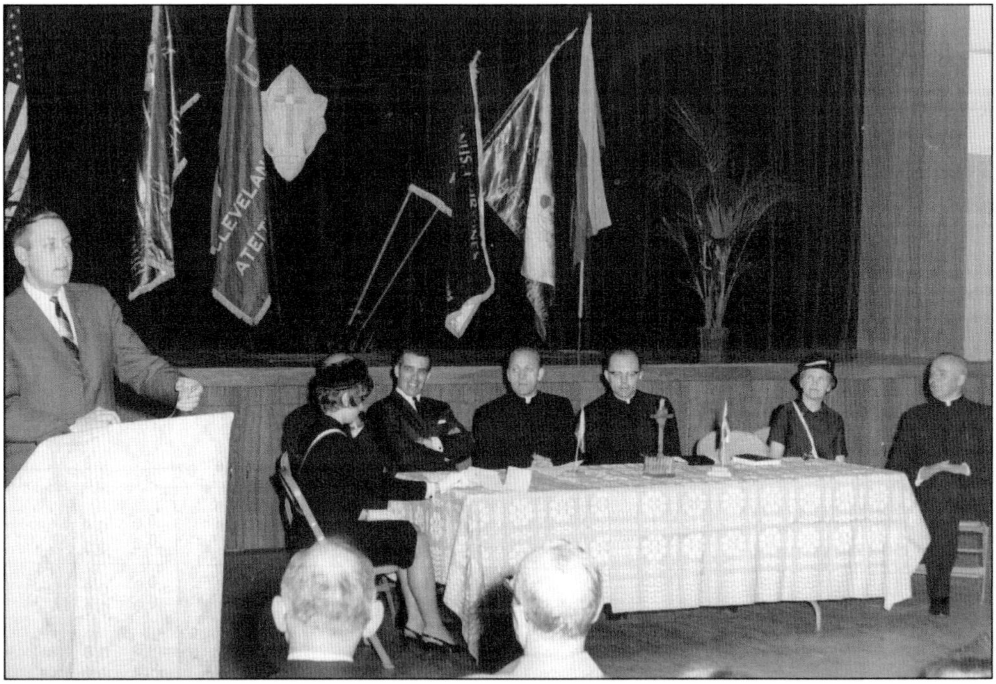

Formed in Lithuania in 1907, the Ateitis Federation, whose members are known as "Ateitininkai," is a Roman Catholic youth organization that had a significant following in Lithuanian secondary schools. It grew in size in the United States with the arrival of political refugees in the second wave. Shown here is A. Sabalis speaking at a yearly Ateitis meeting in Chicago on May 1, 1966. In the 1970s, the Ateitis Foundation established a permanent home when it purchased the onetime estate of Arthur Schmidt in Lemont, Illinois. (LRSC.)

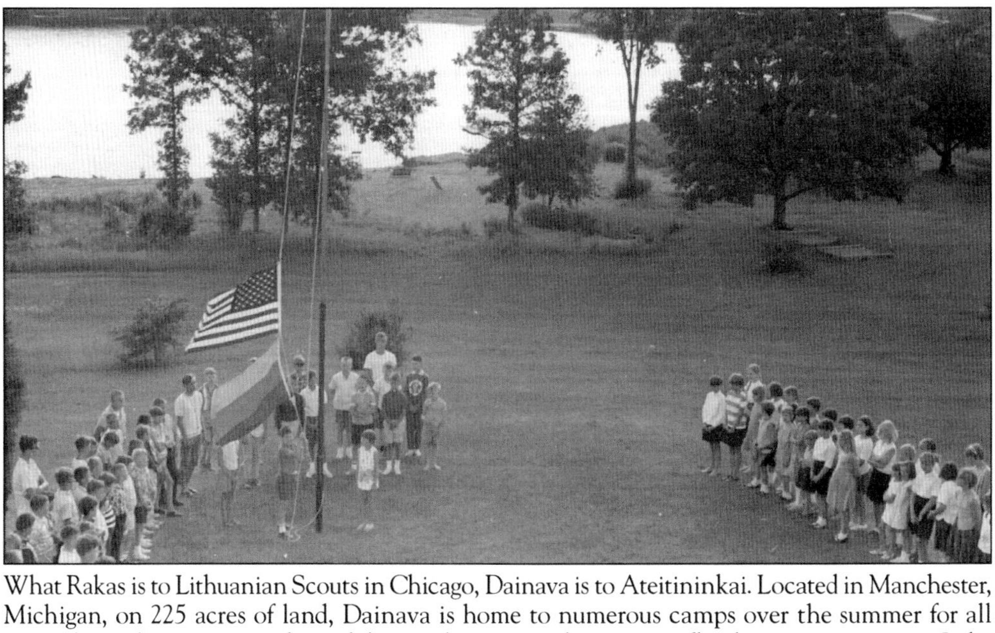

What Rakas is to Lithuanian Scouts in Chicago, Dainava is to Ateitininkai. Located in Manchester, Michigan, on 225 acres of land, Dainava is home to numerous camps over the summer for all ages. Shown here are attendees of the youth camp at the evening flag lowering ceremony. Lake Spiglys is in the background. (LRSC.)

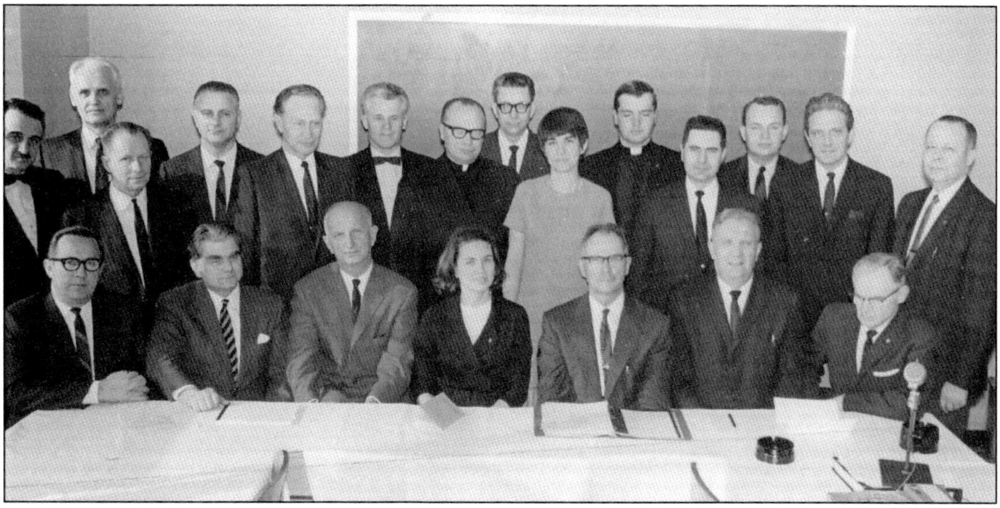

The Lithuanian American Community was founded in 1952 to support the continuation of all aspects of Lithuanian culture in the United States. It has succeeded thus far, supporting numerous Lithuanian schools throughout the country, publications in English and Lithuanian, and sporting events, among other things. All people of Lithuanian ancestry are considered members. Pictured here are Lithuanian American Community members meeting in Chicago on March 17, 1968. (LRSC.)

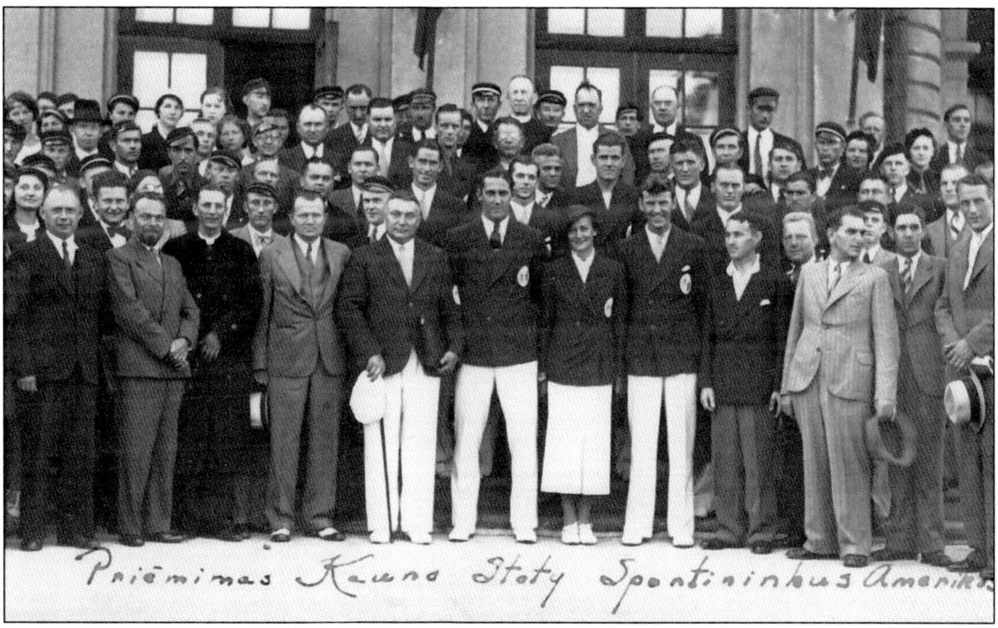

Sports have always played a central role in Lithuanian American life, particularly basketball. In 1935, a delegation of Lithuanian American athletes traveled to independent Lithuania to participate in numerous athletic events to foster good will between the immigrant community and the homeland. Many of these athletes were from Chicago. Here, they are standing in front of the Kaunas train station. The tall gentleman standing front and center of this group photograph is Felix Kriauciunas (Krause), brother of the famous athlete and coach Edward "Moose" Krause. Born and raised in the Back of the Yards, Felix went on to help lead the Lithuanian National Basketball team to championships in the 1937 and 1939 Eurobasket tournaments. (LRSC.)

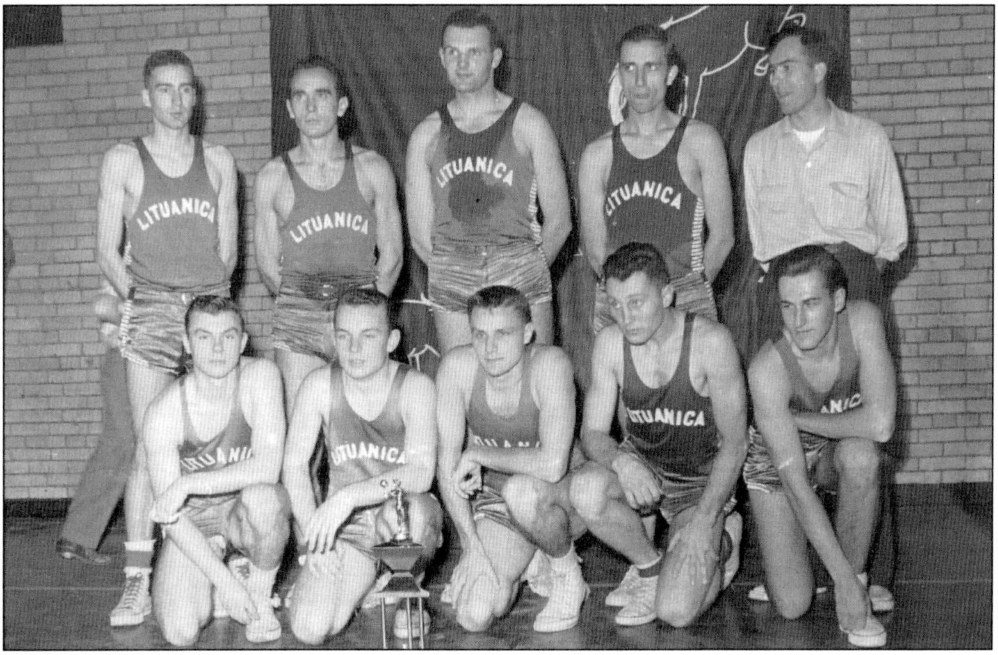

Basketball quickly became one of the most popular sports among the Lithuanian American community. At a yearly tournament hosted by the Lithuanian Athletic Union of North America, various teams throughout communities in the United States and Canada annually get a chance to compete. Chicago has routinely been represented by Lituanica, one of the most successful Lithuanian American basketball programs in North America. Shown here is a Lituanica men's team following a tournament win. (LRSC.)

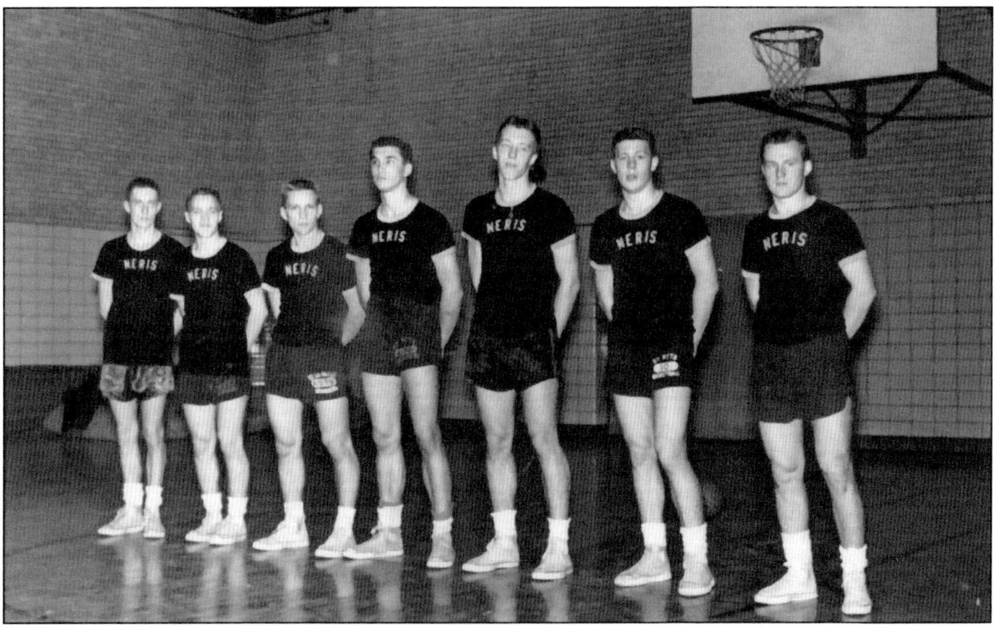

Neris is another Chicago basketball team that has competed in numerous tournaments. Pictured here is a youth team. Note that many of the players are wearing gym shorts from De LaSalle or St. Rita, both high schools with a traditionally high Lithuanian population. (LRSC.)

Five

Preserving Culture in "Little Lithuania"

Assimilating into American society while still maintaining their native language and traditions was the greatest challenge Lithuanian Americans in Chicago faced. Since Lithuania was occupied by foreign powers for most of the 20th century, they felt responsible for ensuring the preservation of their language and traditions. This preservation was done in a variety of ways.

One of the most successful and common methods of keeping Lithuanian culture in the United States alive was through Lithuanian language schools, usually held on Saturdays. In all the Lithuanian neighborhoods of Chicago, each Lithuanian parish often supported a Saturday school staffed by volunteers and nuns from the Sisters of St. Casimir. Such schools still exist in Chicago today and boast high enrollments.

Many groups in Chicago arose with the intention of preserving all things Lithuanian. They were often organized along national levels, with chapters scattered mostly throughout Lithuanian enclaves in the United States and Canada. Although each served a different purpose and represented different views, they were all united by their desire for Lithuanian independence. Taking this into consideration, social groups often were involved in political matters, largely that of promoting Lithuanian independence. As the home of the largest number of Lithuanians outside the country itself, Chicago became the center of cultural activity where many significant Lithuanian social groups had their headquarters and strongest following. The activity in the area resulted in a thriving Lithuanian social and cultural scene.

For much of the 20th century, one could grow up in one of Chicago's Lithuanian neighborhoods quite insulated from the rest of the city. Lithuanians frequented their own taverns, shops, and restaurants and attended Lithuanian operas and comedy shows. In so doing, they managed to create a "Little Lithuania" in Chicago.

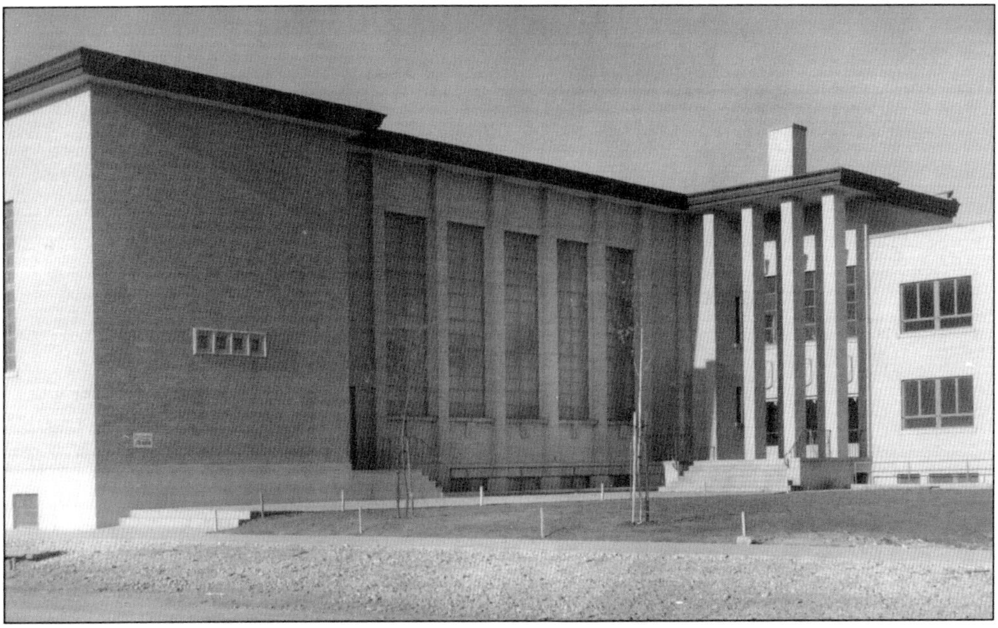

Built by immigrants of the second wave in the mid-1950s, the Lithuanian Youth Center at 5620 South Claremont Avenue is home to numerous culturally significant Lithuanian institutions, including a Lithuanian language school, which holds classes during the school year on Saturdays. The building is shown here in the later stages of construction prior to opening. (LRSC.)

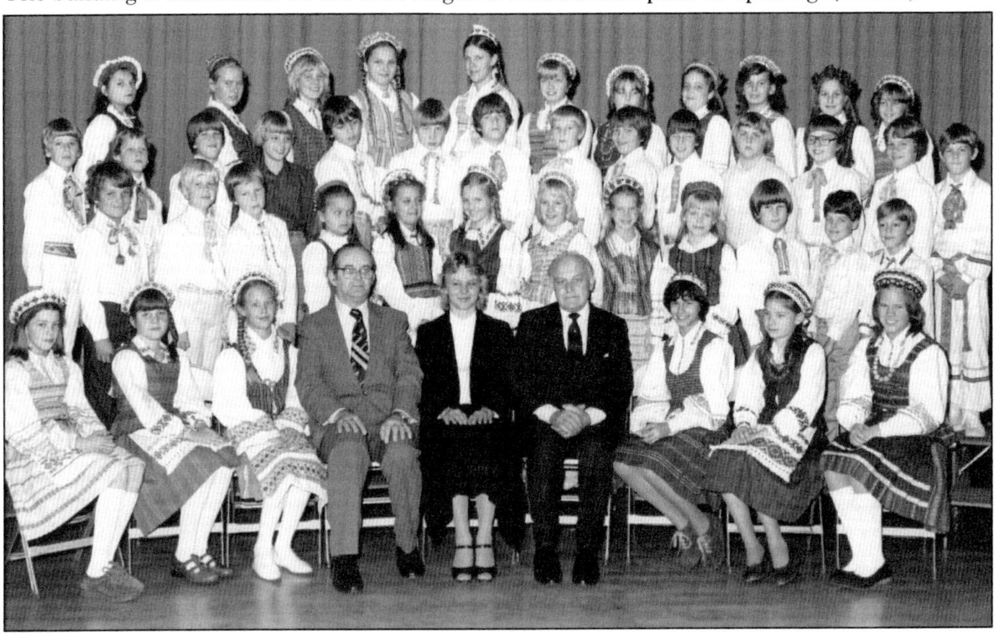

Students attending Lithuanian schools typically take courses in Lithuanian grammar, literature, and history while also participating in traditional folk singing and dancing. Here, the Donelaitis Lithuanian School poses for a group photograph before attending the Lithuanian Song Festival on July 3, 1983, at the University of Illinois at Chicago. The three adults seated in the front row are, from left to right, musician Vytautas Gutauskas, music teacher Audra Alekna, and director of the school Julius Sirka. (LRSC.)

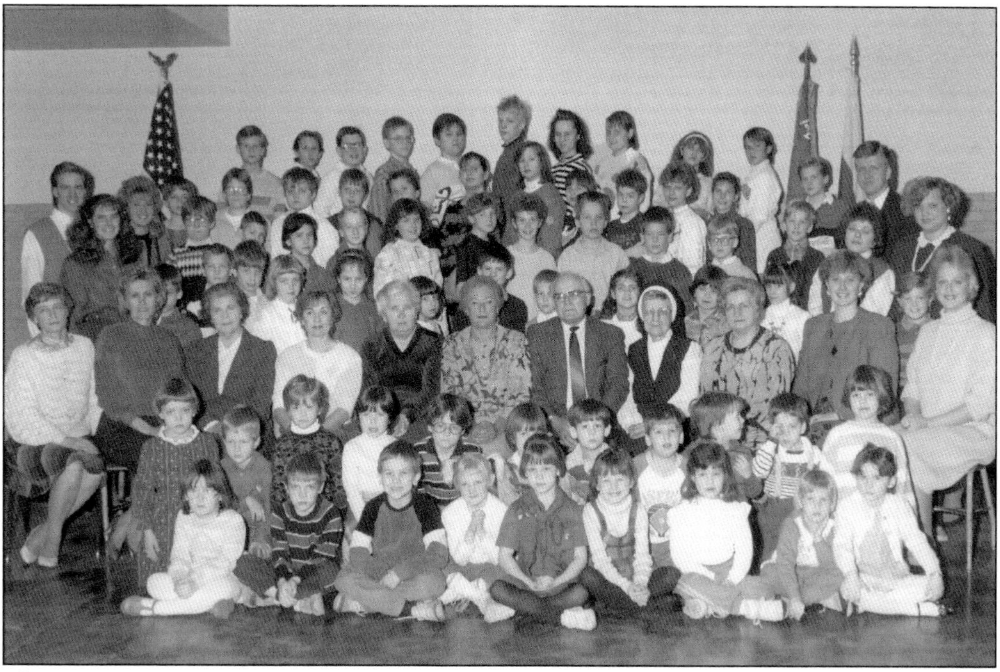

The pupils at Donelaitis Lithuanian School were fortunate to have a knowledgeable staff, shown here in the late 1980s along with students. Classes were held at McKay Public School, located at 6901 South Fairfield Avenue in the Marquette Park neighborhood. Teachers at Lithuanian schools in Chicago were often volunteers consisting of parents and dedicated Lithuanians. (Nijole Riskus-Gierstikas.)

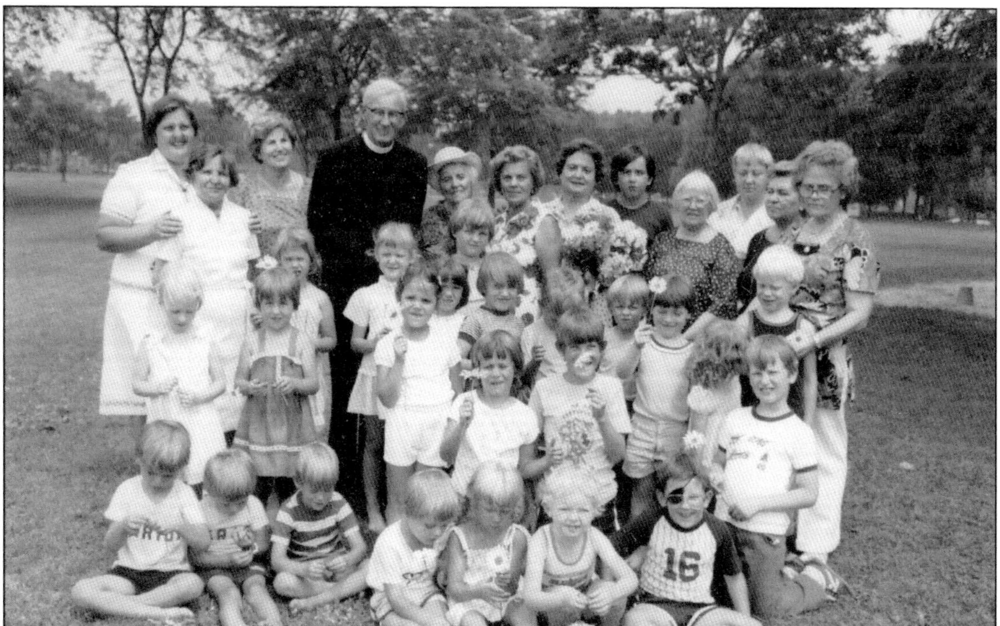

Eager to have them learn Lithuanian, many parents enrolled their children in some type of Lithuanian program at a young age. A popular summer day care, Aikstele was organized by a number of volunteers, including Father Prunskis, standing here in black. (Nijole Riskus-Gierstikas.)

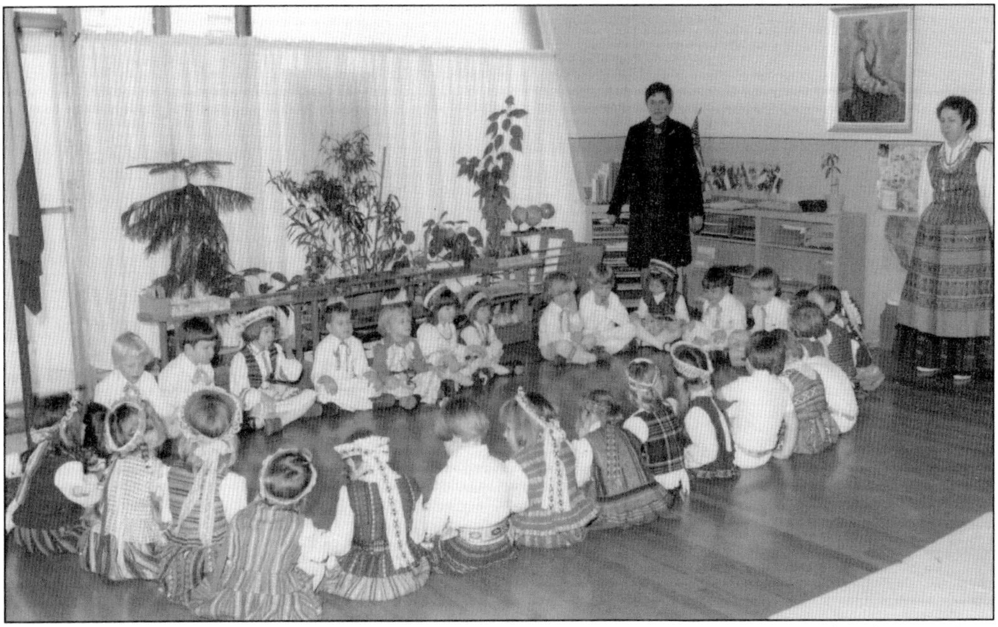

Another example of Lithuanian early childhood education was a Montessori school located on Sixty-ninth Street across from Holy Cross Hospital. Presiding over the children and dressed in Lithuanian national costumes are Dana Dirvonis (left) and a Mrs. Podziunas. The school later relocated to the Lithuanian World Center in Lemont, Illinois. (Nijole Riskus-Gierstikas.)

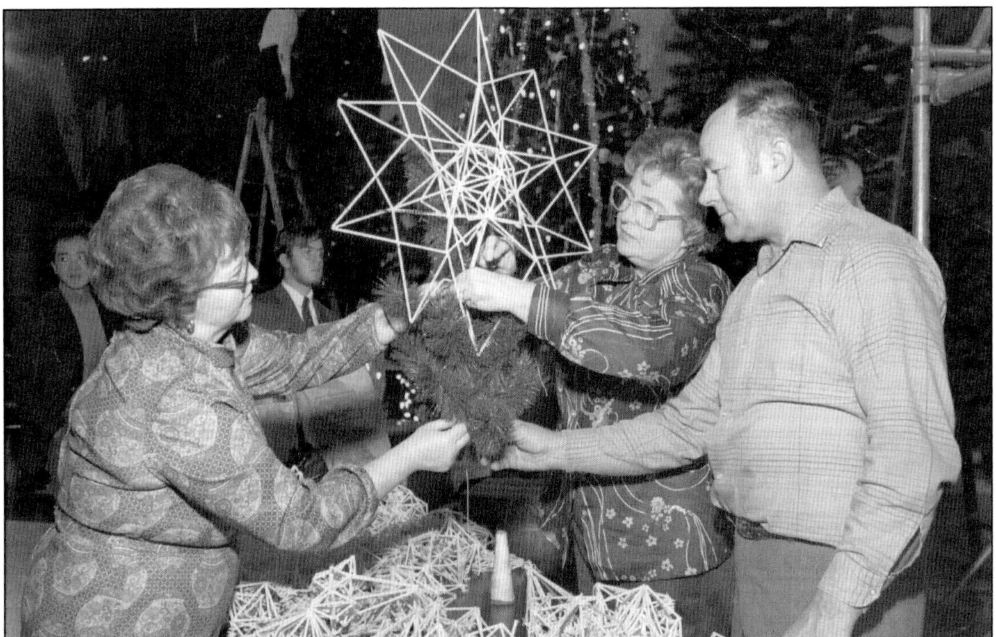

Many Chicagoans will fondly recall the Museum of Science and Industry's annual Christmas Around the World festival, which started in 1942 as a tribute to the allies of the United States. Preparing traditional straw ornaments for the 1972 display's Lithuanian tree are, from left to right, Wanda Radavich, Virginia Kentra, and Ray Kentra. The festival also included in its events a performance by a Lithuanian folk dancing group. (LRSC.)

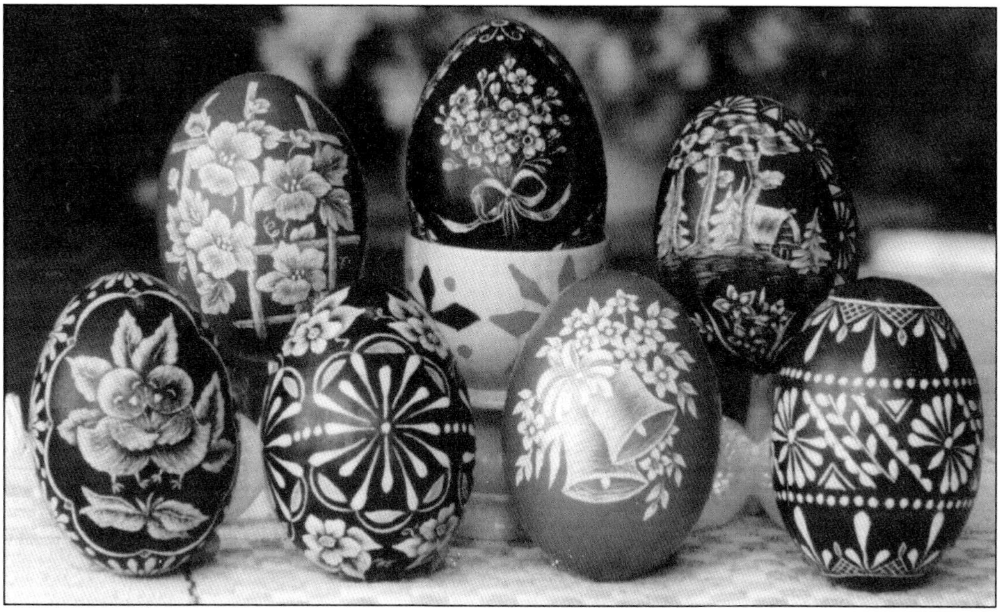

To Lithuanians, nothing says Easter more than traditionally decorated eggs. The sampling shown here demonstrates the many intricate methods and patterns used in decorating. (LRSC.)

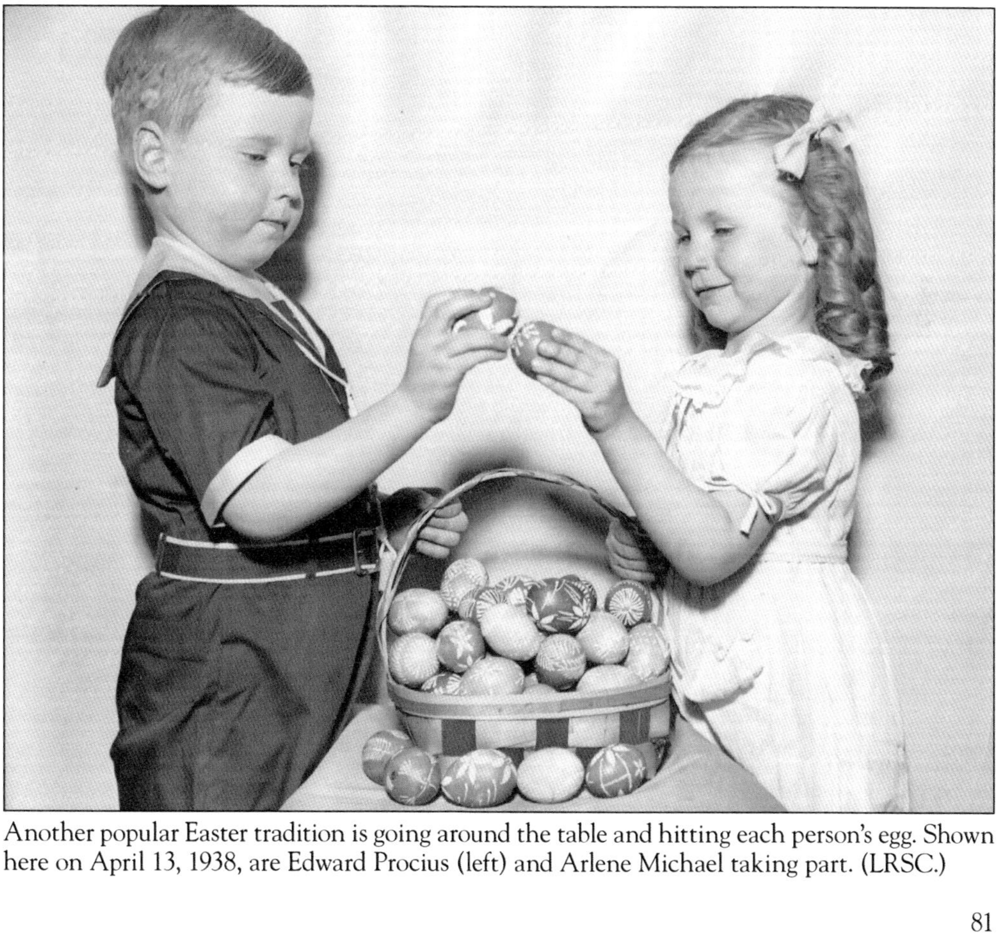

Another popular Easter tradition is going around the table and hitting each person's egg. Shown here on April 13, 1938, are Edward Procius (left) and Arlene Michael taking part. (LRSC.)

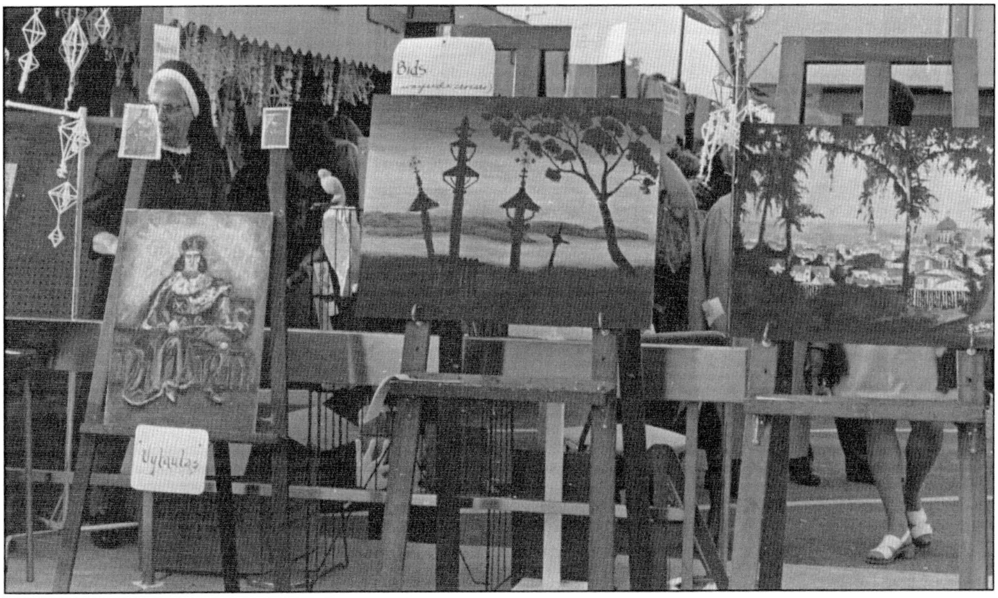

Holidays and festivals were an important way of perpetuating Lithuanian culture in Chicago. The paintings in this image were done by a student from Maria High School and depict traditional Lithuanian rulers and scenes. Festivals like this one, sponsored by the Talman Federal Savings and Loan Association, provided excellent opportunities for Lithuanians to get together. (SSC.)

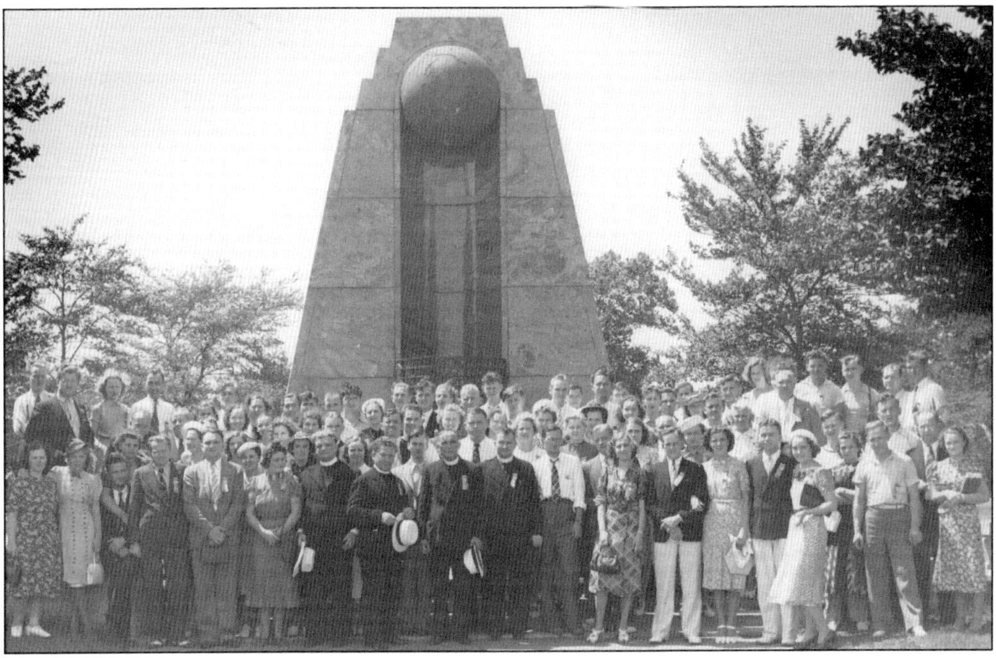

One of the oldest Lithuanian American organizations is the Knights of Lithuania, formed in 1913. Consisting of Roman Catholics of Lithuanian ancestry, the Knights of Lithuania have worked toward preserving Lithuanian culture in the United States for more than a century. Chicago has hosted the national convention on numerous occasions. Pictured here in August 1938 are participants of the 26th National Convention standing in front of the monument to Lithuanian aviators Steponas Darius and Stasys Girenas in Marquette Park. (LRSC.)

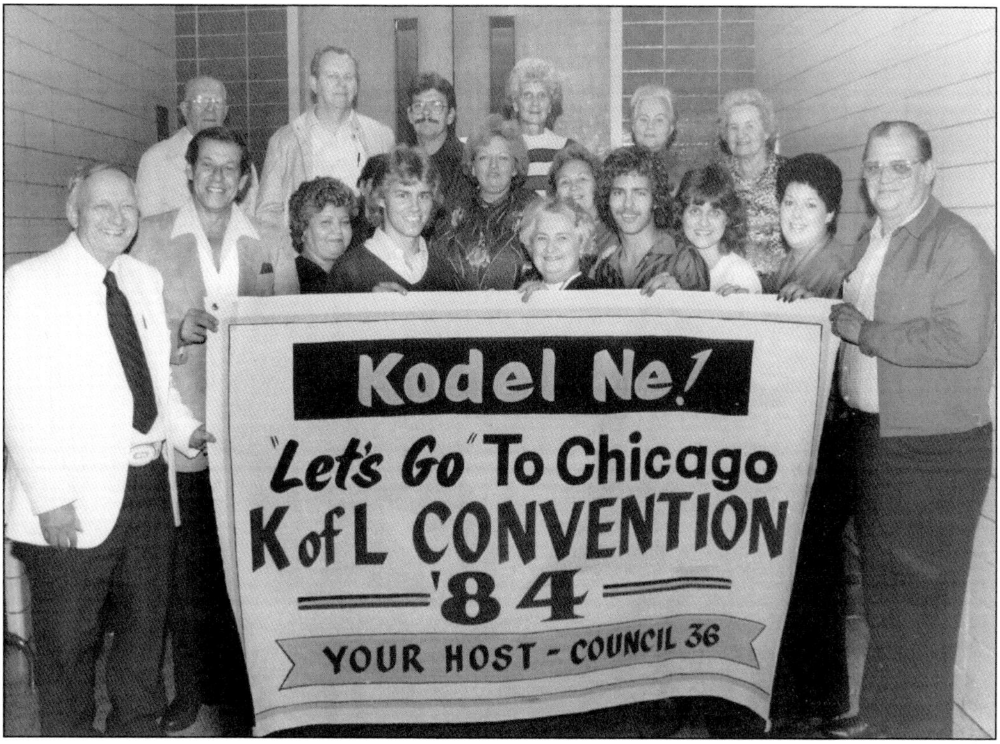

Chicago has been home to many active Knights of Lithuania councils for quite some time. Here, members of Council 36 in Brighton Park successfully lobby to host the 71st National Convention in 1984. (LRSC.)

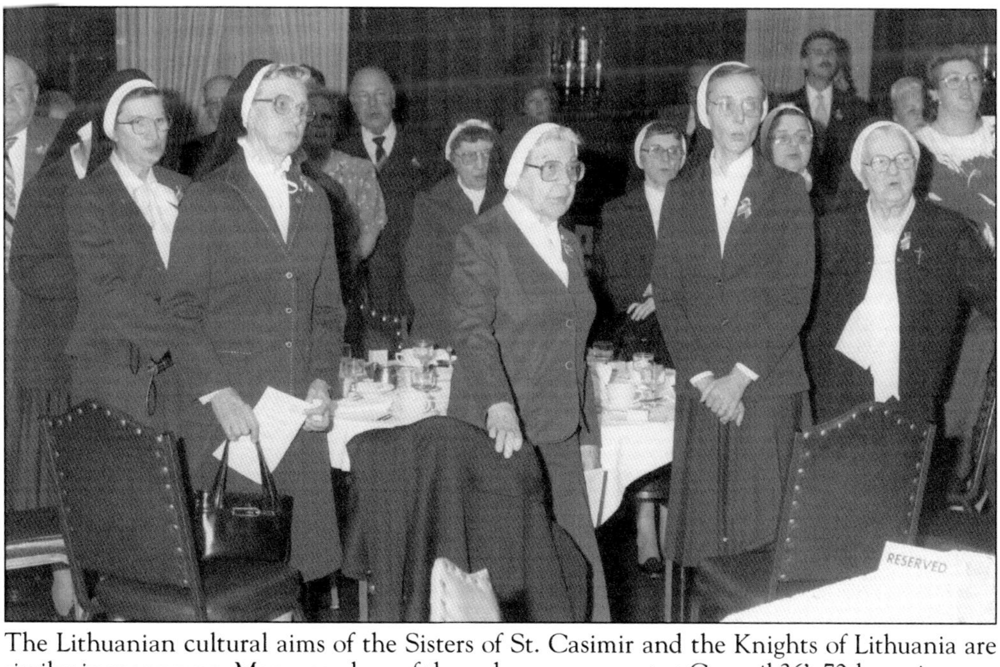

The Lithuanian cultural aims of the Sisters of St. Casimir and the Knights of Lithuania are similar in many ways. Many members of the order were present at Council 36's 70th anniversary banquet in 1982. (LRSC.)

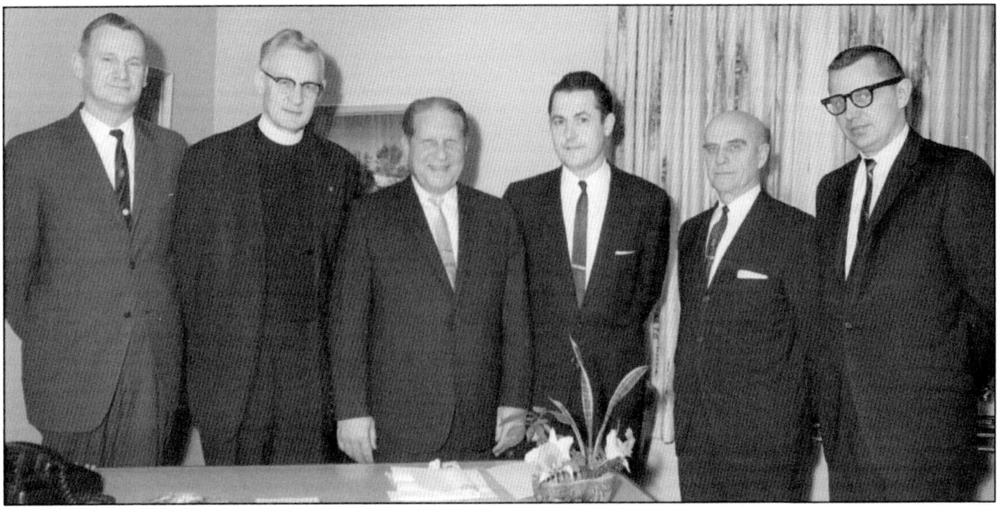

Many organizations in Chicago achieved a large degree of success soliciting donations for Lithuanian activities in Chicago. Founded on March 14, 1962, the Lithuanian Foundation invests donations with the intention of using only the gains to support various causes. Since its creation, it has awarded over $16 million in the name of Lithuanian culture. At this March 23 meeting in the early 1960s, members of the group meet with Lt. Gov. Samuel H. Shapiro to request tax-exempt status. From left to right are Dr. B. Poskus, Fr. Dr. J. Prunskis, Lt. Gov. Samuel H. Shapiro, Dr. A. Razma, A. Reklaitis, and A. Kezelis. (LRSC.)

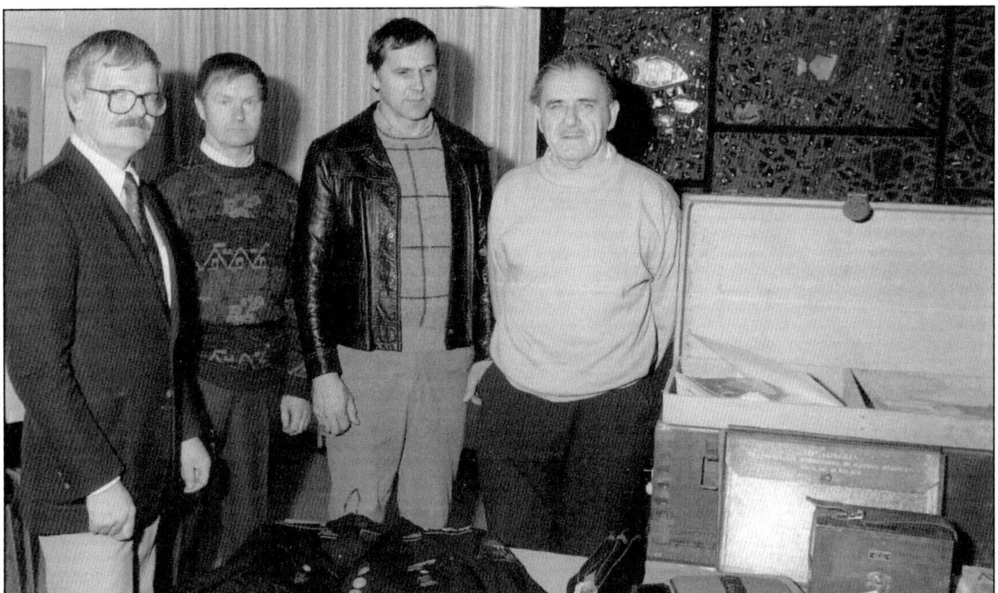

Chicago, with the largest Lithuanian population abroad, is home to numerous archives and libraries. One of the largest is at the Balzekas Museum of Lithuanian Culture, located at 6500 South Pulaski Road close to the Marquette Park neighborhood. Founded in 1966 by owner Stanley Balzekas Jr., the museum boasts numerous exhibits as well as genealogy and archival departments. It also has an extensive collection of artifacts related to aviators Steponas Darius and Stasys Girenas. Standing here with the collection are members of the Darius-Girenas Anniversary Committee. From left to right are Val Ramonis, Jonas Juknius, Edvardas Slusnys, and Gediminas Janula. (LRSC.)

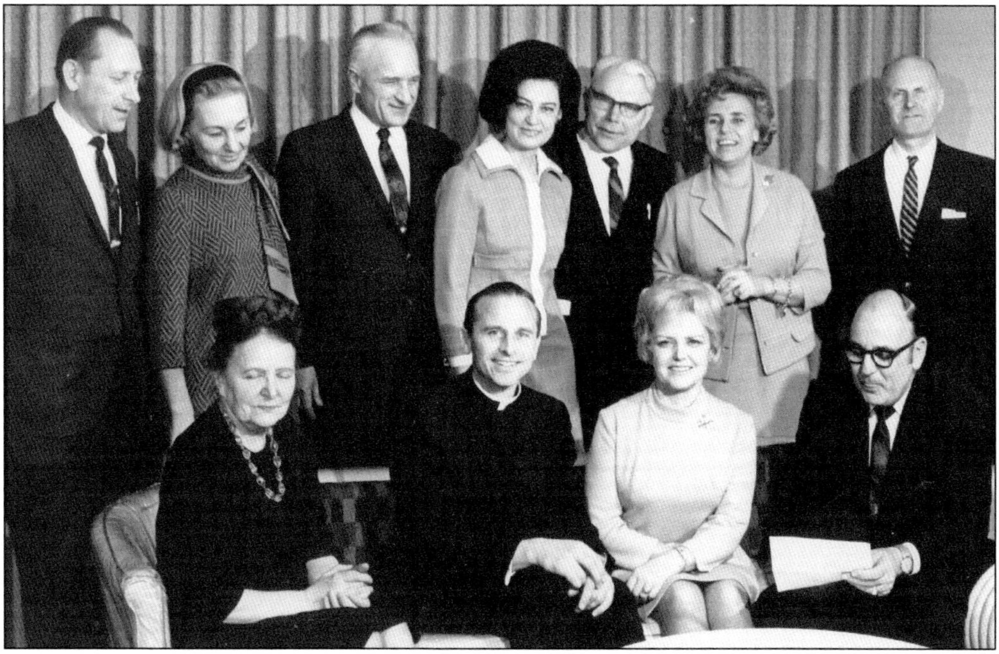

Housed in the Lithuanian Youth Center are the Lithuanian Photo Archives. Shown here are members of the committee that organized the collection, from left to right, (seated) A. Rugyte, Fr. A. Kezys, B. Briediene, and John Evans; (standing) B. Shotas, E. Vilutiene, a Mr. Kancevicius, N. Remiene, J. Janusaitis, J. Grybauskiene, and A. Dzirvonas. (LRSC.)

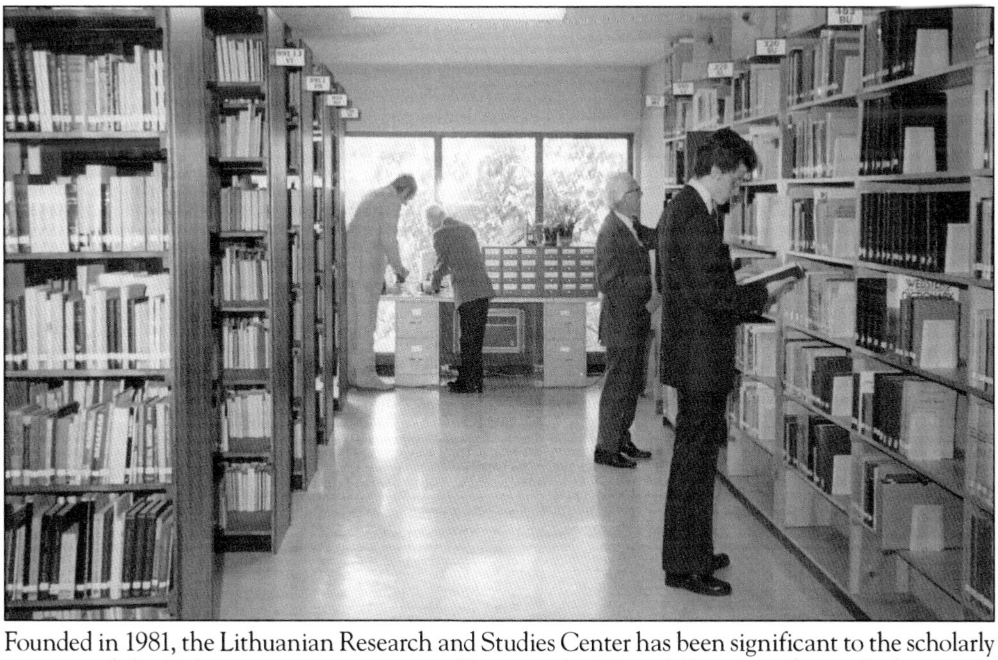

Founded in 1981, the Lithuanian Research and Studies Center has been significant to the scholarly pursuits of the Lithuanian community in Chicago, the United States, and even Lithuania. It maintains numerous collections, included the aforementioned Lithuanian Photo Archives. Shown here are scholars perusing its extensive collections. To date, the center has published more than 50 books on Lithuanian topics. (LRSC.)

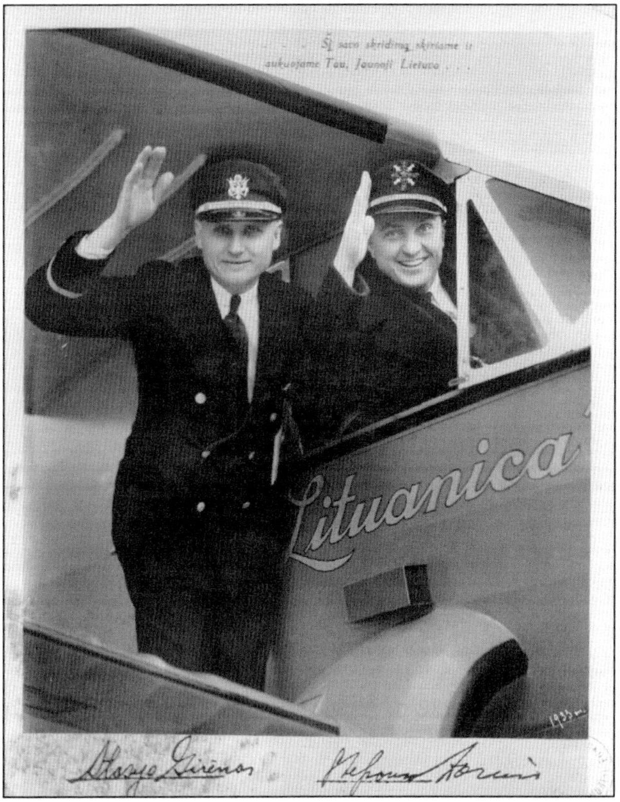

The attempted transatlantic crossing of Lithuanian aviators Steponas Darius and Stasys Girenas was an event significant to Lithuanians around the world. Both men were born in Lithuania and emigrated to Chicago. Their plane *Lituanica* was purchased and modified with funds collected from the Lithuanian American community. Shown here are Lithuanian Chicagoans Stasys Girenas (left) and Steponas Darius (right) prior to their flight. (LRSC.)

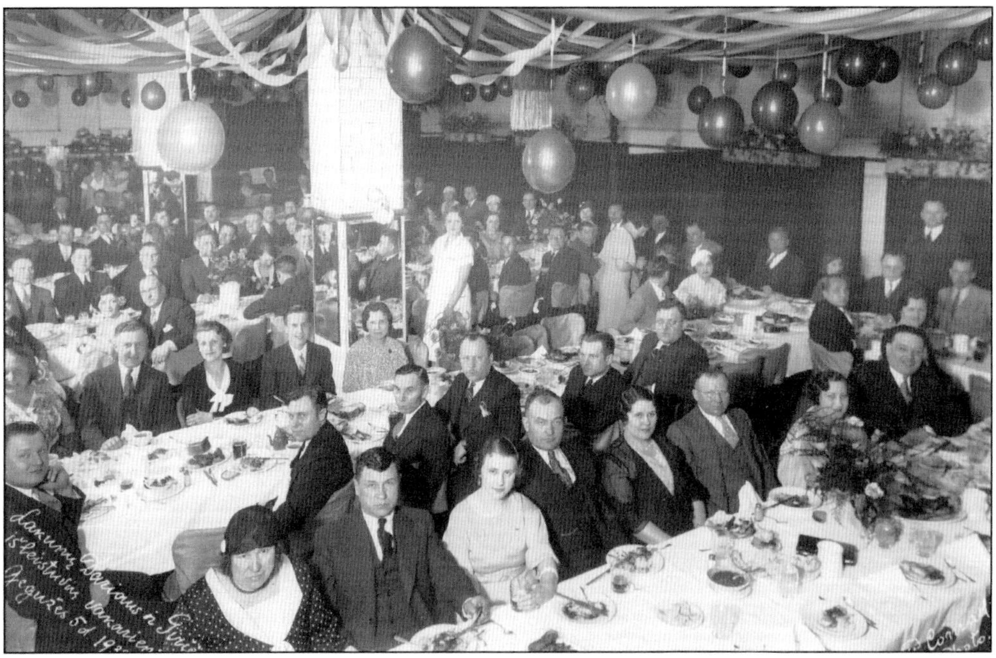

Chicago's Lithuanians must have felt particular civic pride that Stasys Girenas and Steponas Darius lived in their city. Gathered here are Lithuanians attending a going away banquet for the pilots on May 5, 1933, in Chicago. (LRSC.)

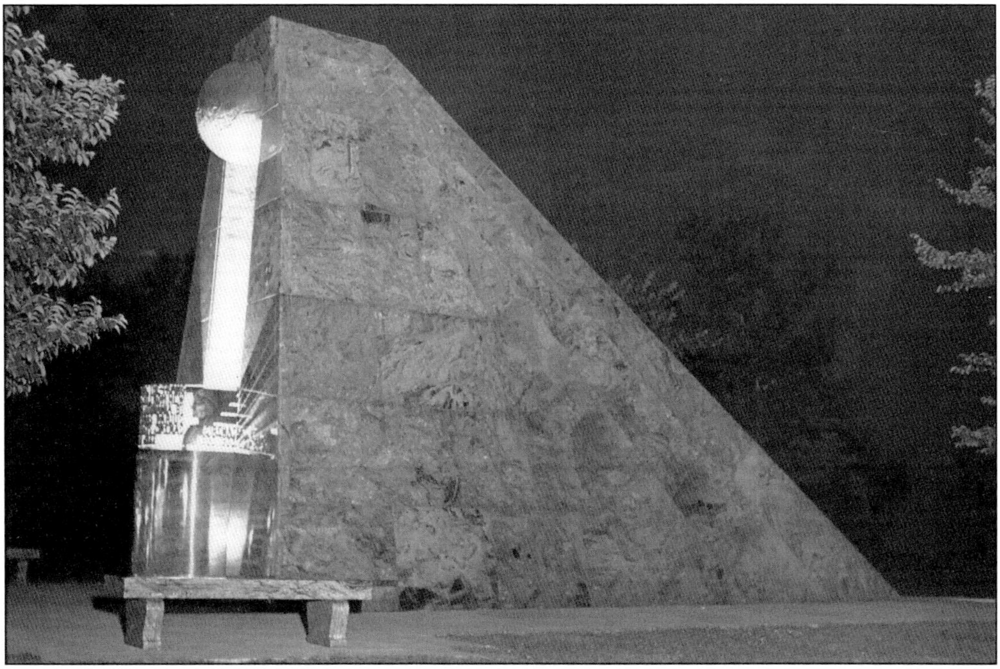

In July 1933, over Germany, the plane in which Darius and Girenas were flying crashed, killing both pilots. Lithuanians around the world were devastated. In honor of the aviators, the Lithuanian community of Chicago raised funds to construct a monument. More than 40,000 people were in attendance at its dedication in July 1935. It is located west of California Avenue and south of West Sixty-seventh Street. Built in the Art Deco style, the monument is shown here lit up at night. (LRSC.)

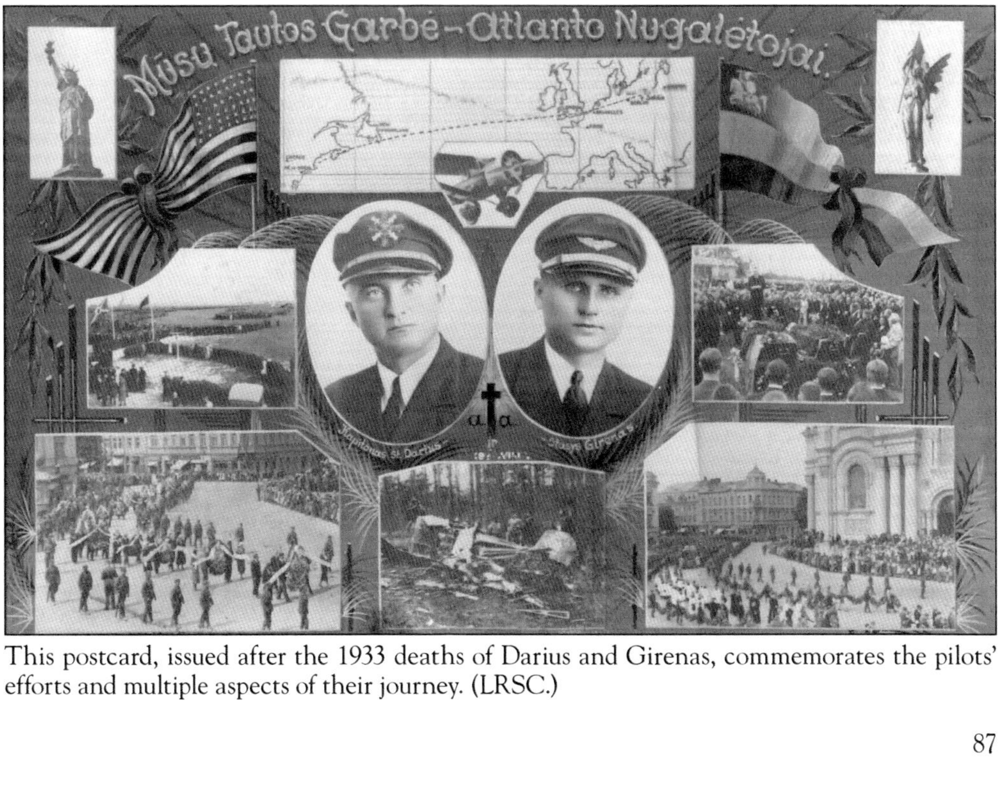

This postcard, issued after the 1933 deaths of Darius and Girenas, commemorates the pilots' efforts and multiple aspects of their journey. (LRSC.)

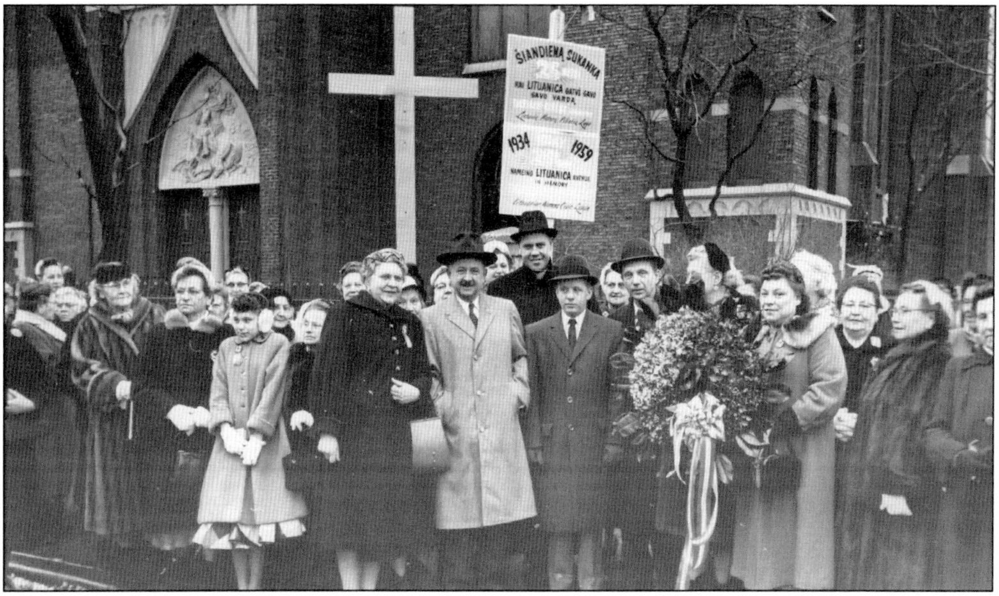

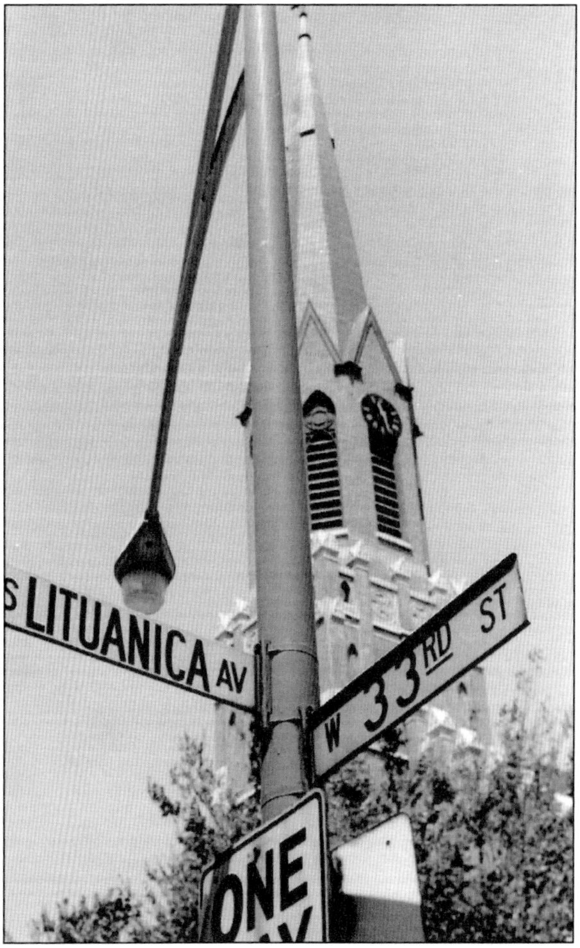

The attempted flight and subsequent death of Darius and Girenas was a culturally significant event to Chicago's Lithuanians. In 1959, the efforts of the Lithuanian Women's Civic League resulted in the naming of Lituanica Avenue. Many braved the cold to attend the ceremony held 25 years after the flight. (LRSC.)

St. George in Bridgeport, the first Lithuanian church in Chicago, was located at Thirty-third Street and Lituanica Avenue. (Eugenijus Butenas.)

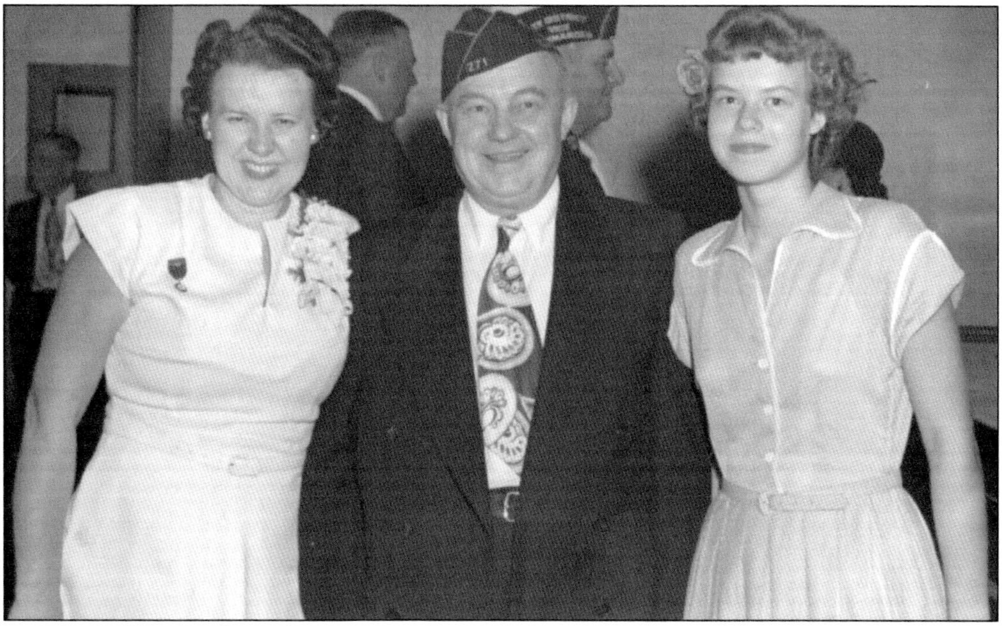

Another tribute to the Lithuanian aviators was the creation of the Darius-Girenas American Legion Post No. 271. Consisting of Lithuanian American veterans, numerous social events hosted by the group are fondly recalled by Lithuanians in Chicago. On July 17, 1949, Antoinette Ezerski was installed as the post chaplain. Photographed are Antoinette Ezerksi (left), her husband, Joseph (center), and their daughter, Loretta. (Michael and Loretta Ezerski.)

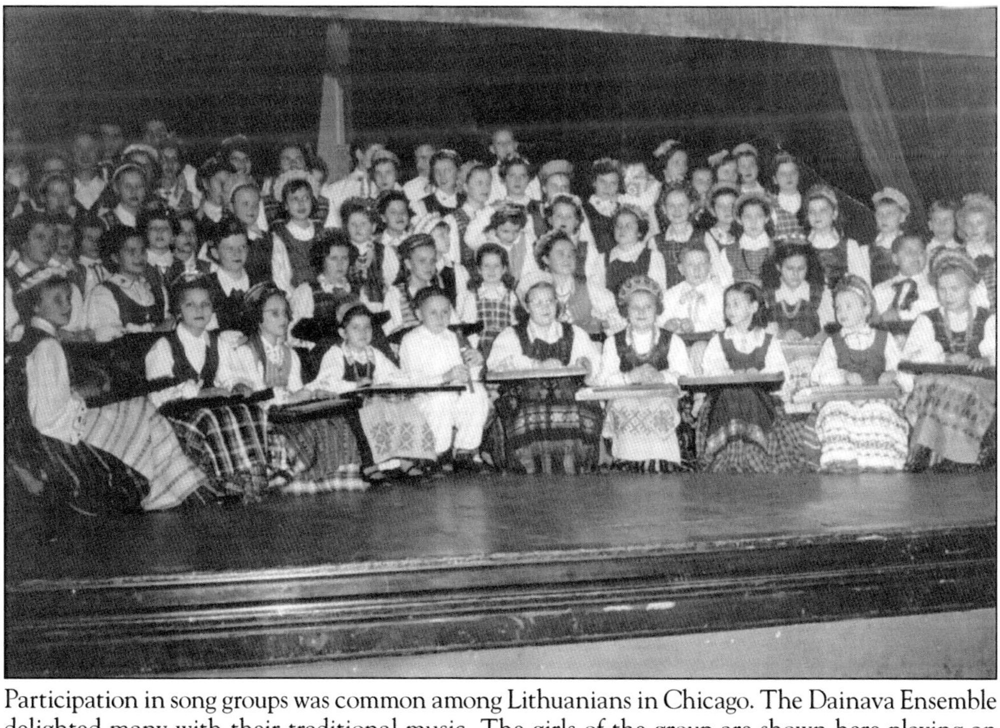

Participation in song groups was common among Lithuanians in Chicago. The Dainava Ensemble delighted many with their traditional music. The girls of the group are shown here playing an ancient Lithuanian instrument known as the *kankles*. (Nijole Riskus-Gierstikas.)

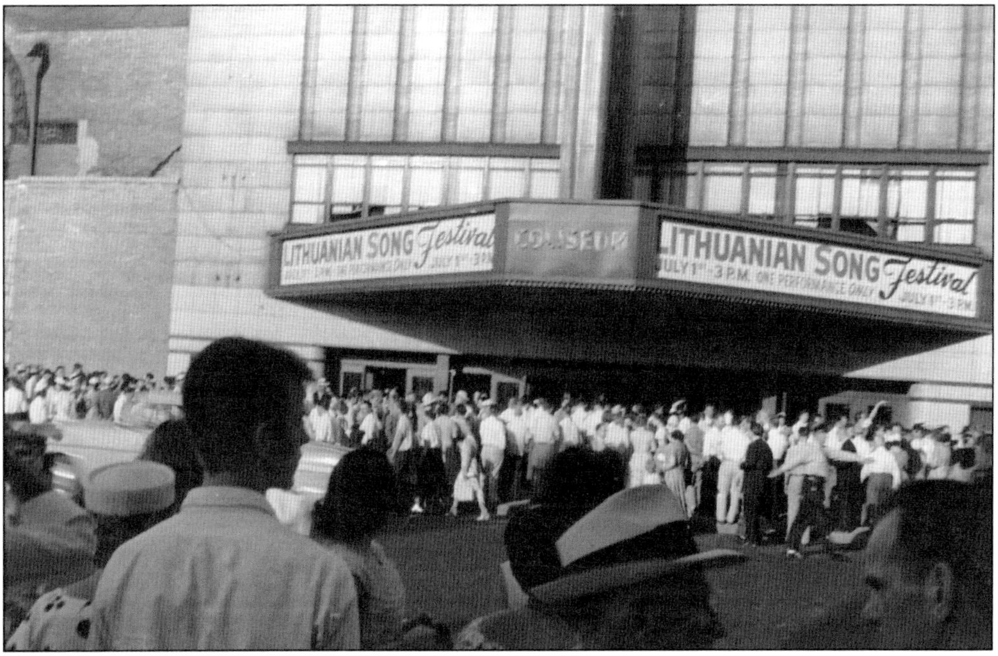

Every four or more years, the Lithuanian communities in the United States and Canada host the Lithuanian Song Festival. To date, great numbers of Lithuanian Americans have taken part in the event or attended it. The first one in the United States was held at the Chicago Coliseum on July 1, 1956. Shown here are festivalgoers underneath the marquee of the stadium. (LRSC.)

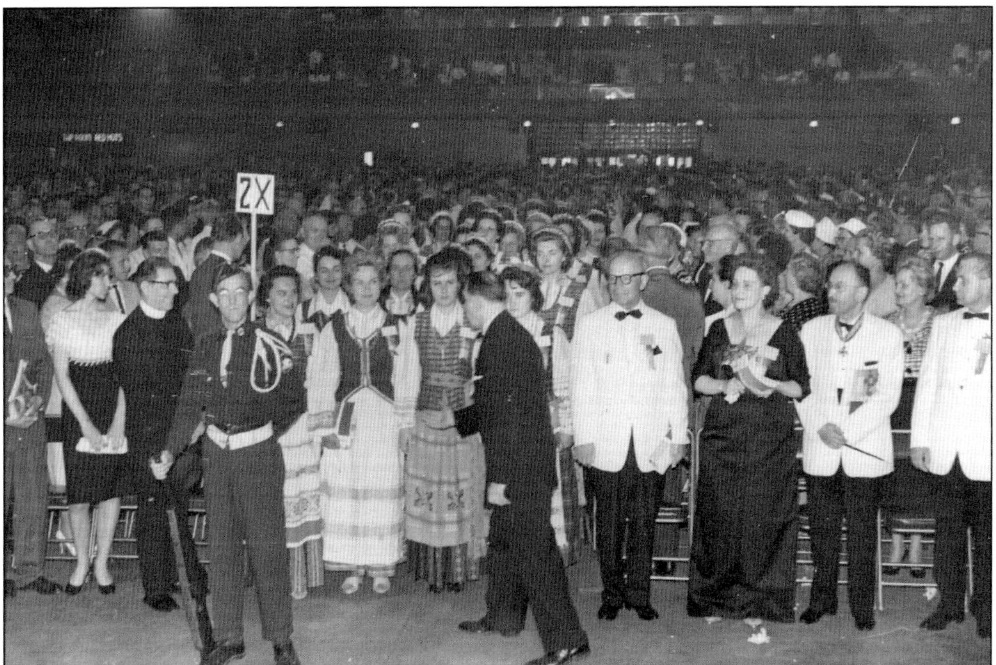

The 1956 Lithuanian Song Festival was a great success, as can be seen from the vast crowd of people in attendance. Chicago continued to host the event many more times, albeit at a different venue. (LRSC.)

To many, folk dancing was part of the Lithuanian American experience. Many schools and organizations sponsored groups. Ramute Juodkaite (left) and Danguole Prismantaite from Holy Cross in the Back of the Yards demonstrate their talents in this image taken at the International Amphitheater during the Lithuanian Dance Festival on June 10, 1957. (LRSC.)

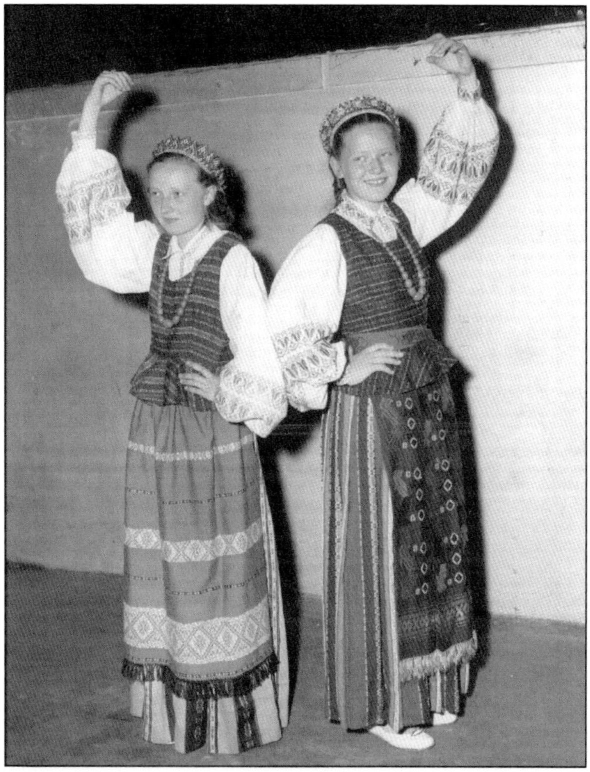

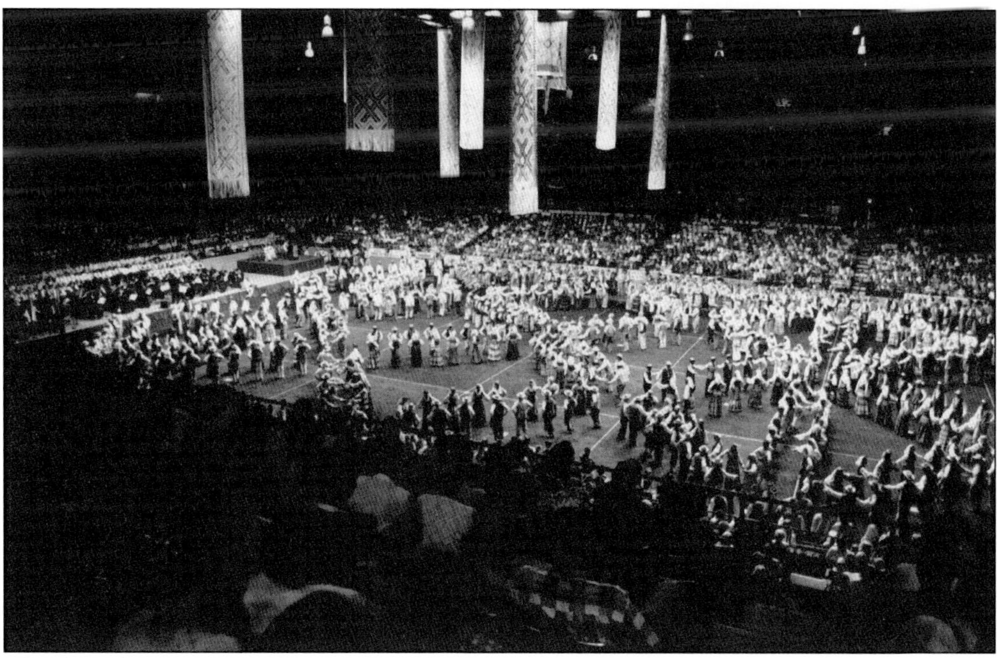

Like the Lithuanian Song Festival, the Lithuanian Dance Festival is held approximately every four years in various cities with a significant Lithuanian presence in the United States and Canada. Lithuanian folk dancing often utilizes large numbers of dancers to form geometric patterns, as shown at this dance festival in Chicago, date unknown. (LRSC.)

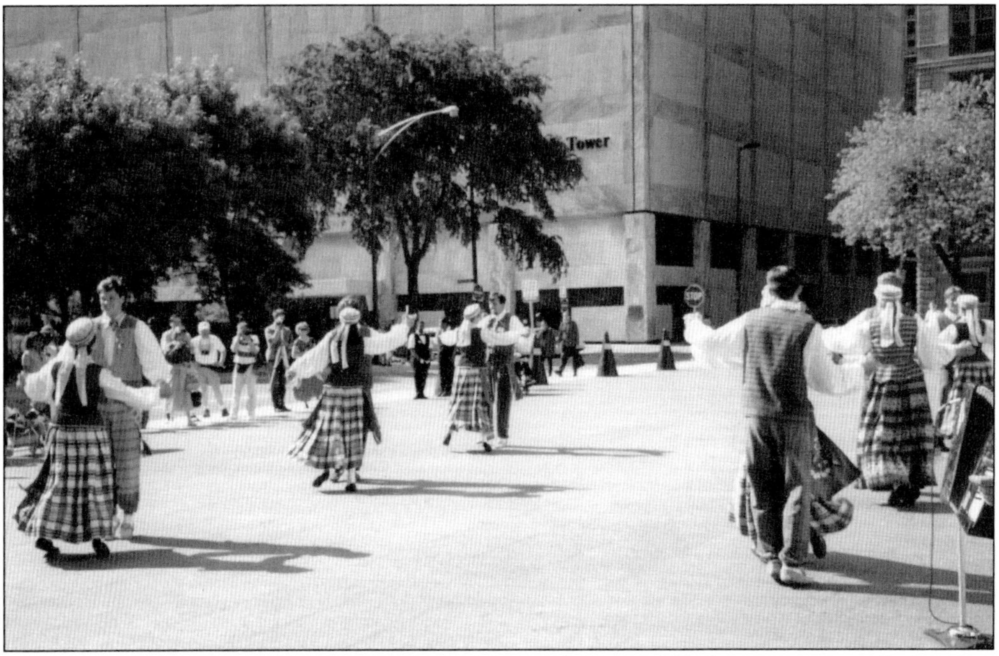

Chicago and its surrounding area is home to many Lithuanian folk dance groups, including one sponsored by the Knights of Lithuania known as Vyciai. Here, the group performs in front of the Museum of Contemporary Art on June 21, 1997. Other groups include Gija, Grandis, Letunas, Spindulys, and Suktinis. (LRSC.)

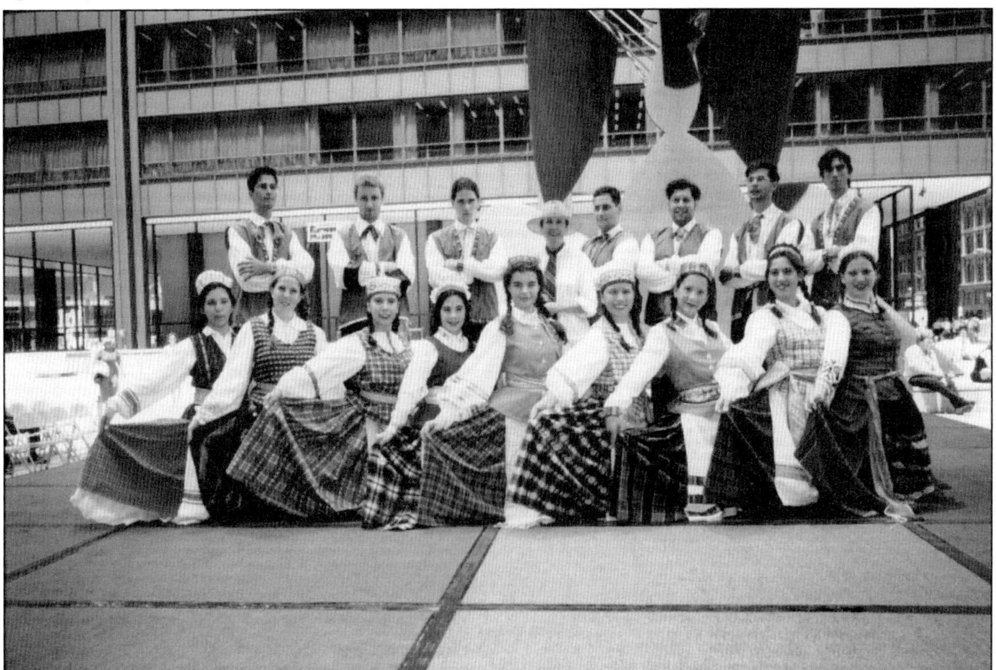

The success of numerous Lithuanian dance festivals in Chicago has led to the participation of dance groups from all around the world. Pictured here in Daley Plaza on July 10, 1996, are dancers from Brazil and Argentina. (LRSC.)

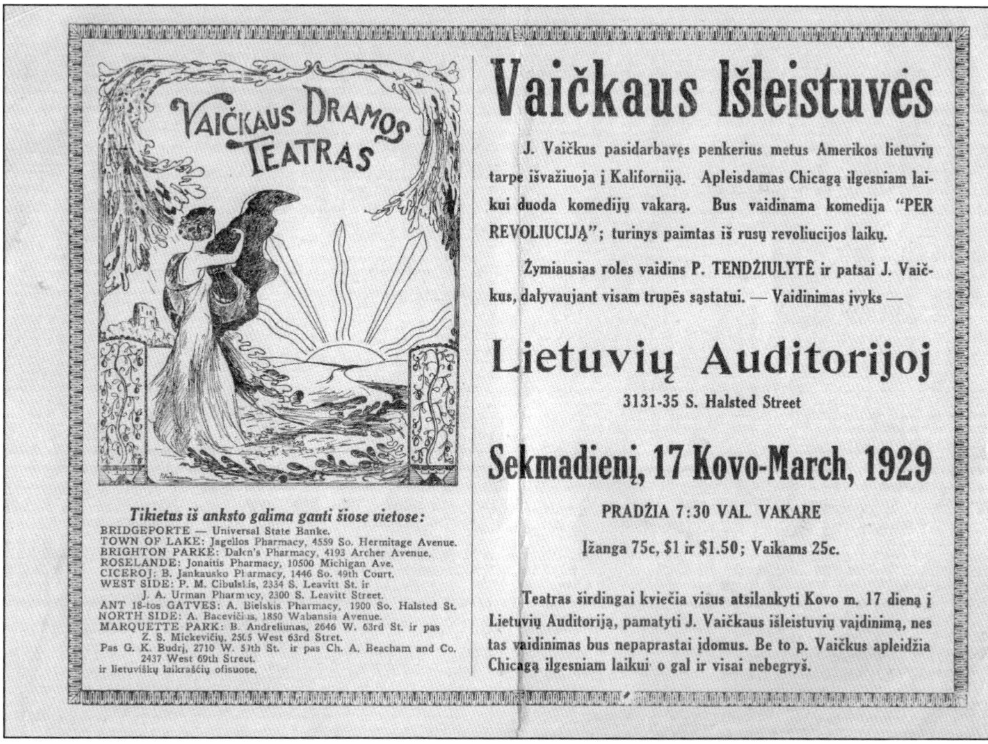

Aside from traditional Lithuanian entertainment, the community in Chicago has always enjoyed the diverse talents of its members. This poster advertises a drama, featuring actress P. Tendiulyte, held on Sunday, March 17, 1929, at Chicago Lithuanian Auditorium in Bridgeport. (LRSC.)

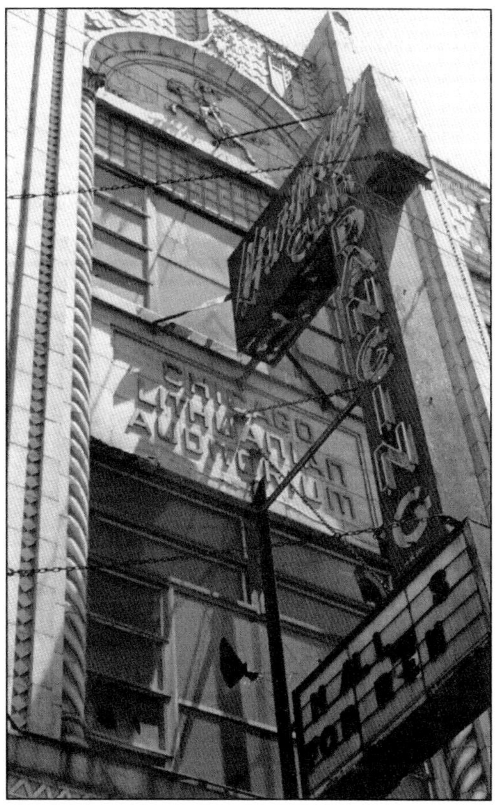

Bridgeport's Chicago Lithuanian Auditorium at 3133 South Halsted Street was a well-known and popular venue for entertainment. For many years, the location hosted some sort of Lithuanian cultural activity nearly every night of the week. Although no longer in use by the community, the name and Lithuanian symbols emblazoned on the facade serve as reminders of the area's large Lithuanian presence. (LRSC.)

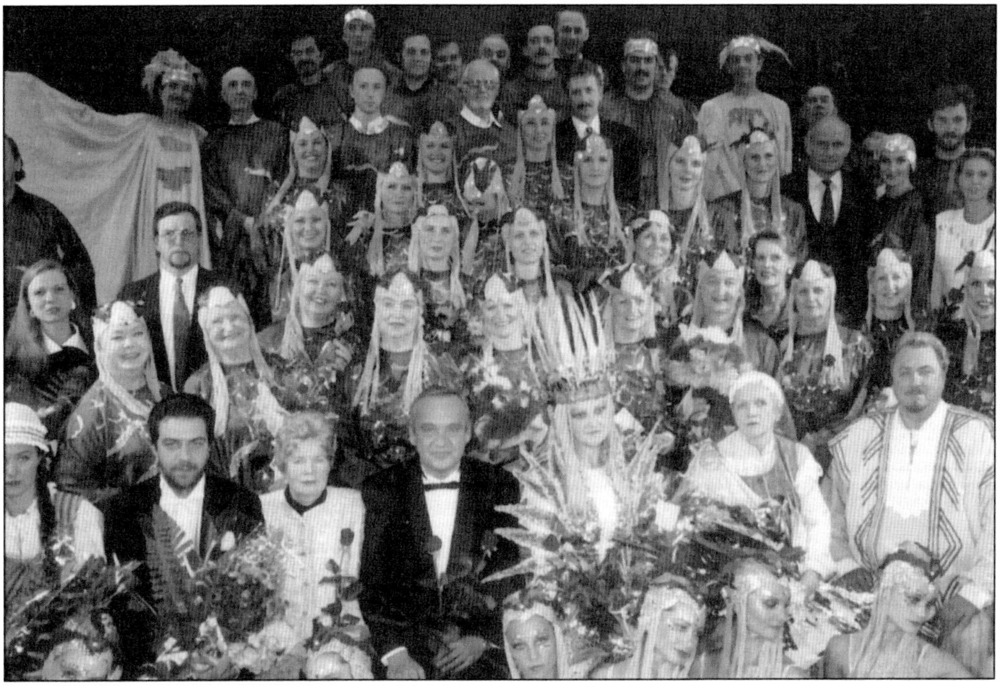

On March 21, 1966, a total of 1,500 people attended the Lithuanian Opera Company of Chicago's presentation of *LaTraviata*. Originating as a men's chorus in the early 1950s, the company stages elaborate performances with production costs sometimes running as high as $45,000. Shown above is the cast for a performance in the early 2000s. (Grazina Biciunas-Santoski.)

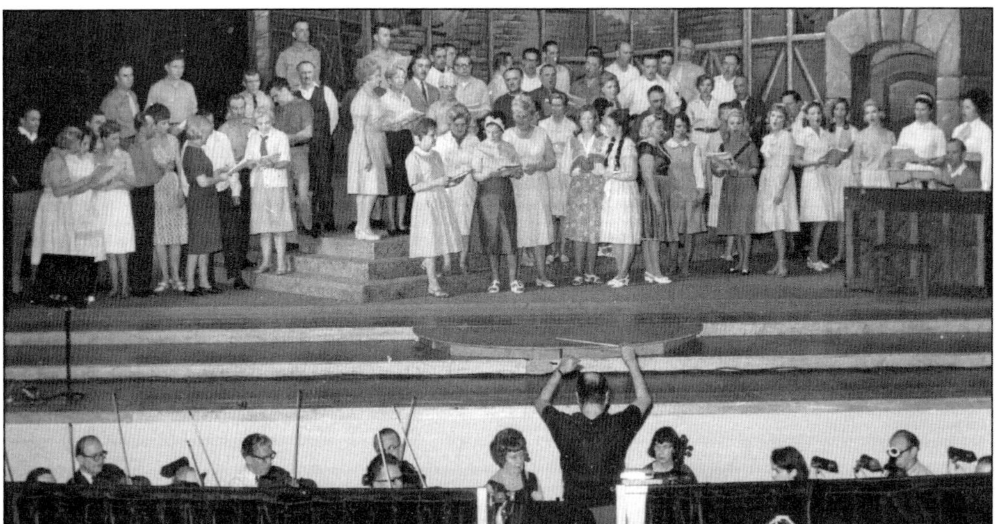

The Lithuanian Opera Company of Chicago has demonstrated its merits by staging many varied productions since its founding and catering performances to its Lithuanian audience exceptionally well. Shown here at Maria High School in the Marquette Park neighborhood is the company performing the opera *Dana* by Julius Gaidelis about life in displaced person camps throughout Europe after World War II. Most Lithuanian immigrants of the second wave lived through such an experience themselves and likely made up a majority of the audience in this picture. (Grazina Biciunas-Santoski.)

Many attempts were made among the Lithuanian community in Chicago to support artists in Soviet-occupied Lithuania. As restrictions lessened, talented performers such as Gintare Jautakaite were able to come to the United States and perform. This poster advertises the artist's performance at the Lithuanian Youth Center on May 22, 1988. (LRSC.)

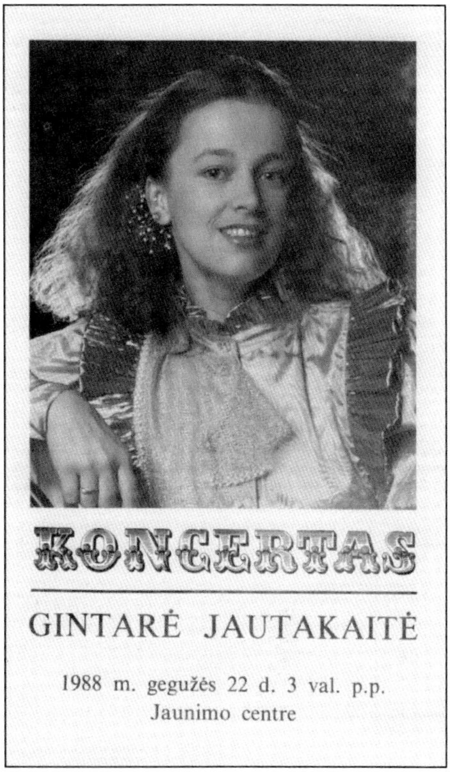

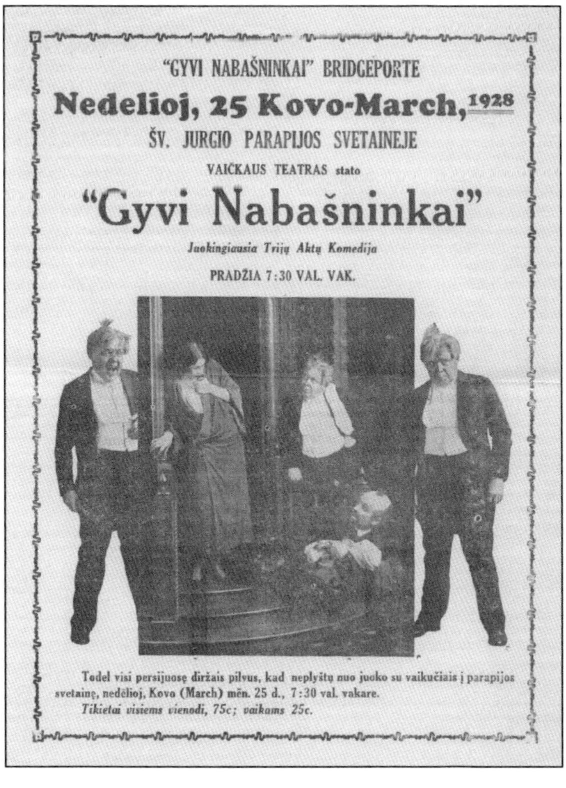

The wide variety of entertainment available was evidence of the cultural richness of Lithuanian Chicago. On March 25, 1928, St. George Parish in Bridgeport hosted the self-proclaimed "Funniest Comedy in Three Acts" by the Vaickaus Theater group. Apparently the show was appropriate for children, as an approximate translation of the advertisement reads "be sure to tighten your belts so when your stomach bursts from laughing your pants don't split with children present." Admission was 75¢ for adults and 25¢ for children. (LRSC.)

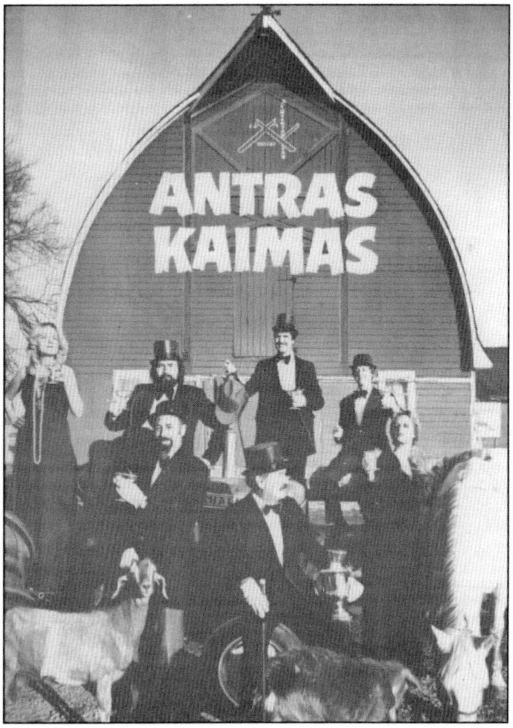

Following in the footsteps of the comedic shows of Vaickaus Theater in the 1920s was the sketch comedy group Antras Kaimas. Based on Chicago's Second City (the name Antras Kaimas translates to "second farm" and also refers to Chicago having the second largest Lithuanian population outside Vilnius), the group was formed in 1963 and began performing for audiences in Union Pier, Michigan, and various Lithuanian bars in Chicago, such as the Gintaras Club in Marquette Park. Antras Kaimas eventually went on to perform in all Lithuanian communities throughout the United States and Canada. This was the poster for the 1980 cast. From left to right are (first row) Romas Stakauskas, Algirdas Titus Anatanaitis (director), and Dana Mikuzis; (second row) Jurate Jakstys, Eugenijus Butenas, Jurgis Riskus, and Juozas Kapacinskas. (Romas Stakauskas.)

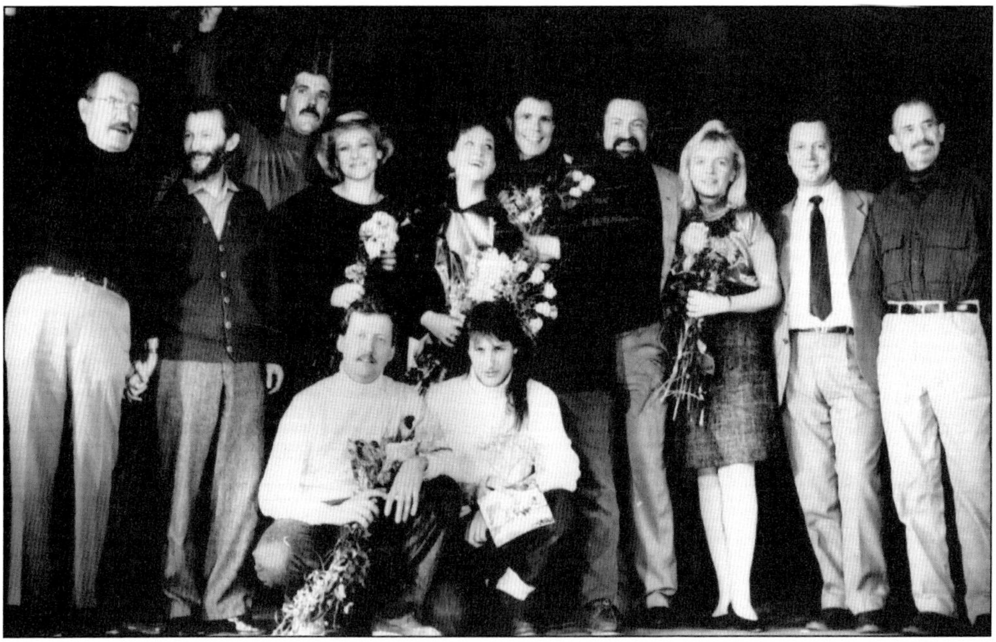

In 1989, the cast of Antras Kaimas traveled to Soviet Lithuania. In three weeks time, they performed over 21 shows in 17 locations throughout the country. The trip was a success and demonstrated how well the Lithuanian community in America had kept up ties with the homeland. Shown here on stage are, from left to right, (kneeling) Juozas Kapacinskas and Joe Ulevicius; (standing) Algirdas Titus Antainaits, unidentified, Jurgis Riskus, Vida Gylvydiene, Alida Vitaite, Edvardas Tuskenis, Eugenijus Butenas, Jurate Jakstys, unidentified, and Romas Stakauskas. (Romas Stakauskas.)

Six

Politics, Patriotism, and the Fight for Independence

Lithuanian Chicago has always been active in politics, a tradition that continues to this day. Throughout the years, numerous Lithuanian Americans have run for office in Illinois and other candidates have routinely courted the community for support. They often found it amongst the many Lithuanian organizations that existed in Chicago. When there was a need for political action, these organizations increased their activities to accomplish a specific purpose, often related to the issue of Lithuanian independence, the common factor that united Lithuanian political action and organizations.

The short lived period of Lithuanian independence ended in 1940 when the country was alternately occupied by both Nazi Germany and the Soviet Union during World War II. As the United States entered the war in 1941, large numbers of Lithuanian Americans volunteered or were drafted into the armed forces and proved their loyalty to the United States. To many, the war doubtlessly had special significance as its course would determine the fate of Lithuania. Upon their return, these veterans established their own organizations that often took part in political activities.

To Lithuanians in Chicago, the biggest political issue of the 20th century was their ancestral homeland's fight for independence. At the end of World War I, they lobbied hard for the United States to recognize Lithuanian sovereignty and promoted their cause by seeking the attention of Pres. Woodrow Wilson and Pres. Warren G. Harding. From 1918 to 1939, they sought to increase their ties to newly independent Lithuania and provide it with any help they could. During and after World War II and throughout the Cold War, Chicago's Lithuanians once again took up the cause and made sure that the American public did not forget the importance of freedom and democracy abroad. As the Soviet Union lost its hold on Lithuania, Lithuanian Chicagoans were quick to promote the country's interests and rejoiced when the small nation regained its independence in 1990.

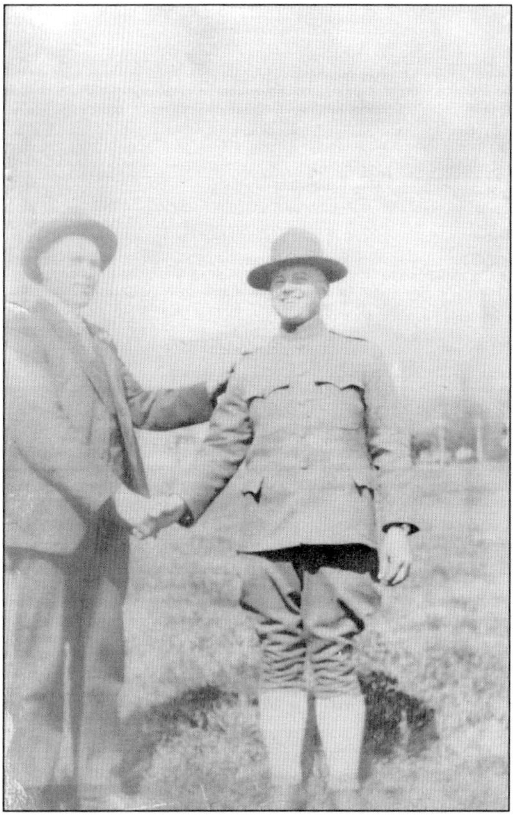

By the time the United States entered World War I in 1917, an estimated 50,000 Lithuanians were living in Chicago. Many of them were called upon to fight for their adopted homeland. In this photograph is Joseph Ezerski (right) from the Back of the Yards looking smart in his uniform as he shakes the hand of an unidentified acquaintance. (Michael and Loretta Ezerski.)

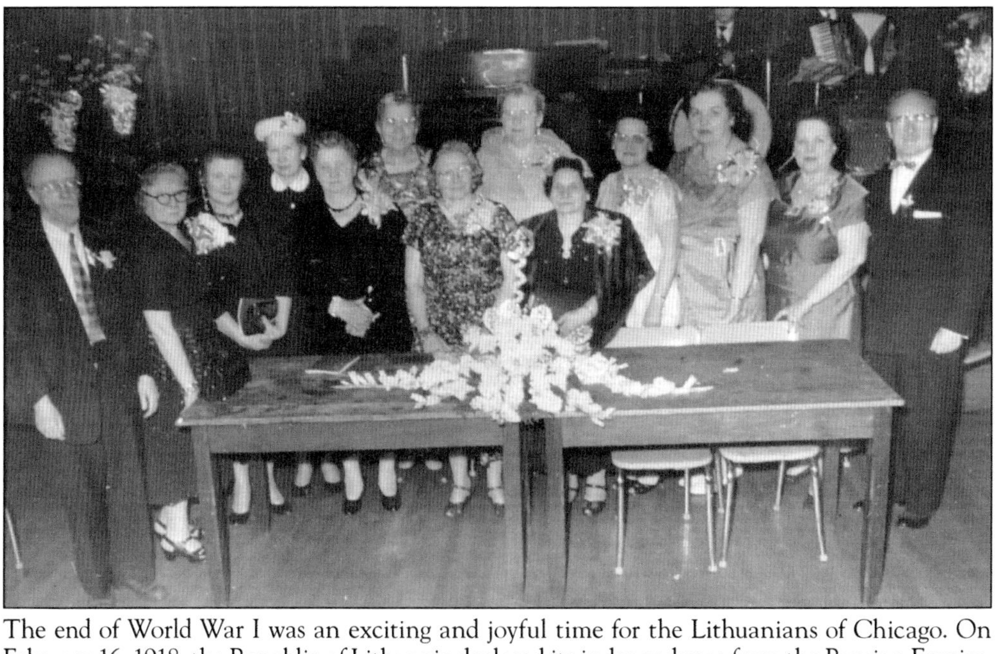

The end of World War I was an exciting and joyful time for the Lithuanians of Chicago. On February 16, 1918, the Republic of Lithuania declared its independence from the Russian Empire. Chicago's large Lithuanian population resulted in the opening of a Lithuanian consulate in the city in 1924, the staff of which is pictured here possibly sometime in the 1940s. (LRSC.)

One of the most influential figures of the Lithuanian period of independence from 1918 to 1940 was Antanas Smetona, whose portrait is pictured here. His term as the first president of Lithuania ended in 1920, but he regained power in a coup and ruled the country from 1926 to 1940. A staunch nationalist, Smetona fled Lithuania for fear of Soviet reprisals in 1940 and made his way to the United States, spending time in Chicago before settling in Cleveland, Ohio. He died in a house fire in 1944. (LRSC.)

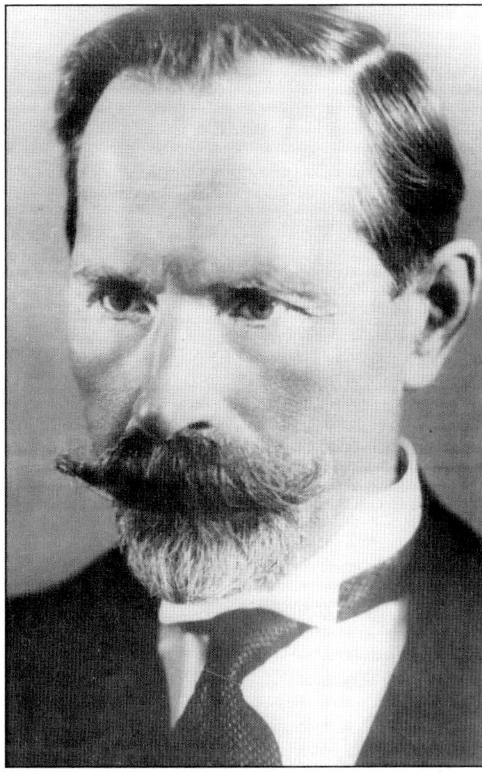

February 16 became an important day to Lithuanian communities around the world when the country declared its independence in 1918. The event was marked annually with celebrations and commemorations. On February 16, 1938, the Lithuanian consul of Chicago, Dr. Petras Dauzvardis, and his wife, Josephine, invited the Latvian and Estonian consuls to celebrate with them. Standing in the center are Josephine Dauzvardis and her husband, Petras. Such celebrations would take on a more somber tone in the years to come. (LRSC.)

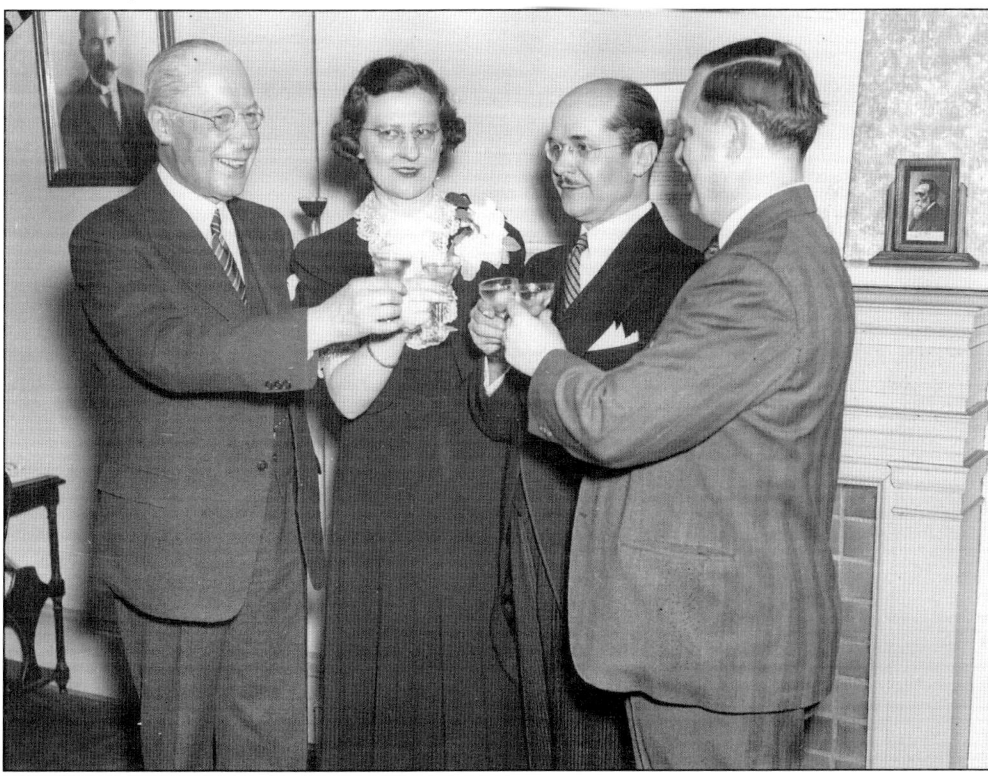

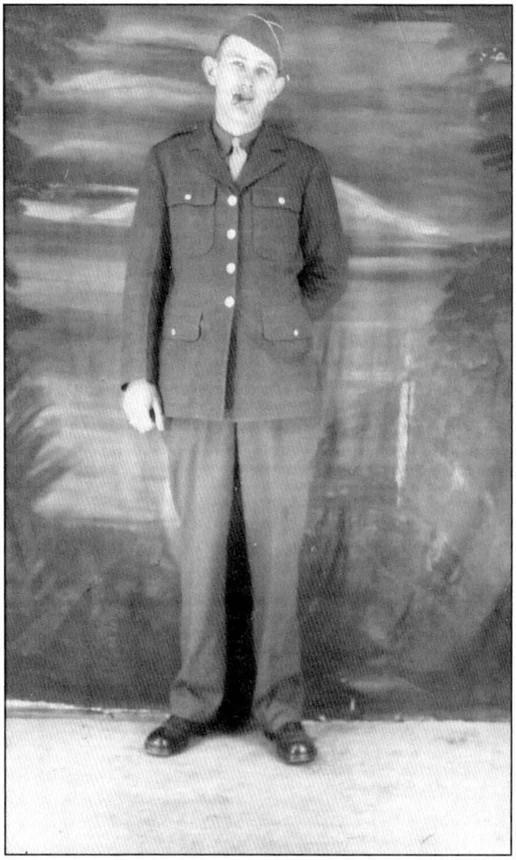

Like in World War I, many Lithuanian Chicagoans served their country proudly during World War II. Pictured here is Vincent Pavilionis after his successful completion of boot camp in 1942. (Rodney Pavilionis.)

In 1943, Vincent Pavilionis took part in the invasion of Kiska Island in Alaska, which had been occupied by the Japanese a year earlier. He can be seen here, second from the left, holding a captured Japanese flag with his fellow soldiers. (Rodney Pavilionis.)

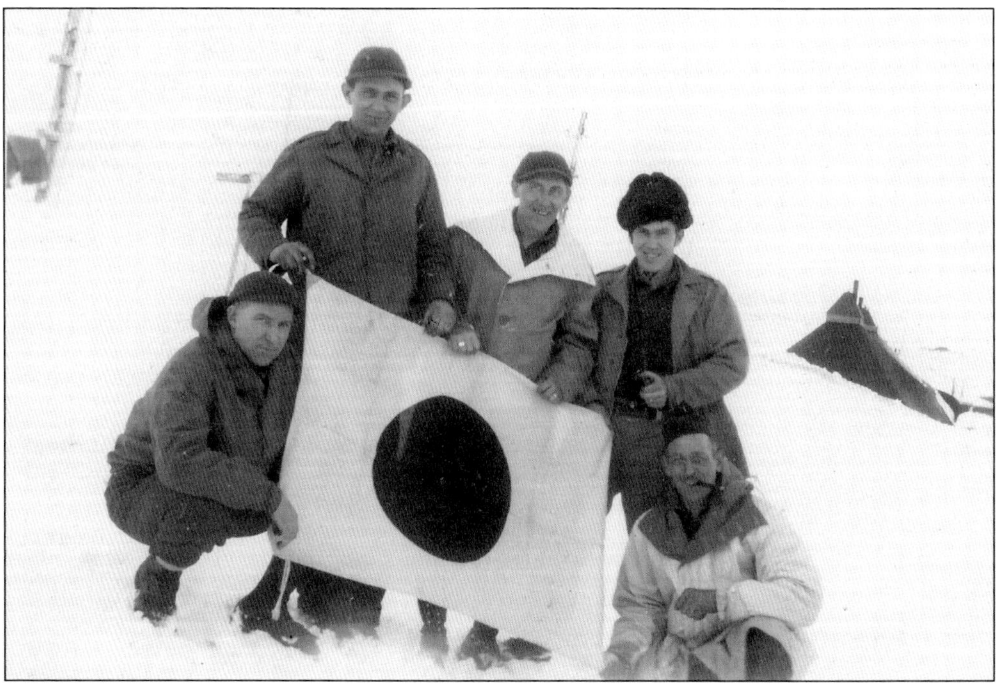

The Lithuanian community of Chicago was unable to escape the costs of World War II. Jack Eudeikis, pictured here in his Army uniform, was killed on February 8, 1945, in Germany during the Battle of the Bulge. Buried in Belgium, a memorial mass was held for him at Holy Cross Church on June 9, 1945, in the Back of the Yards neighborhood where he grew up. (Stack family.)

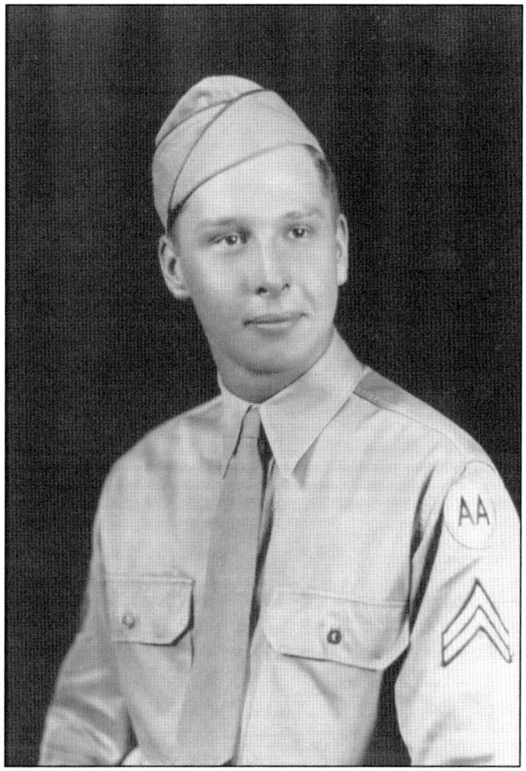

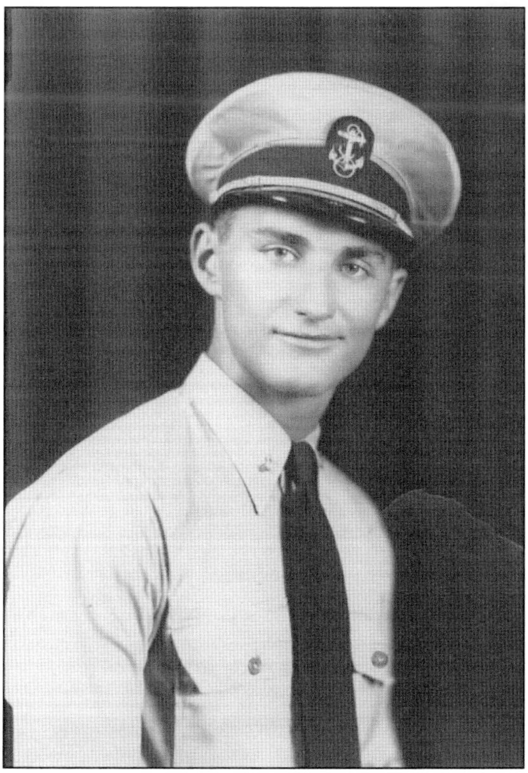

One of Jack Eudeikis's longtime friends was Frank Stack, pictured here in his naval uniform. Frank began his military career as a pilot in the Naval Air Corps and later went into the United States Army. Upon his return to the Back of the Yards, he joined the Chicago Police Department. (Stack family.)

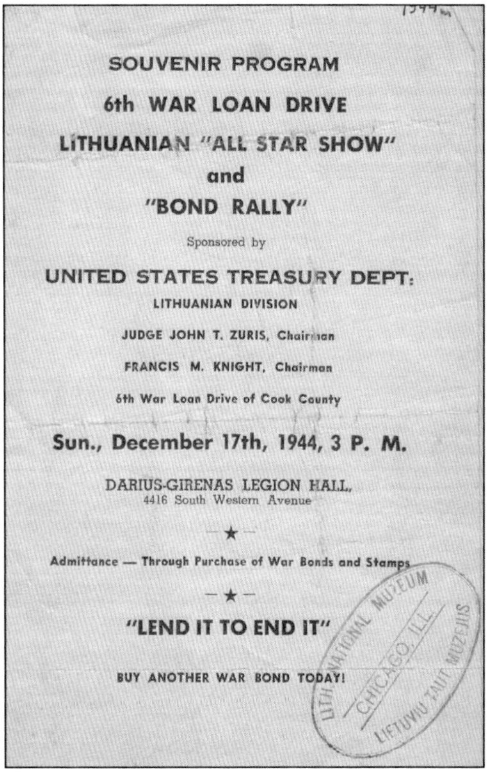

SOUVENIR PROGRAM

6th WAR LOAN DRIVE

LITHUANIAN "ALL STAR SHOW"

and

"BOND RALLY"

Sponsored by

UNITED STATES TREASURY DEPT:

LITHUANIAN DIVISION

JUDGE JOHN T. ZURIS, Chairman

FRANCIS M. KNIGHT, Chairman

6th War Loan Drive of Cook County

Sun., December 17th, 1944, 3 P. M.

DARIUS-GIRENAS LEGION HALL,
4416 South Western Avenue

★

Admittance — Through Purchase of War Bonds and Stamps

★

"LEND IT TO END IT"

BUY ANOTHER WAR BOND TODAY!

During World War II, Lithuanians in Chicago directed their energies towards the war effort. This poster advertises a bond rally with the promise of entertainment, hosted by the Lithuanian Division of the US Treasury Department at the Darius-Girenas Legion Hall at 4416 South Western Avenue. (LRSC.)

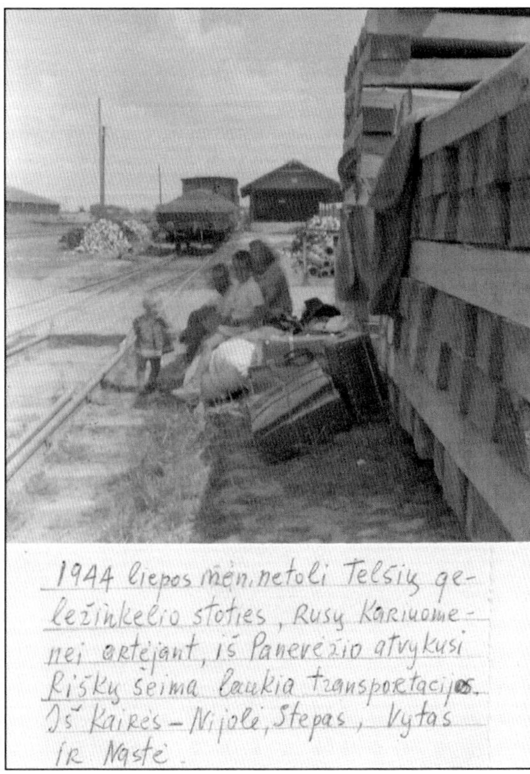

As Lithuanians in Chicago concerned themselves with the war effort, many in Lithuania were fleeing the advance of the Soviet Union along the eastern front. Having experienced the Soviet brutality of 1940, great numbers of people fled west. In this July 1944 photograph, the Riskus family waits for a train near the Lithuanian town of Telsiai to take them away from the impending front. From left to right are Nijole, Stepas, Vytas, and Anastasia Riskus. After the war, such refugees would constitute the second wave of Lithuanian immigration to Chicago. (Nijole Riskus-Gierstikas.)

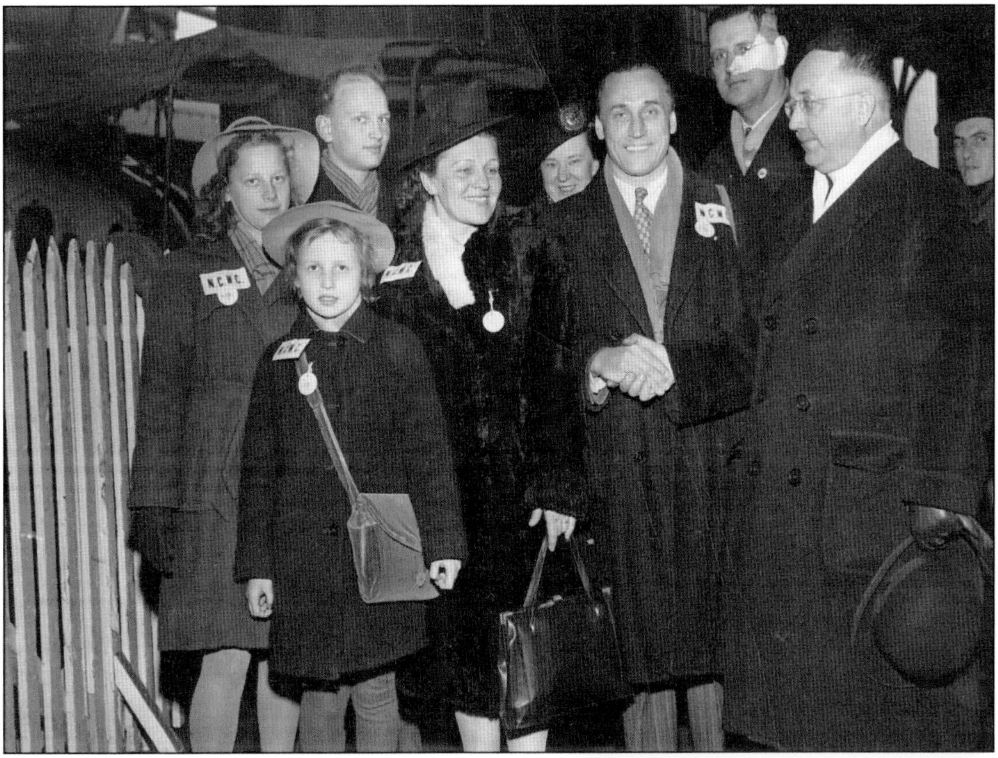

Towards the end of World War II and in the years immediately after, Lithuanians in Chicago supported organizations such as the United Lithuanian Relief Fund of America. In the 20 years after the war, the United Lithuanian Relief Fund of America distributed nearly $7 million in goods and money to Lithuanians in need. Even more important was the organization's efforts to prevent the forced repatriation of Lithuanians to the Soviet Union. Shown here to the far right is the Rev. Dr. Jouzas Koncius, president of the organization, greeting a Lithuanian family who was displaced after the war. Many such families eventually settled in the Lithuanian neighborhoods of Chicago. (LRSC.)

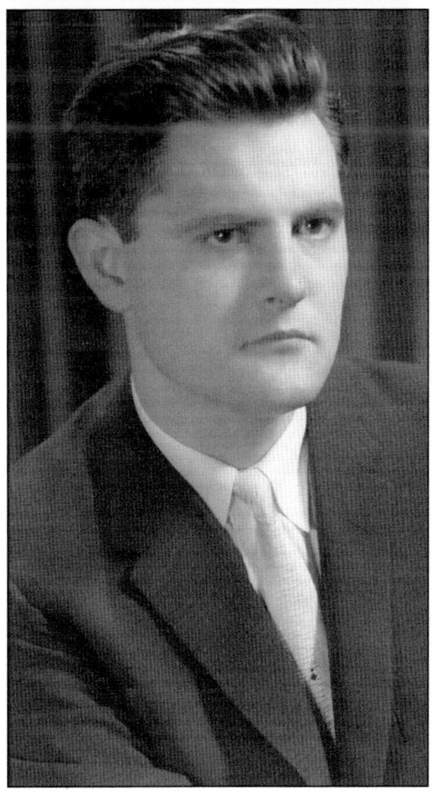

Many of the displaced persons who came to the United States from Lithuania after World War II were dedicated to regaining their homeland's freedom. Valdas Adamkus, whose portrait from the late 1940s or early 1950s can be seen here, was no exception. While studying engineering at the Illinois Institute of Technology, the future president of Lithuania organized a petition signed by 40,000 people encouraging the United States to intercede on behalf of the large numbers of Lithuanians languishing in the Soviet Gulag. (LRSC.)

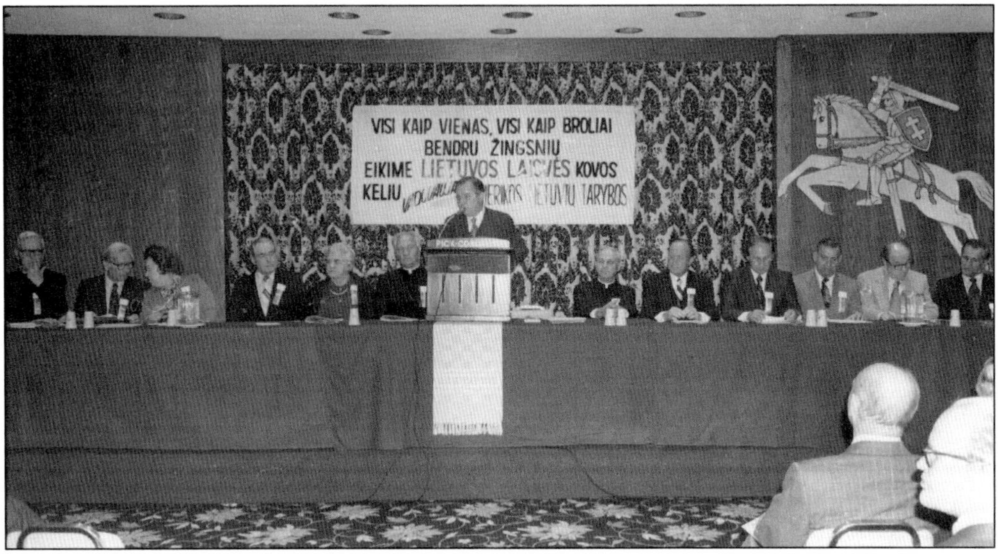

The Lithuanian American Council has represented Lithuanian interests for nearly a century. Based in Chicago, the organization has played a key political role in Lithuania's struggle for independence and current issues affecting the country and communities abroad. This banner at a meeting of the organization in the 1950s or 1960s explains that the road to Lithuanian freedom is through unity with the Lithuanian American Council leading the way. (LRSC.)

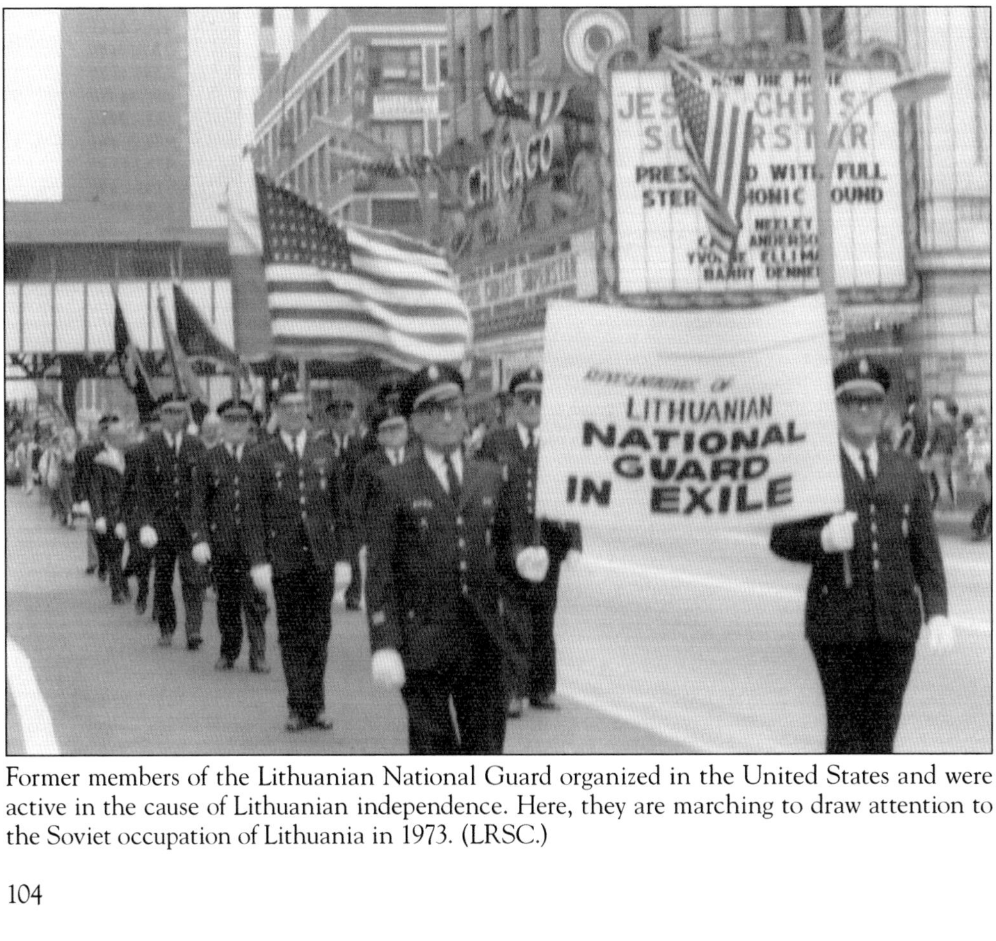

Former members of the Lithuanian National Guard organized in the United States and were active in the cause of Lithuanian independence. Here, they are marching to draw attention to the Soviet occupation of Lithuania in 1973. (LRSC.)

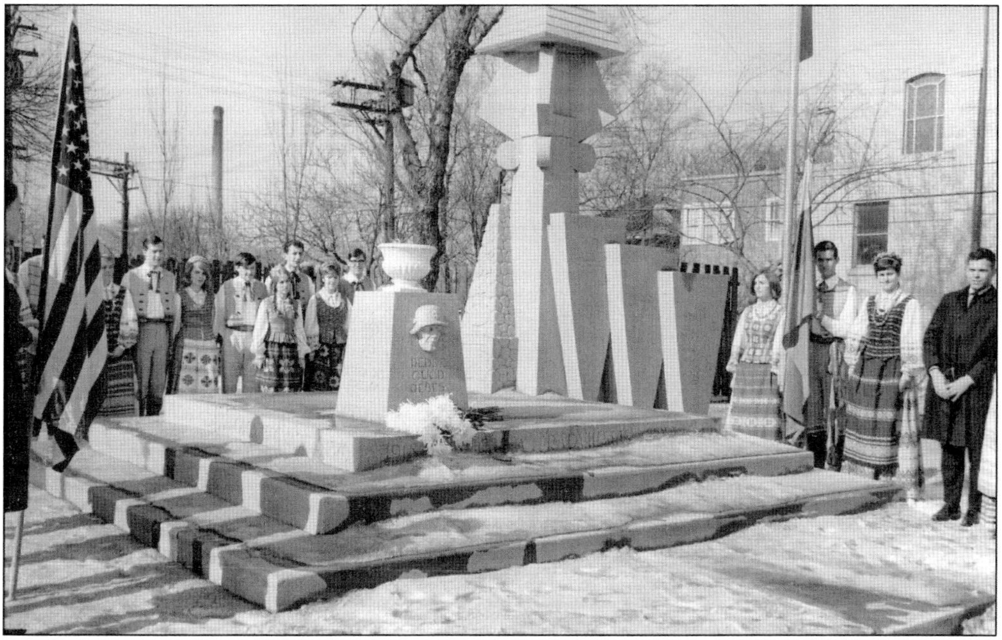

Commemorating Lithuanian independence and its suffering under Soviet occupation was a constant theme in Lithuanian Chicago. The memorial at the Lithuanian Youth Center in Gage Park was often the sight of such events. In this photograph, unidentified students in Lithuanian national costume brave the cold weather at a ceremony honoring those who died for Lithuania's freedom. (LRSC.)

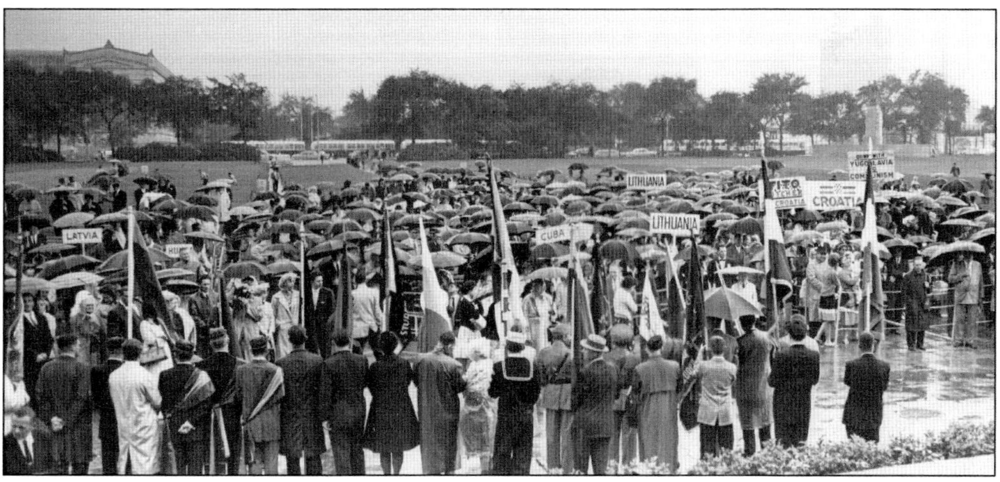

Lithuanians were not the only staunchly anticommunist ethnic group in Chicago. On many occasions, rain or shine, Lithuanians would cooperate with other nationalities in the name of democracy and freedom. This anticommunist rally in Grant Park around 1960 includes representatives from Croatia, Cuba, Hungary, Latvia, Lithuania, and Yugoslavia. (LRSC.)

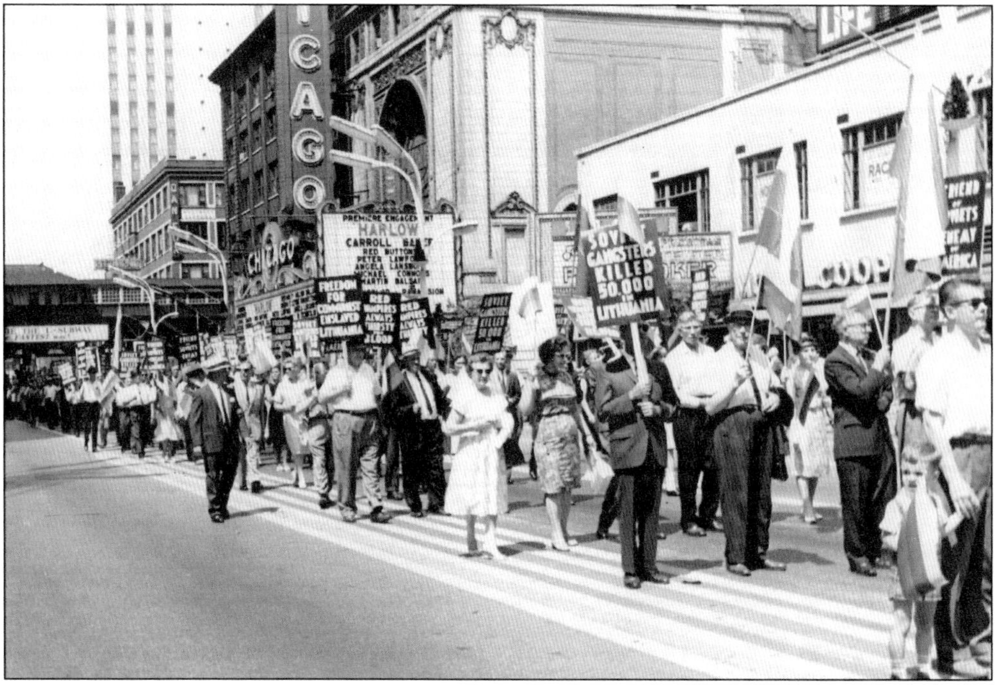

Lithuania's political situation during the Cold War made this time period particularly personal for Lithuanian Americans. Using strongly worded signs that reveal their thoughts of the Soviet Union, Lithuanians march in downtown Chicago in 1965 to generate awareness of Soviet atrocities. (LRSC.)

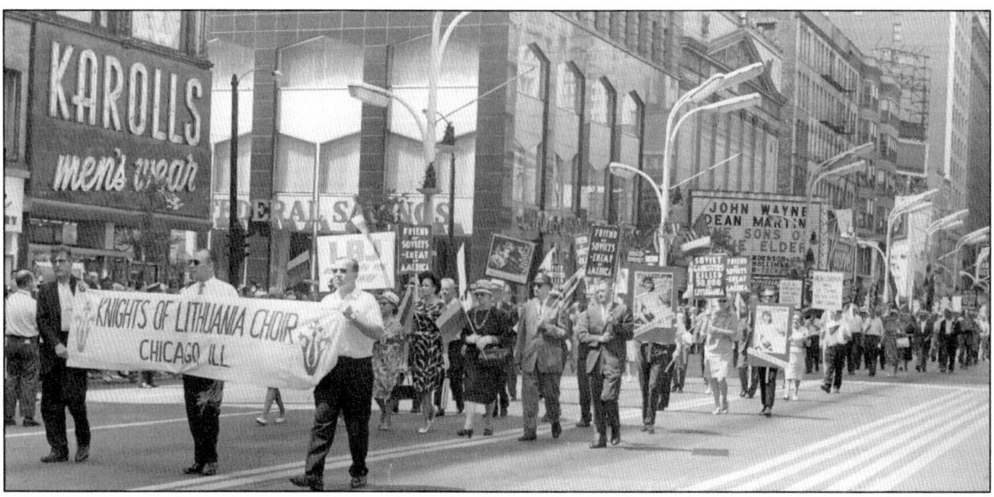

Many Lithuanian social organizations in Chicago took part in demonstrations to support Lithuanian independence. This 1965 march downtown includes the Knights of Lithuania Choir. (LRSC.)

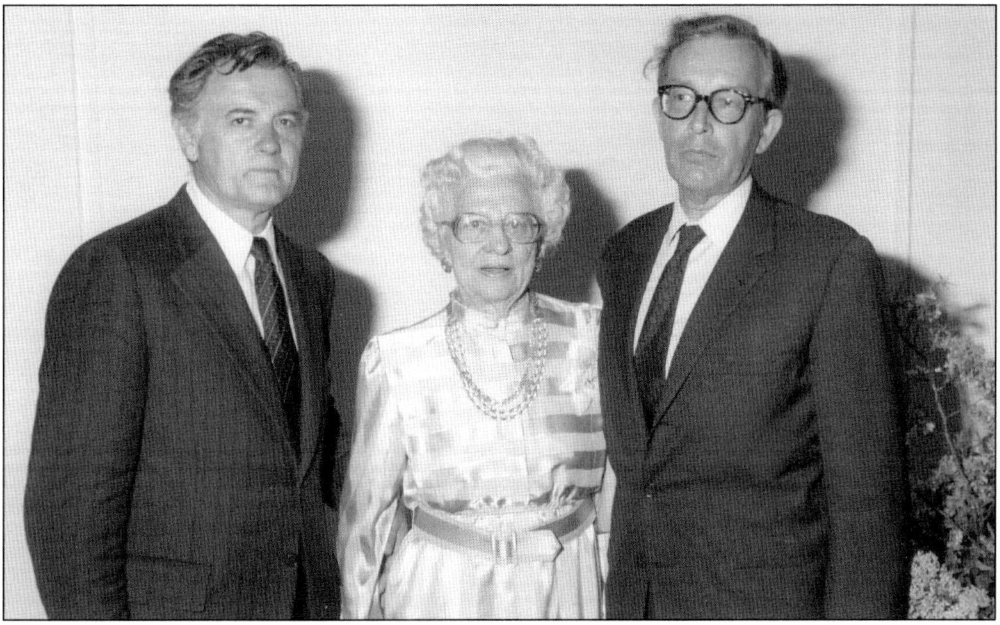

Having been appointed to the Lithuanian consulate in Chicago during the country's period of independence, Dr. Petras Dauzvardis remained at his post, representing the government of the Republic of Lithuania in exile from 1940 to his death in 1971. Dr. Dauzvardis and his wife, Josephine, were respected members of the community. In this photograph, taken sometime in the late 1960s or early 1970s, Valdas Adamkus (left) poses with Josephine Dauzvardis and Stasys Lozoraitis, the former foreign minister of Lithuania in the 1930s. (LRSC.)

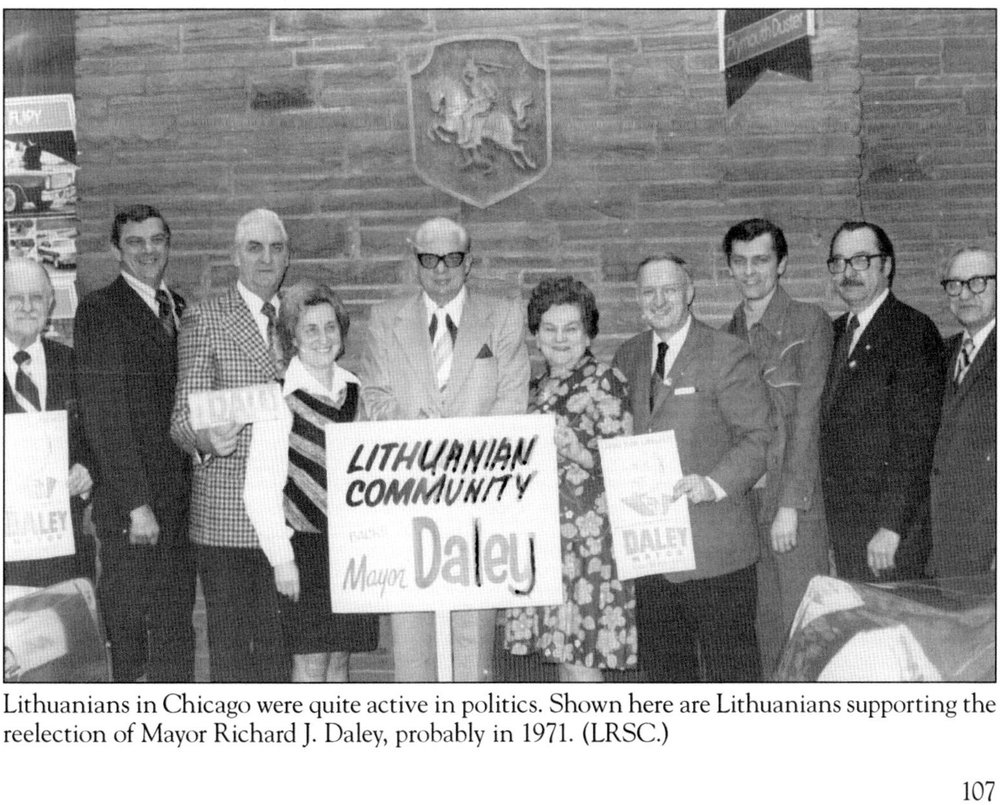

Lithuanians in Chicago were quite active in politics. Shown here are Lithuanians supporting the reelection of Mayor Richard J. Daley, probably in 1971. (LRSC.)

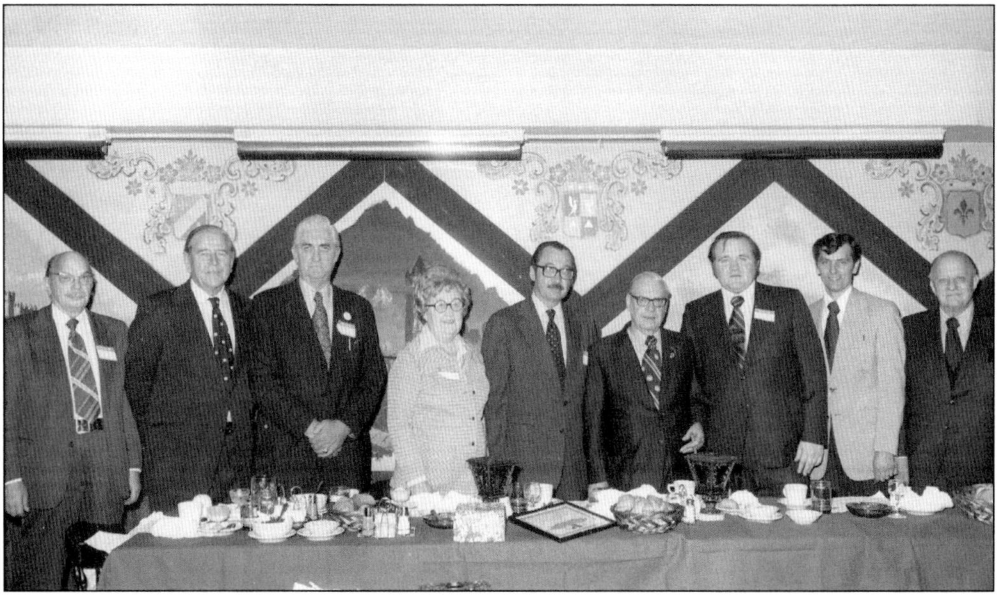

When Sen. LeRoy W. Lemke worked towards government funding for ethnic dance and art groups, he gained the support of many influential Lithuanians in Chicago. He was honored with a luncheon at the Golden Ox Restaurant at Archer and Kostner Avenue on October 25, 1976. Pictured at the luncheon are, from left to right, John Drevin, Adolph Baliunas, Harry Petraitis, Euphrosine Mikuzis, Stanley Balzekas Jr., Congressman John G. Fary, Senator Lemke, Joe Katauskas, Jr., and Charles A. Beacham. (LRSC.)

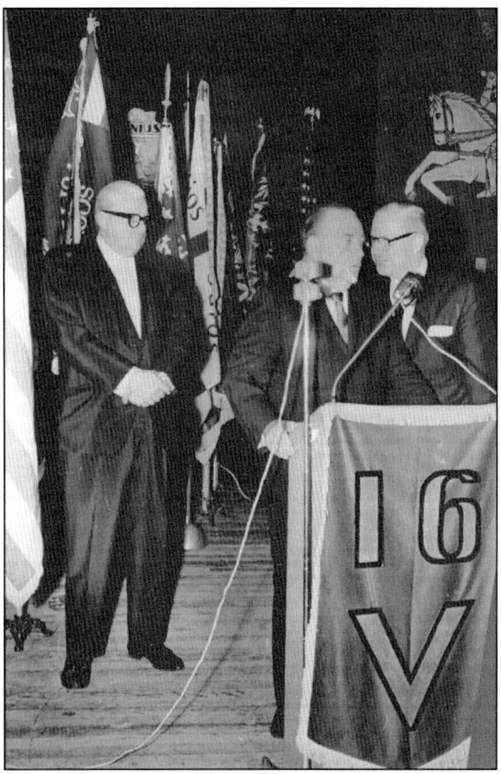

Lithuanian Independence Day commemorations commonly drew large crowds and influential people. Here, Mayor Richard J. Daley addresses a group of Lithuanians. The "V" emblazoned on the banner hanging on the podium is for the month of February (in Lithuanian, Vasaris). (LRSC.)

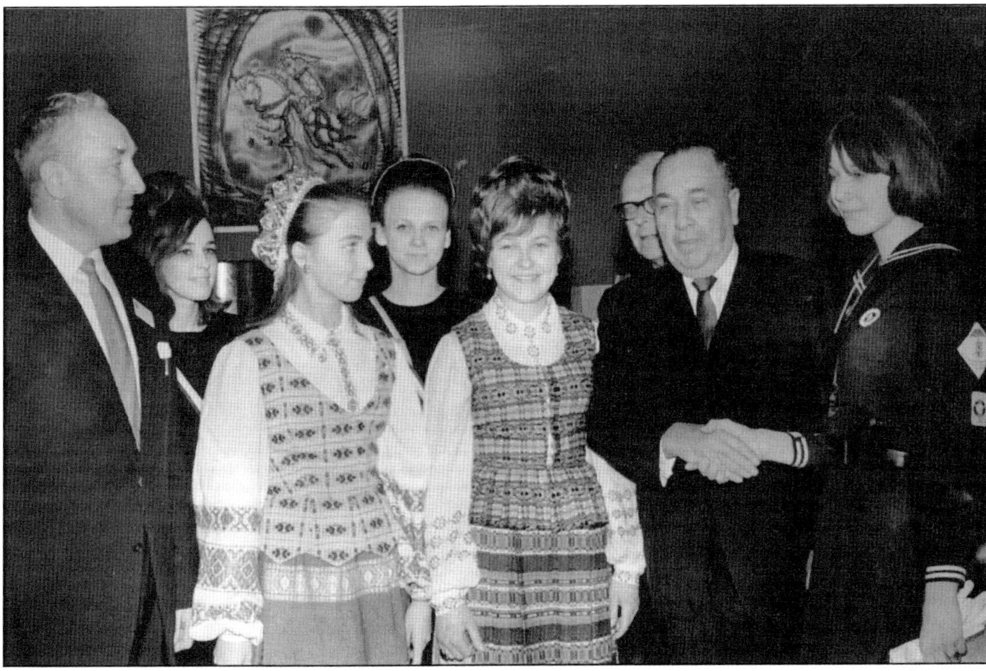

Following his speech, the mayor takes time to meet with unidentified representatives of various Lithuanian organizations in Chicago, including Neo-Lithuania and the Scouts. (LRSC.)

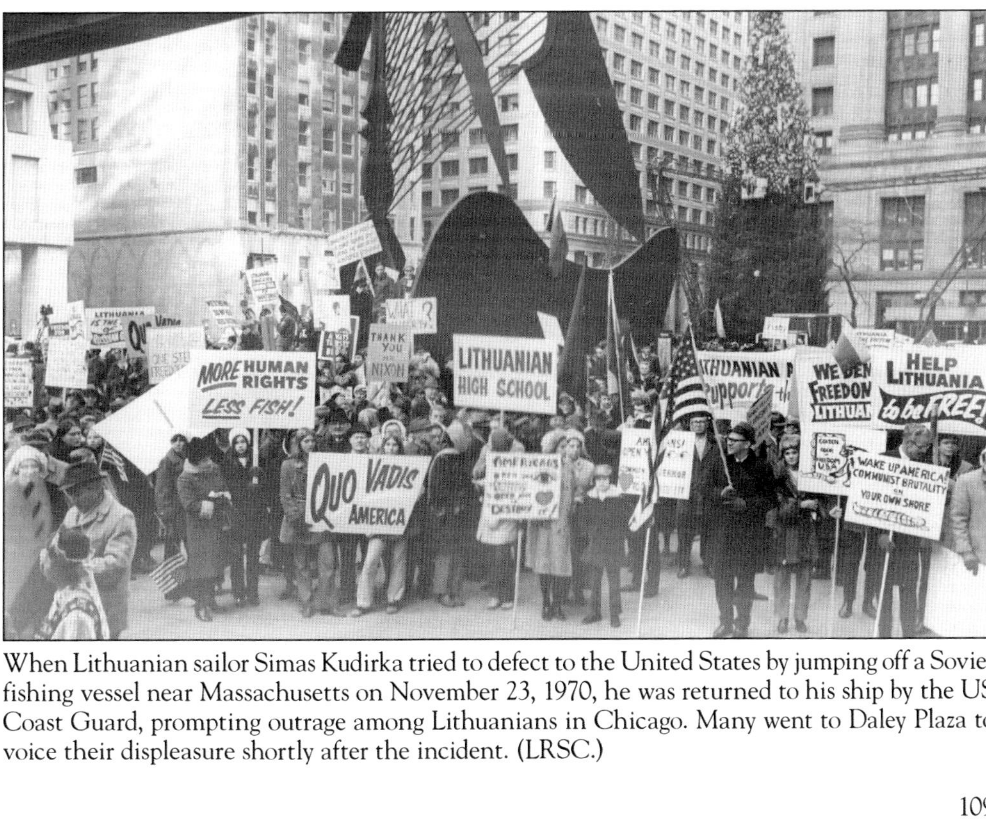

When Lithuanian sailor Simas Kudirka tried to defect to the United States by jumping off a Soviet fishing vessel near Massachusetts on November 23, 1970, he was returned to his ship by the US Coast Guard, prompting outrage among Lithuanians in Chicago. Many went to Daley Plaza to voice their displeasure shortly after the incident. (LRSC.)

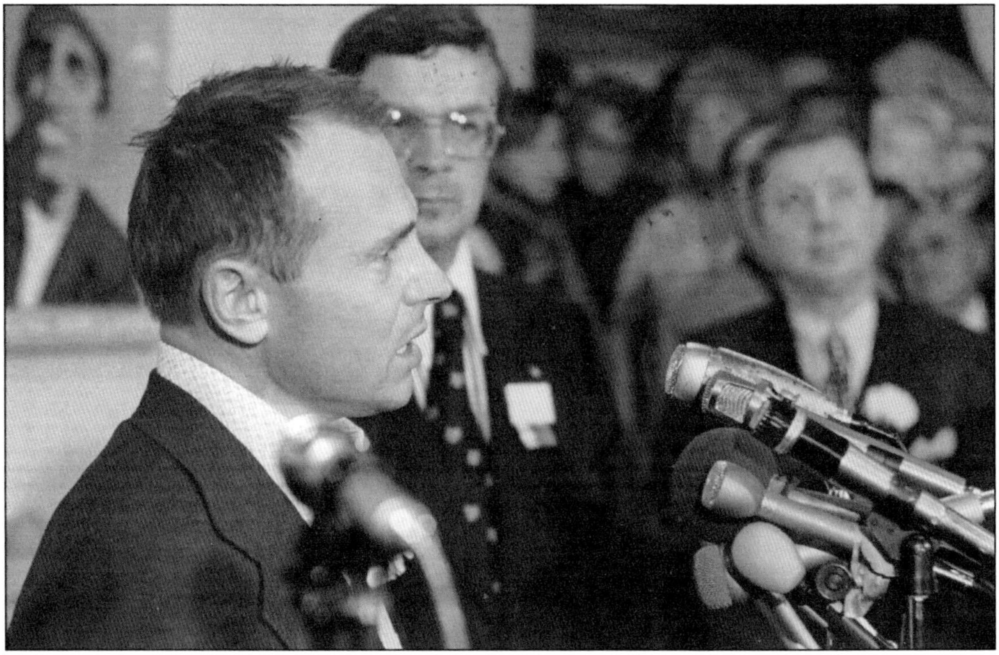

Simas Kurdirka avoided hard labor in a Soviet labor camp due to his mother having been an American citizen. After his ordeal, he was allowed to immigrate to the United States in 1974. Here, Kurdirka addresses reporters at Midway Airport around the time of his arrival to the United States. (LRSC.)

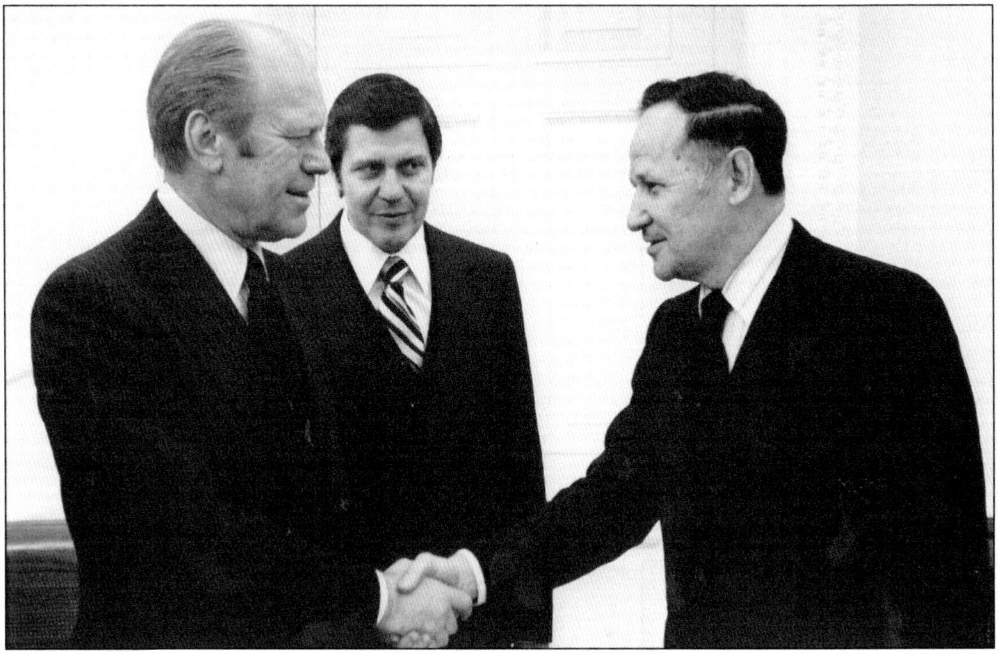

Many Lithuanians in Chicago were politically involved themselves, such as Casimir G. Oksas, a veteran of multiple wars who was at one time the Republican party nominee for Cook County recorder of deeds. He later served as a Cook County jury commissioner. Shown here is Oksas shaking hands with Pres. Gerald Ford as special assistant to the president Myron Kuropas looks on. (LRSC.)

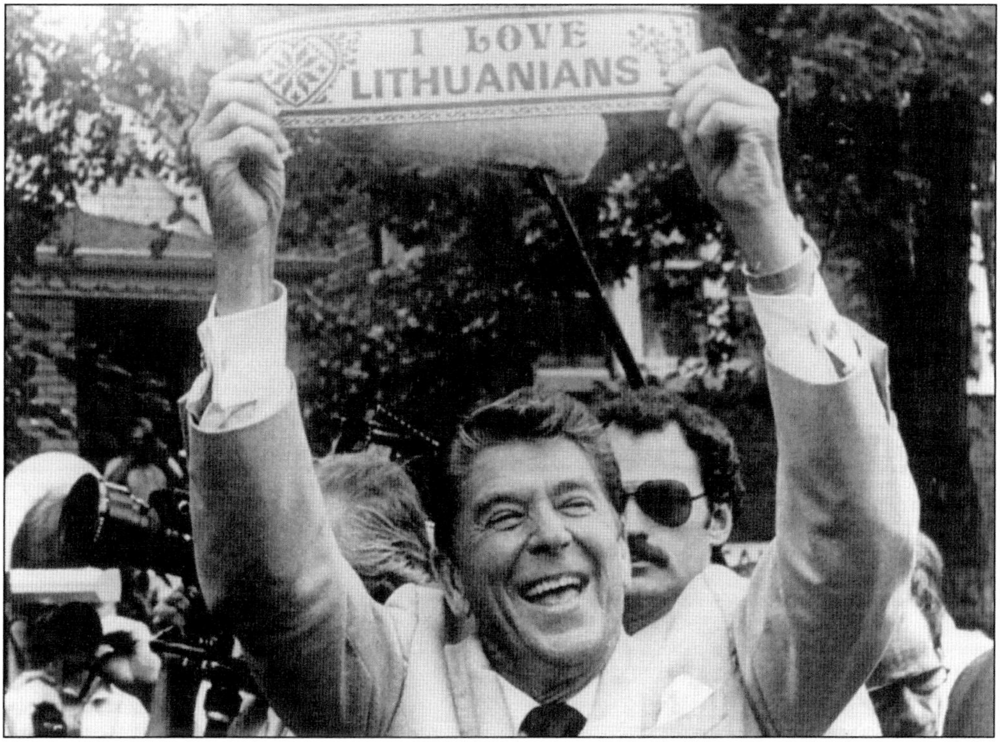

Pres. Ronald Reagan's tough stance towards the "evil empire" of the Soviet Union was quite popular with many Lithuanians. At a campaign stop at the Lithuanian Festival held in Marquette Park in the summer of 1981, Reagan reciprocated their support. (LRSC.)

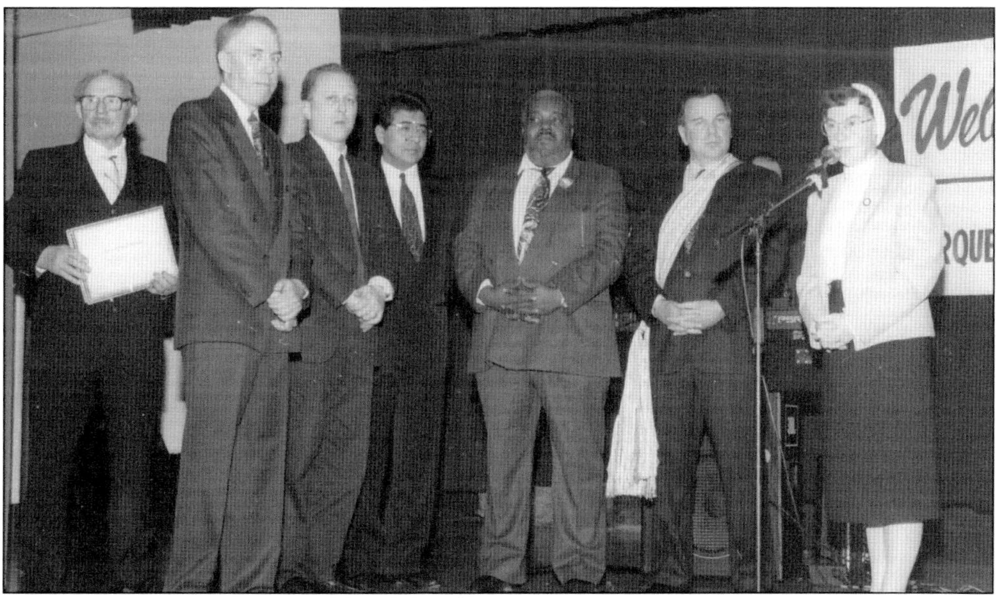

Like his father, Mayor Richard M. Daley also reached out to the Lithuanian community. Shown here at an event in Marquette Park in the mid- to late 1990s are, from left to right, Juozas Bagdzius, Joe Kulys, Alderman Jim Laski, Cook County commissioner Joseph Moreno, Alderman Virgil Jones, Mayor Daley, and Sr. Margaret Petcavage of the Sisters of St. Casimir. (SSC.)

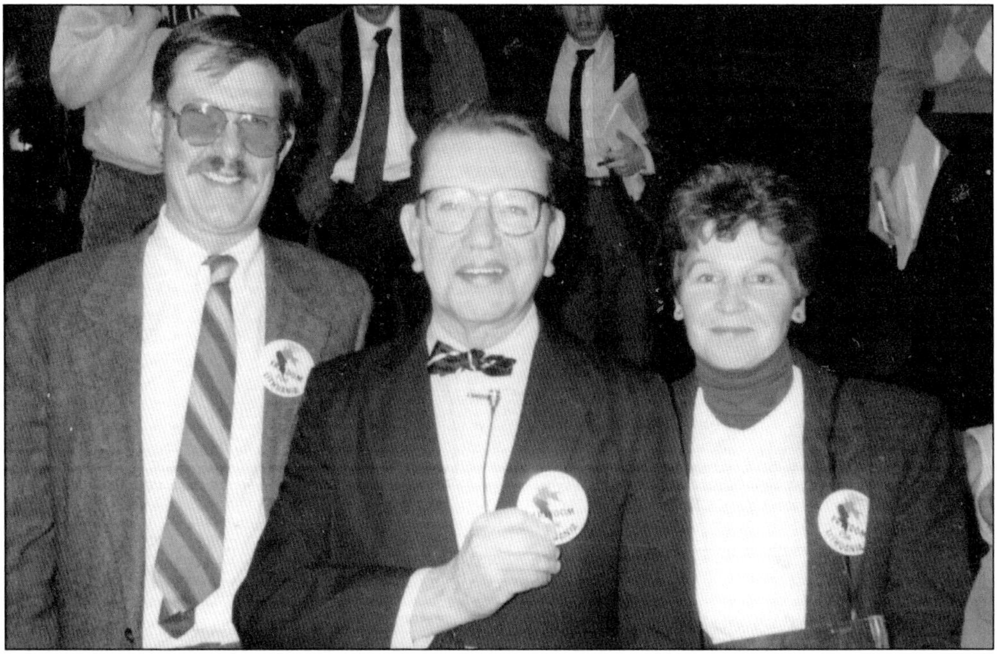

Lithuania's demands for independence from the Soviet Union in the late 1980s led to significant political activism among Lithuanian organizations in Chicago. Jurgis Augius (left), a supporter of Americans for Lithuanian Freedom, stands with US senator Paul Simon of Illinois around 1989. The woman to the right is unidentified. (LRSC.)

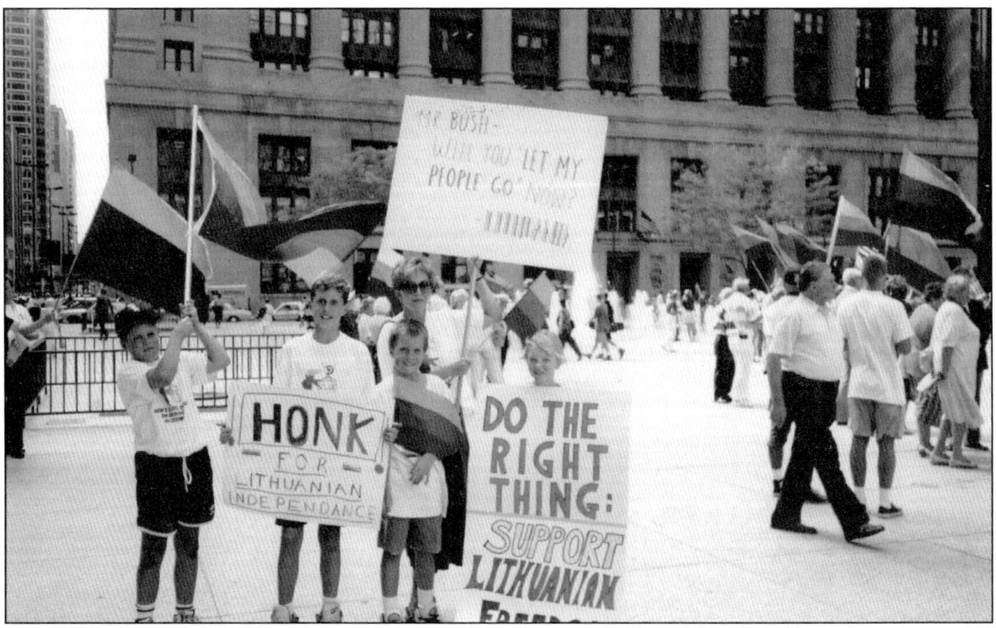

As the political situation in Lithuania intensified and began to cause Soviet crackdowns, Lithuanians in Chicago did what they could to generate as much publicity as possible. The summer following Lithuania's declaration of independence from the Soviet Union on March 11, 1990, was particularly busy. Wearing activist shirts, and armed with flags and signs, whole families came to lend their support. Standing with the Vygantas family in Daley Plaza is Justin Riskus (left). (LRSC.)

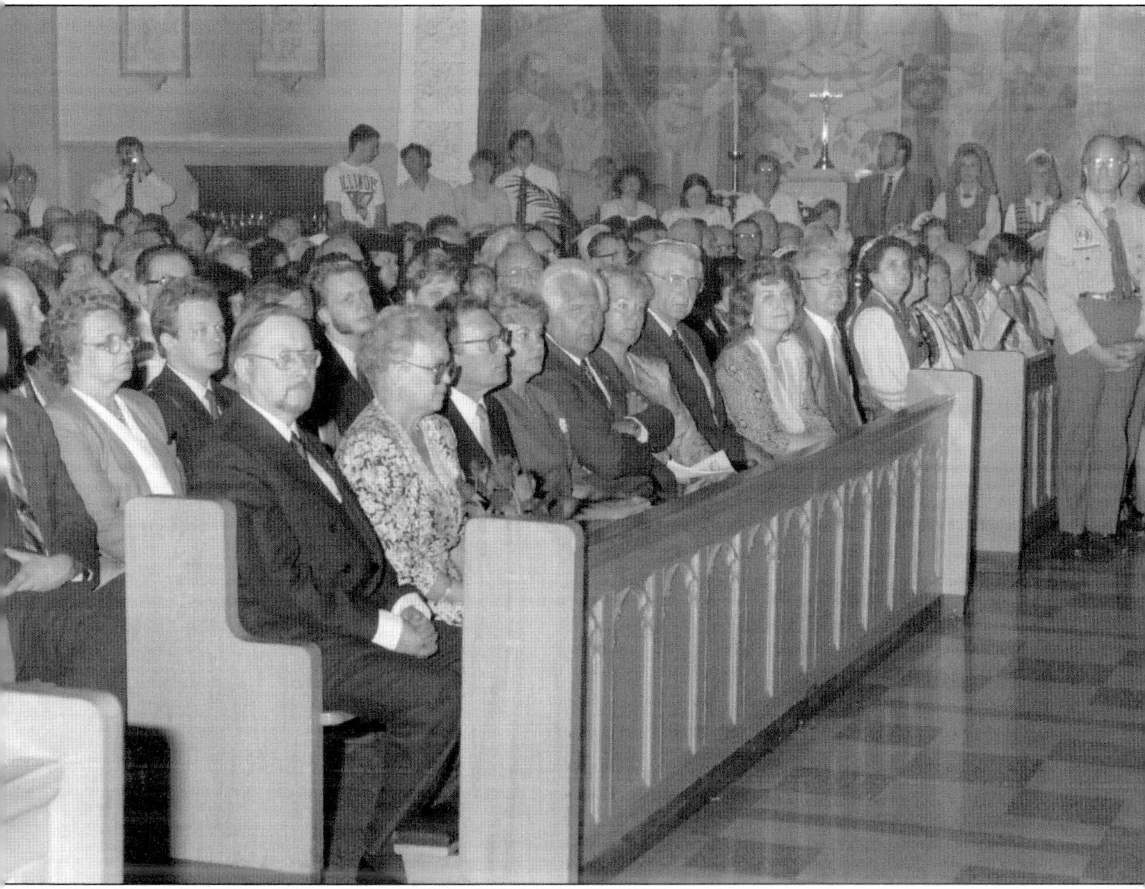

On September 2, 1991, Pres. George H.W. Bush expressed American support for Lithuanian independence. Upon the Soviet Union acknowledging Lithuania's freedom a few days later, the more than 50-year struggle was over. Pres. Vytautas Landsbergis's visit on Sunday, May 12, 1991, to Nativity BVM Church in Marquette Park was widely attended. He is seen here sitting at the right end of the front pew. (LRSC.)

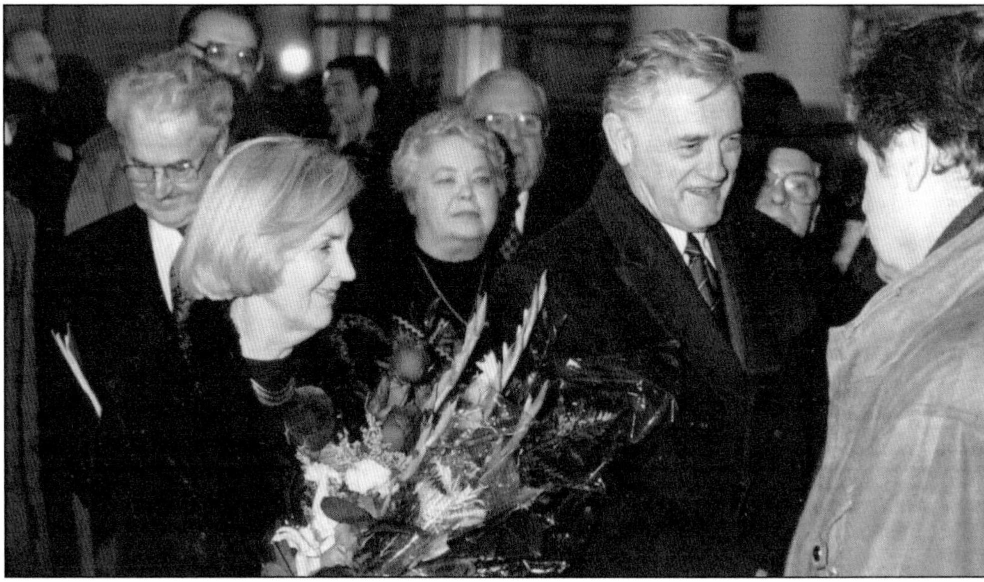

The Lithuanian community of Chicago has always maintained close ties with Lithuania. As a former resident of the area, Valdas Adamkus's election to the office of the president of Lithuania in 1998 demonstrates this. Regarded as an active and respected member of the Lithuanian American community, he was popular with many Lithuanians in the United States, particularly in Chicago. He can be seen here on one of his many visits to Chicago. Standing to Pres. Valdas Adamkus's right holding a bouquet of flowers is his wife, Alma. (LRSC.)

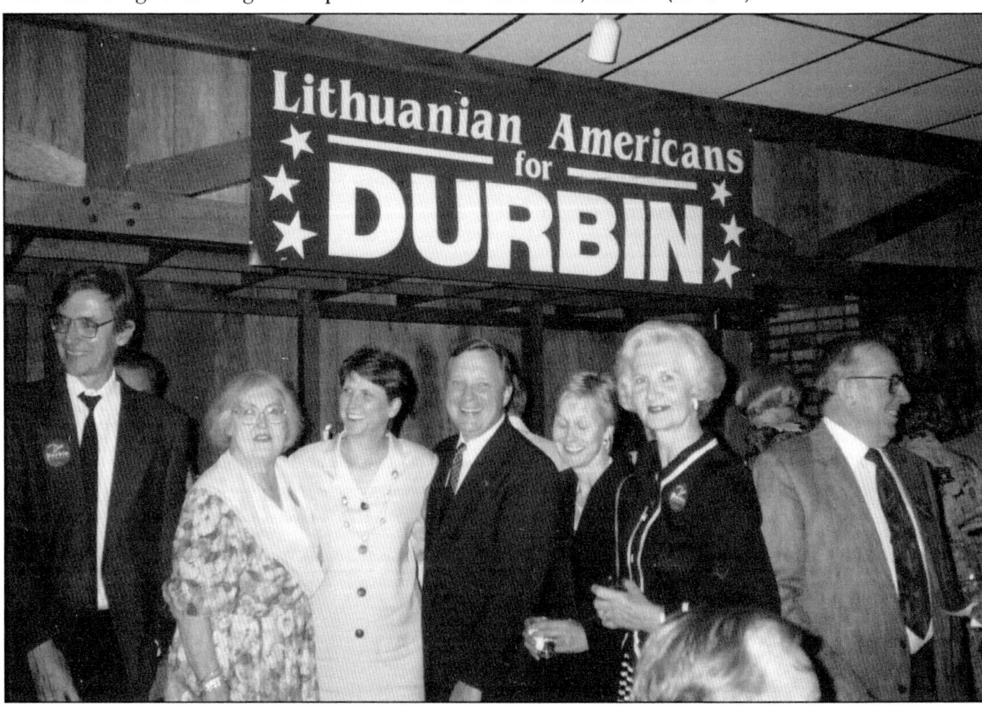

Richard Durbin's support for Lithuanian causes has made him popular with the Lithuanians of Chicago. He is also of Lithuanian descent, his mother having been born in Lithuania. He is shown here at a fundraising event in Lemont, Illinois.

Seven

Moving to the Suburbs

From the late 1800s until the 1960s, Chicago was home to a thriving Lithuanian community. Lithuanian enclaves in Back of the Yards, Bridgeport, Brighton Park, and Marquette Park, among others, had flourished for more than half a century and were home to numerous Lithuanian churches, businesses, and social and political organizations. The latter half of the 20th century, accelerating in the 1970s, saw the movement of Lithuanians from the neighborhoods of the city to the suburbs of Chicago. This movement was not new, as Lithuanians had already established communities in places like Cicero and Waukegan, but differed in its size and scope. While numerous Lithuanian institutions still exist and are successfully supported by Lithuanians in Chicago, the focus of the Lithuanian community has shifted outside of the city.

The purchase of a former seminary on 14 acres of land in Lemont, Illinois, in 1988 provided a new home for Lithuanian activities. Called the Lithuanian World Center, the compound includes a Roman Catholic Church, a Lithuanian school held on Saturdays, a Lithuanian-language Montessori, several banquet halls, and multiple gymnasiums. Many Lithuanian organizations also utilize the space for their activities. The Lithuanian World Center's location has drawn many Lithuanian families to Lemont and the west suburbs, particularly those that arrived in the United States following the collapse of the Soviet Union.

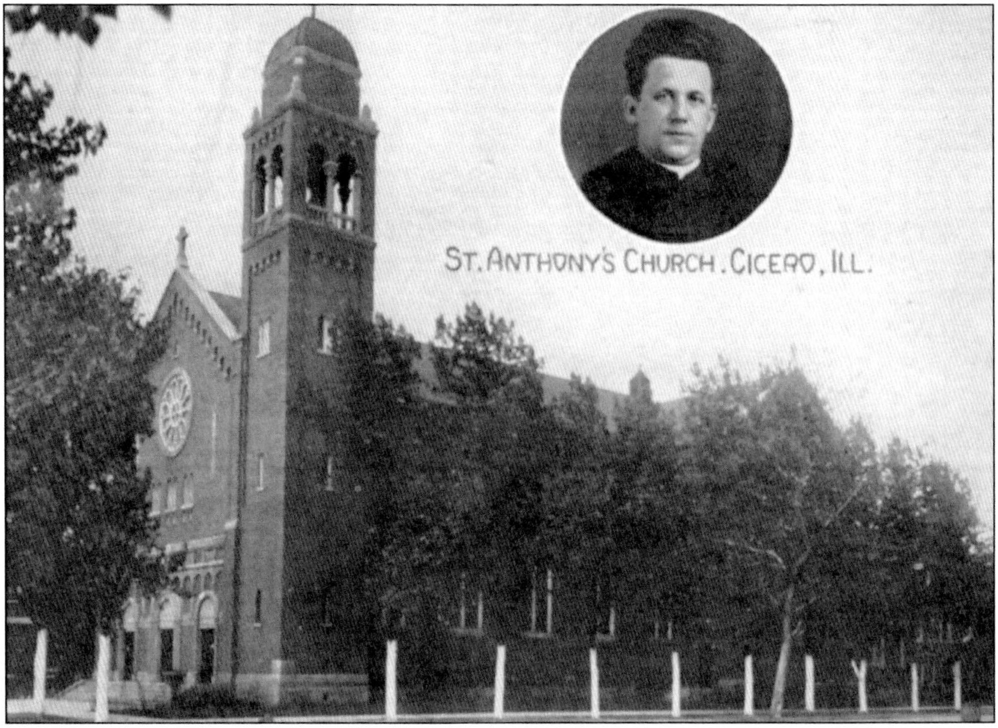

One of the oldest Lithuanian communities in the suburbs of Chicago is in Cicero. This postcard, dated December 22, 1931, is of St. Anthony's Church. Like neighborhoods in the city, Lithuanians in Cicero were highly involved in their local parish. (LRSC.)

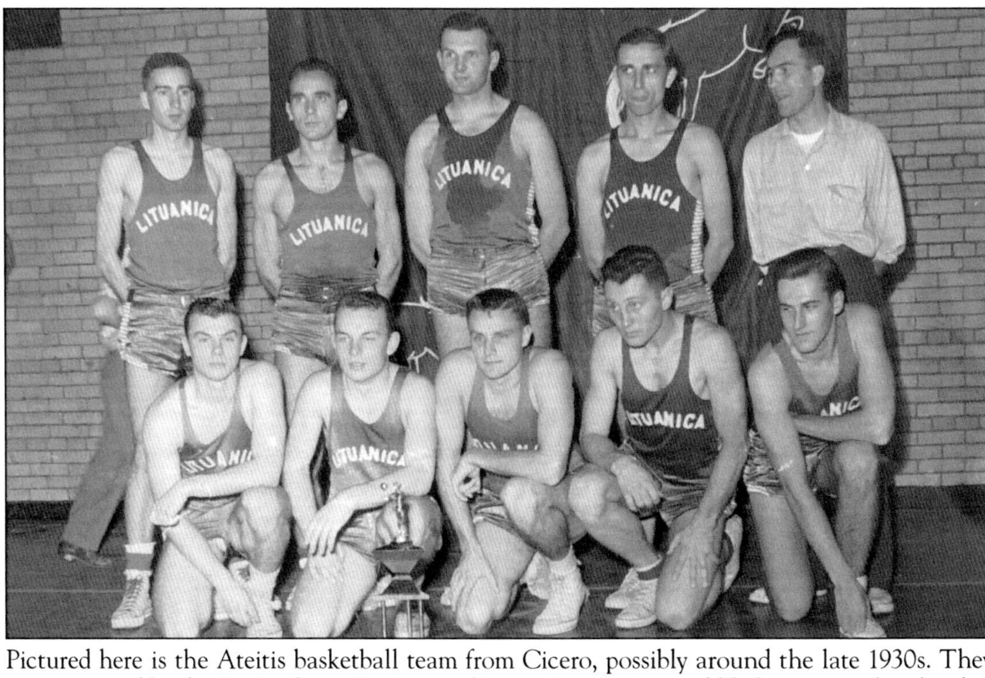

Pictured here is the Ateitis basketball team from Cicero, possibly around the late 1930s. They are sponsored by the St. Anthony Savings and Loan Association and likely competed with other Lithuanian teams in Chicago. (LRSC.)

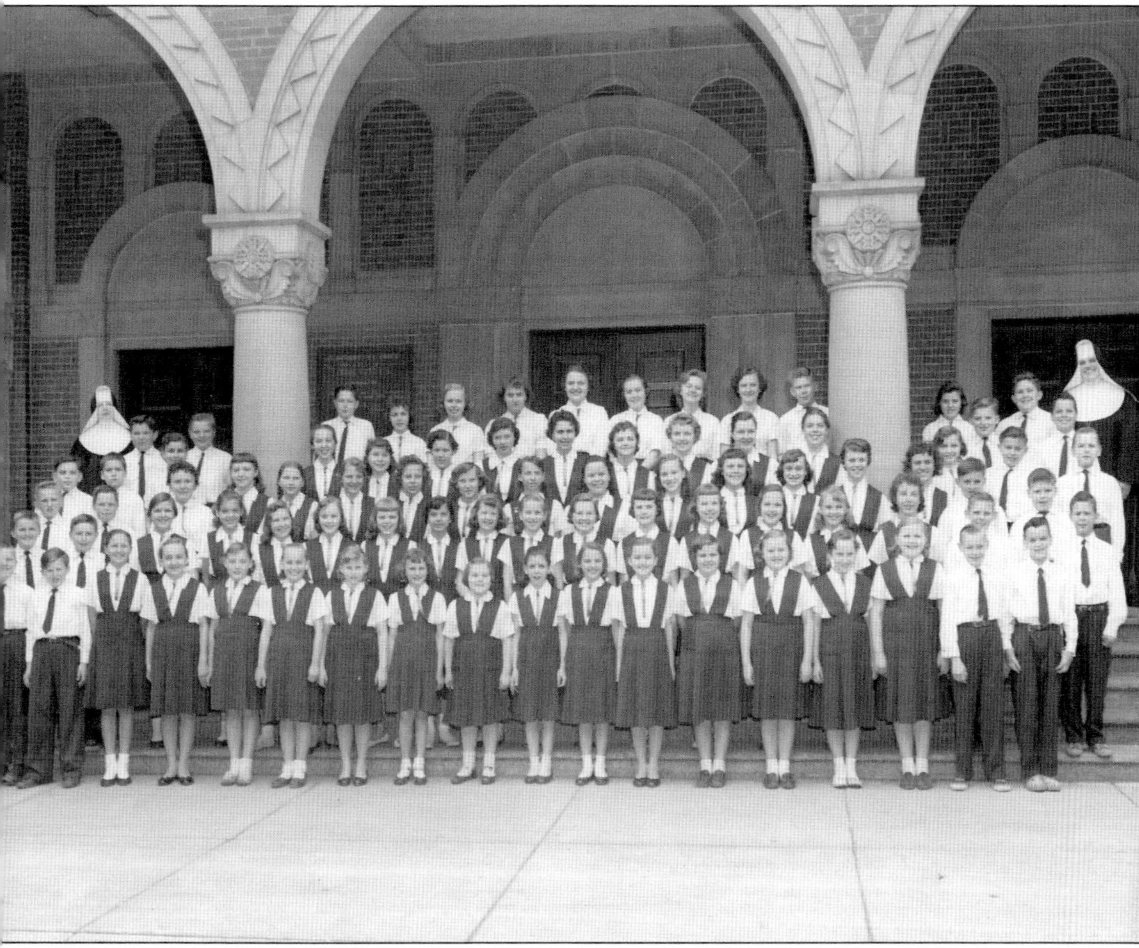

The Lithuanians of Cicero were highly active and involved. This group photograph from June 30, 1957, is of students from St. Anthony School who participated in the Lithuanian Song Festival. They are being led in their endeavors by two Sisters of St. Casimir. (SSC.)

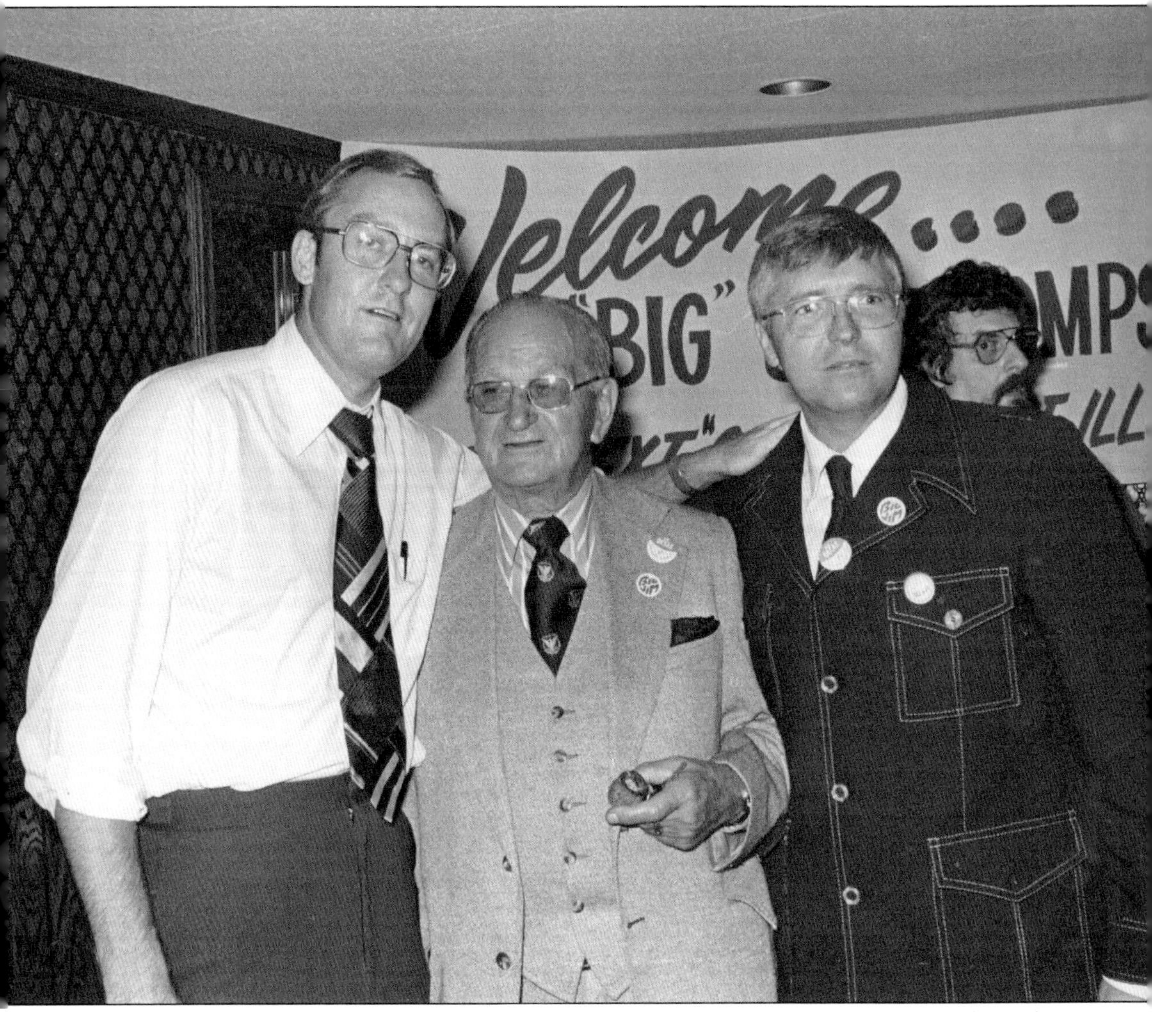

Like their neighbors in the city, Cicero's Lithuanians often were involved in politics. Shown here at a reception at St. Anthony's Parish on October 3, 1976, are, from left to right, then gubernatorial candidate Jim Thompson, Jonas Kimbarkas, and Edvardas Sumanas. (LRSC.)

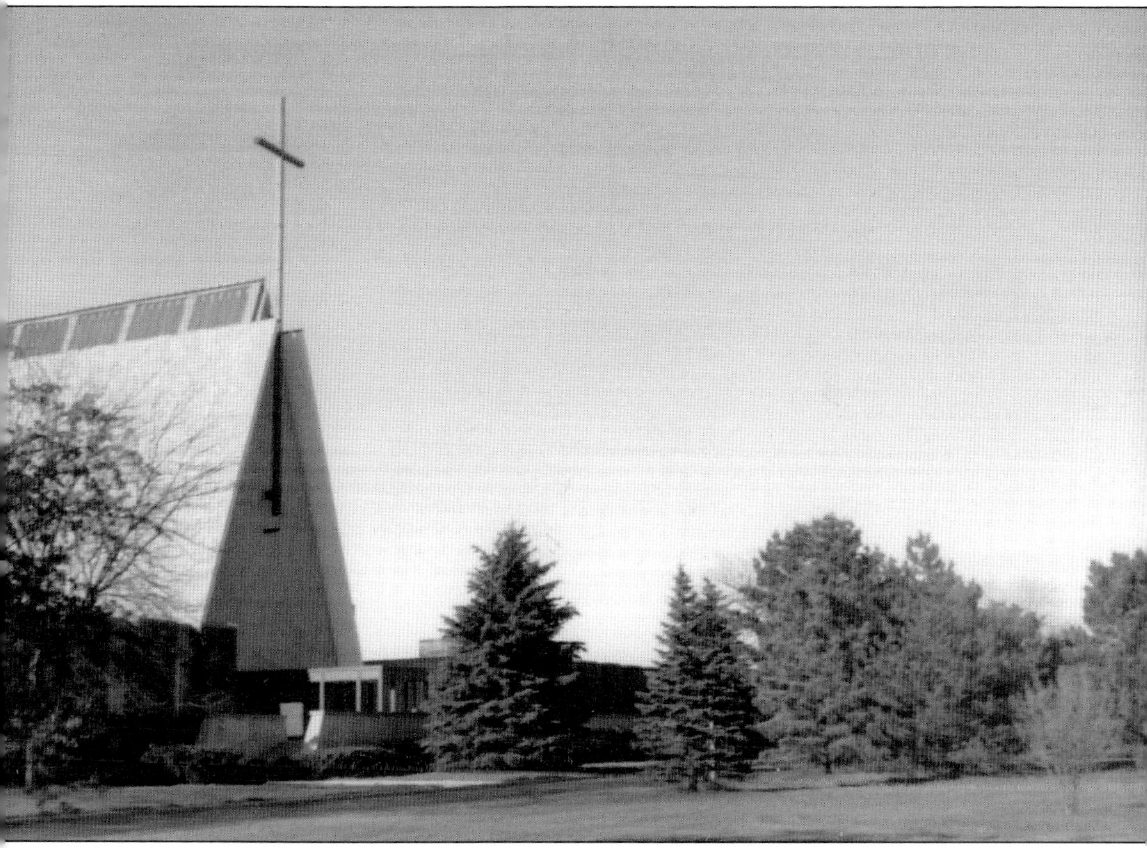

Purchased in 1988 for $800,000, the Lithuanian World Center provided an important focal point for the Lithuanian community in the suburbs of Chicago. The building, a former seminary, is located at 14911 127th Street on 14 acres of land in Lemont, Illinois. Seen here is the front of the center featuring the Blessed Jurgis Matulaitis Catholic Mission and Church. (LRSC.)

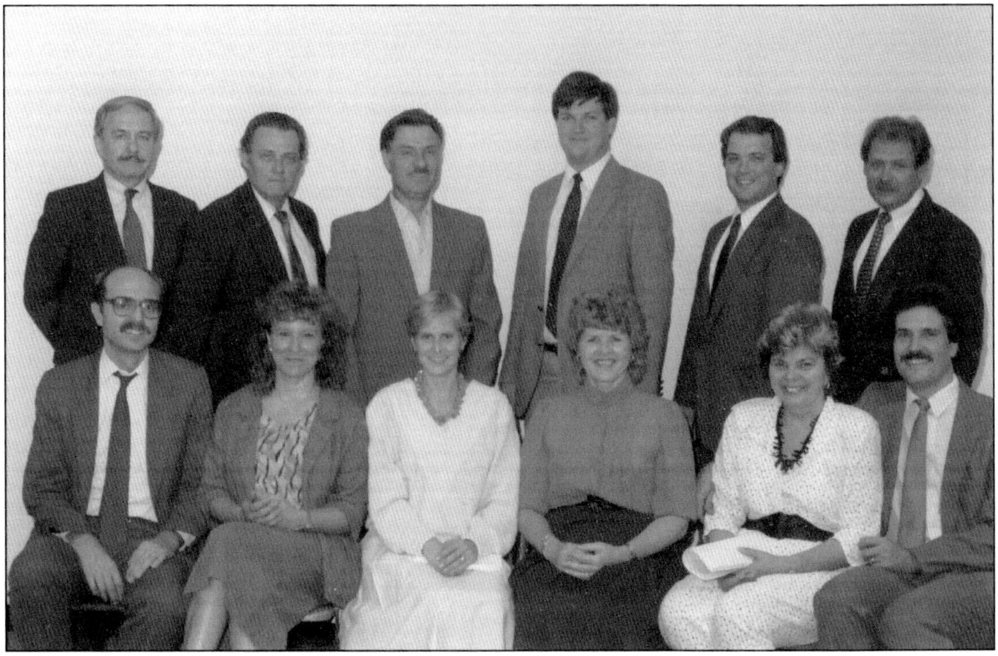

Many have played a key part in helping the Lithuanian World Center thrive. Pictured here is the board of directors not long after the building was purchased in 1988. From left to right are (seated) R. Domanskis, A. Katiliskyte, R. Susinskiene, D. Dundziliene, G. Rimkiene, and J. Riskus; (standing) M. Jakaitis, L. Slenys, V. Soliunas, L. Norusis, R. Burba, and V. Januskis. (LRSC.)

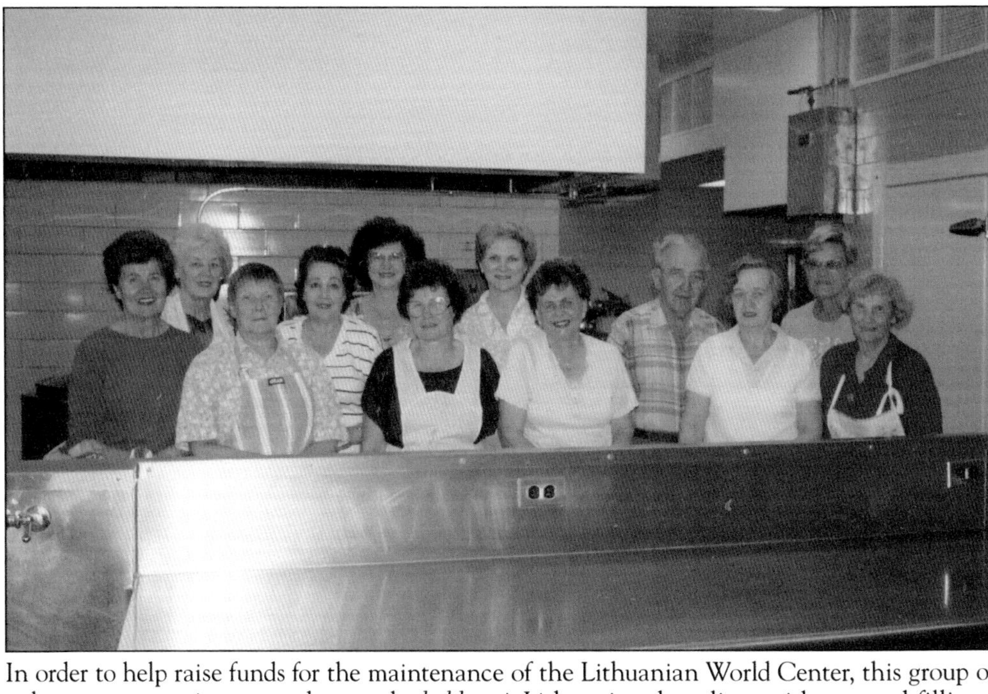

In order to help raise funds for the maintenance of the Lithuanian World Center, this group of volunteers met twice a month to make *koldunai*, Lithuanian dumplings with assorted fillings. With their expertise, more than 6,000 *koldunai* could be made in three hours. These were then frozen and sold to eager customers. (LRSC.)

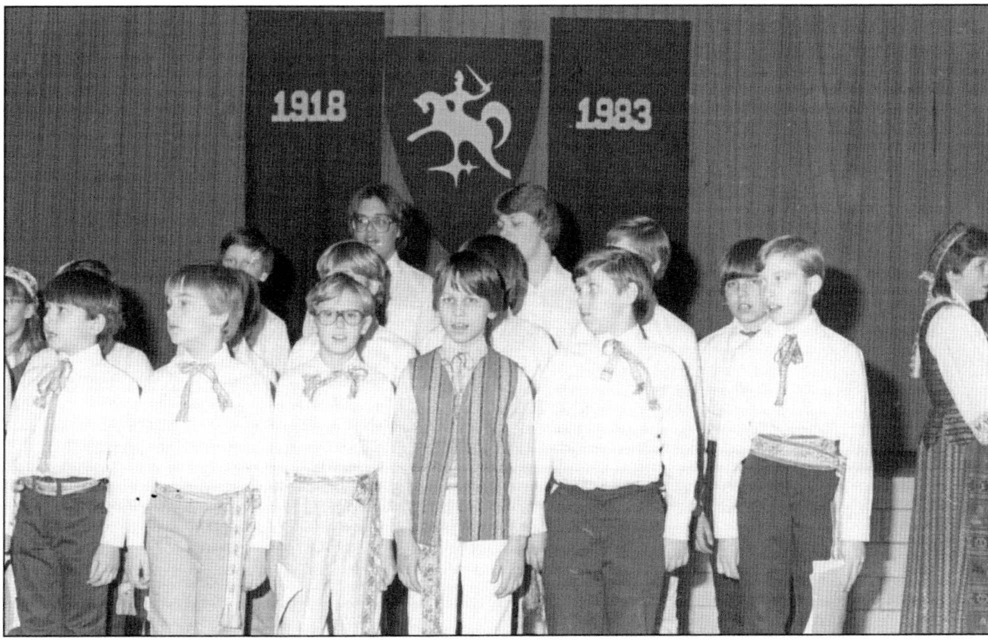

The Lithuanian World Center soon became home to numerous organizations like the Maironis Lithuanian School. Shown here, unidentified students prepare for an upcoming Lithuanian independence day ceremony on February 12, 1983. Prior to being located at the center, the Maironis School met at a public school in Lemont. (LRSC.)

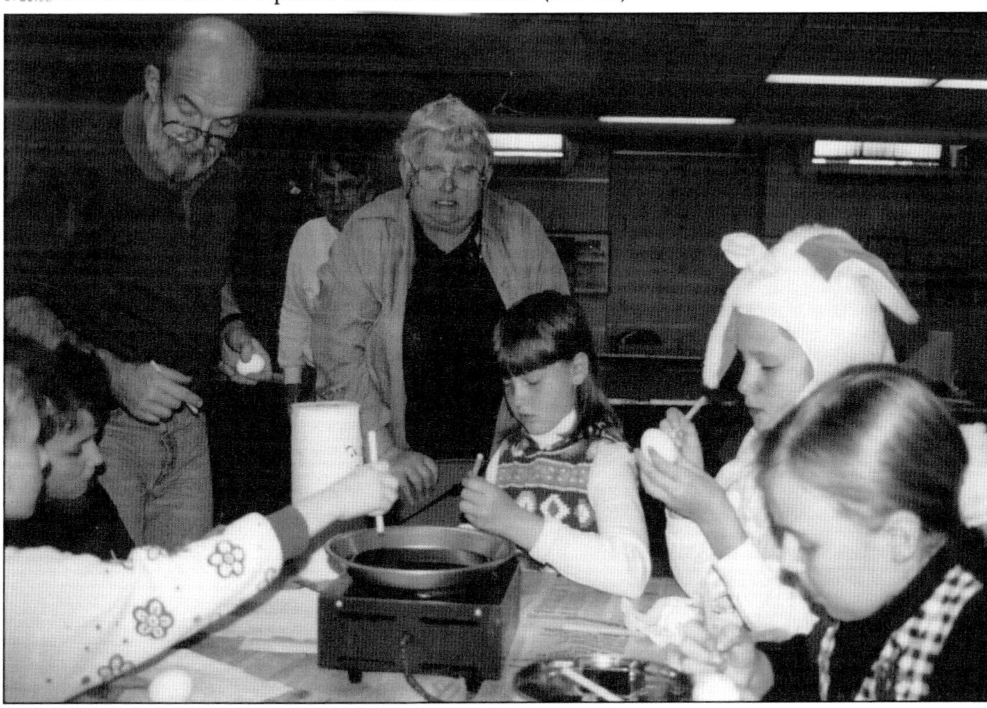

Maironis Lithuanian School is a place where children from kindergarten to 10th grade learn the Lithuanian language and traditions. Lou Volodka, standing far left, instructs eager students in the art of decorating Lithuanian eggs in 1996. (LRSC.)

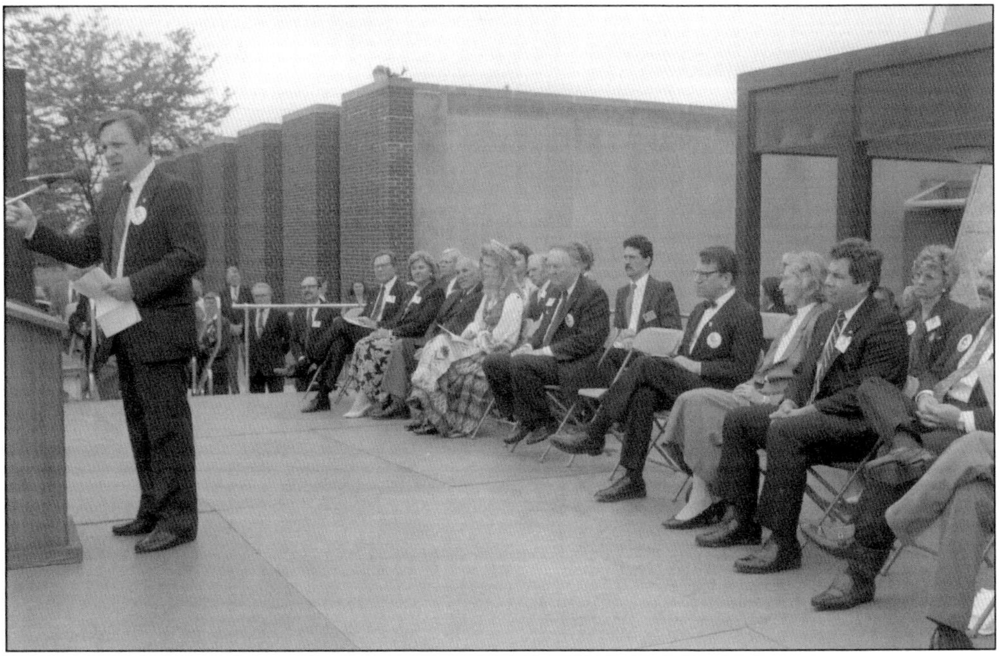

Around the time of Lithuania's independence, the Lithuanian World Center became a hotbed of political activity. This included many visits from dignitaries, such as Congressman Richard Durbin, himself a Lithuanian American. He can be seen above giving a speech in support of Lithuanian independence around 1990. (LRSC.)

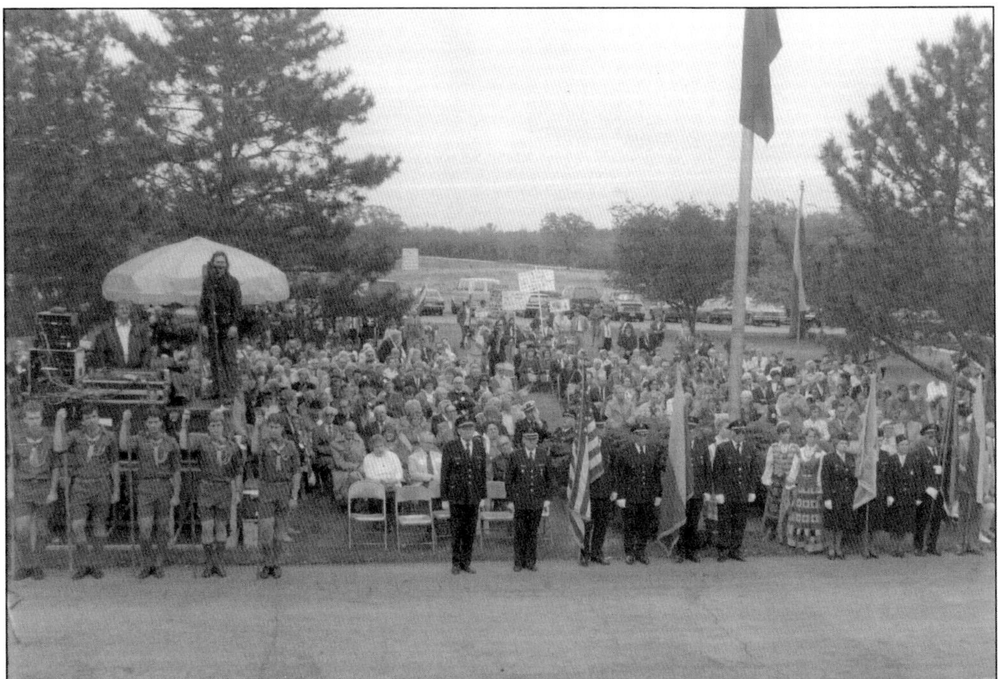

Eager to show their support, Lithuanians in the suburbs often attended events such as the one above in significant numbers. (LRSC.)

During the time of Lithuania's independence in the early 1990s, the Lithuanian World Center was the headquarters for two organizations that greatly helped the country's cause: Lithuanian Hotline and Lithuanian Mercy Lift. Lithuanian Hotline was created in 1990 to generate publicity and to provide the American media with accurate information regarding Lithuania's situation. Lithuanian Mercy Lift gathered much needed medical supplies to aid Lithuanians after the fall of the Soviet Union. At right is Paul Simon standing with a hotline member in 1990. Below are members of Lithuanian Mercy Lift, which by 2004 had shipped nearly $124 million worth of supplies to Lithuania. (Both, LRSC.)

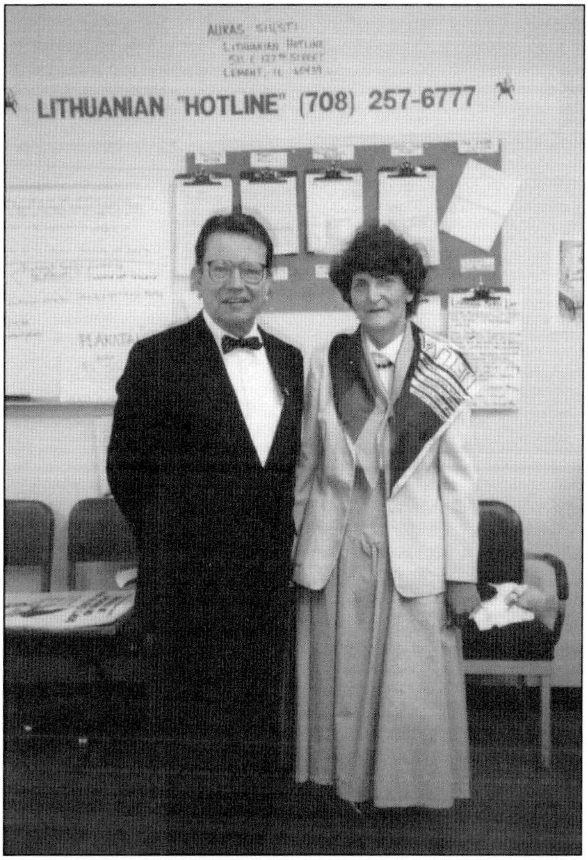

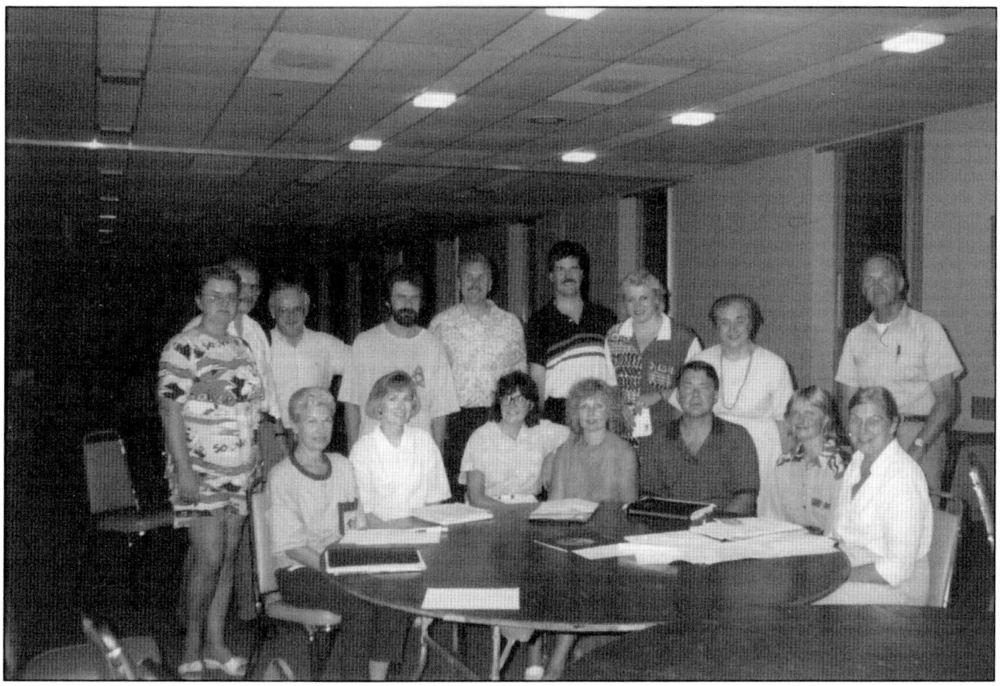

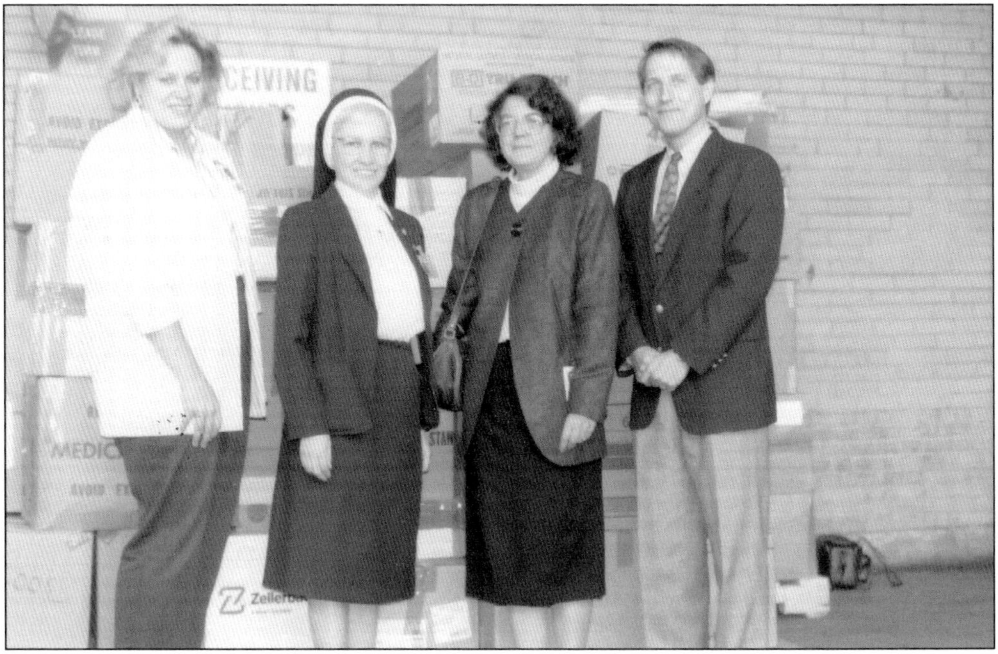

Many of the supplies donated to Lithuanian Mercy Lift came from Lithuanian-affiliated organizations like Holy Cross Hospital, administered by the Sisters of St. Casimir. Shown here with supplies donated by the hospital in 1993 are, from left to right, Rita Riskus, Sister Juline, Jackie Cimino, and Mark Clement. (LRSC.)

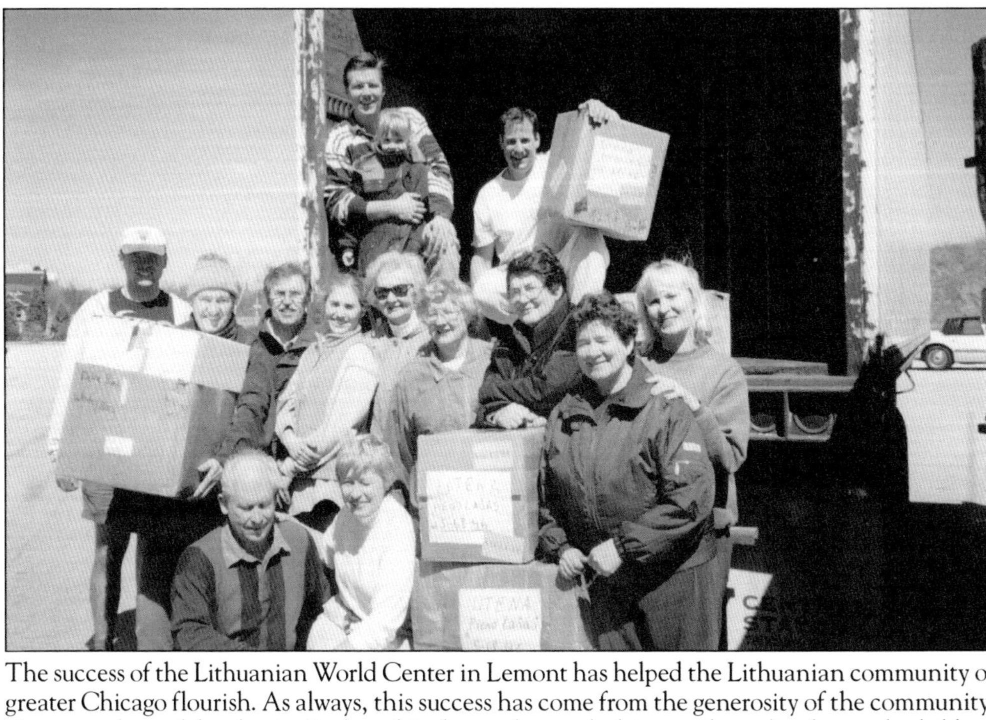

The success of the Lithuanian World Center in Lemont has helped the Lithuanian community of greater Chicago flourish. As always, this success has come from the generosity of the community. Here, members of the charity Saulute ship donated toys, clothing, and supplies for needy children in Lithuania on April 5; the year is unknown. (LRSC.)

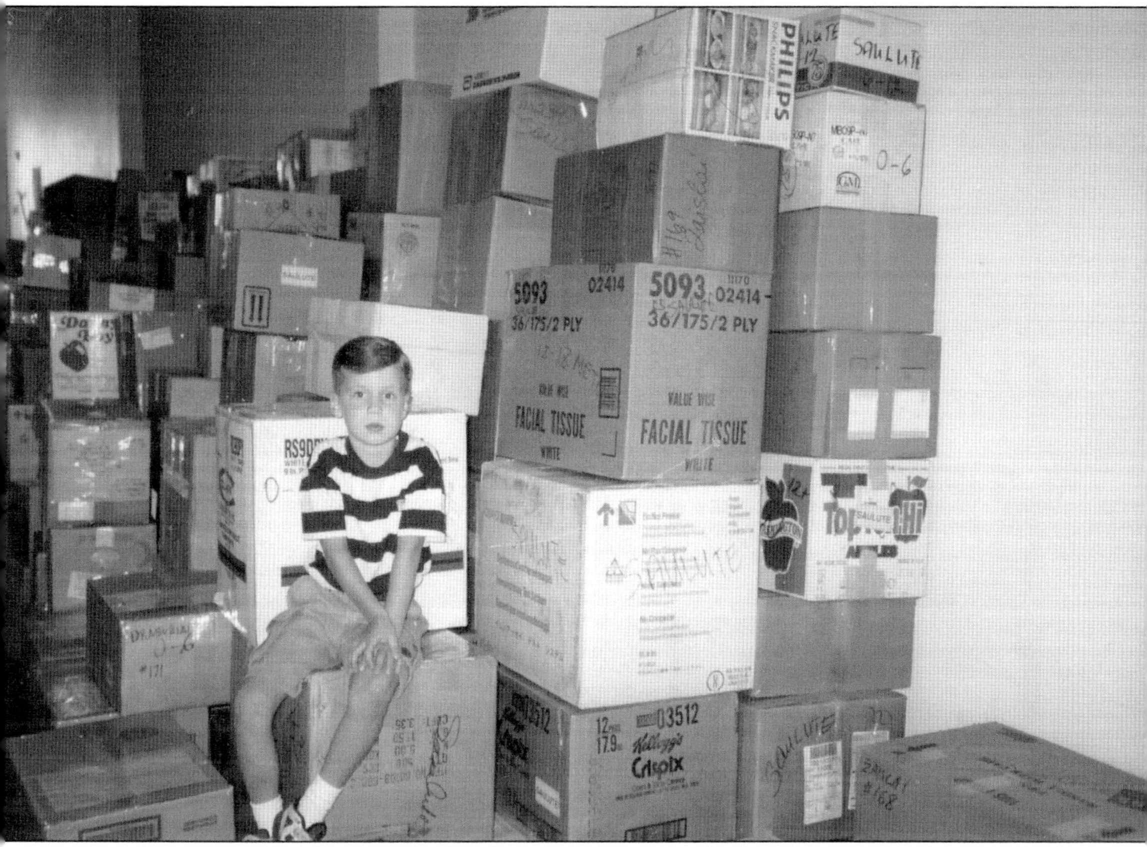

Saulute has been quite successful in collecting and donating goods to needy children in Lithuania, largely thanks to volunteers like Aleksas Siliunas, shown here after taking part in an August shipment. (LRSC.)

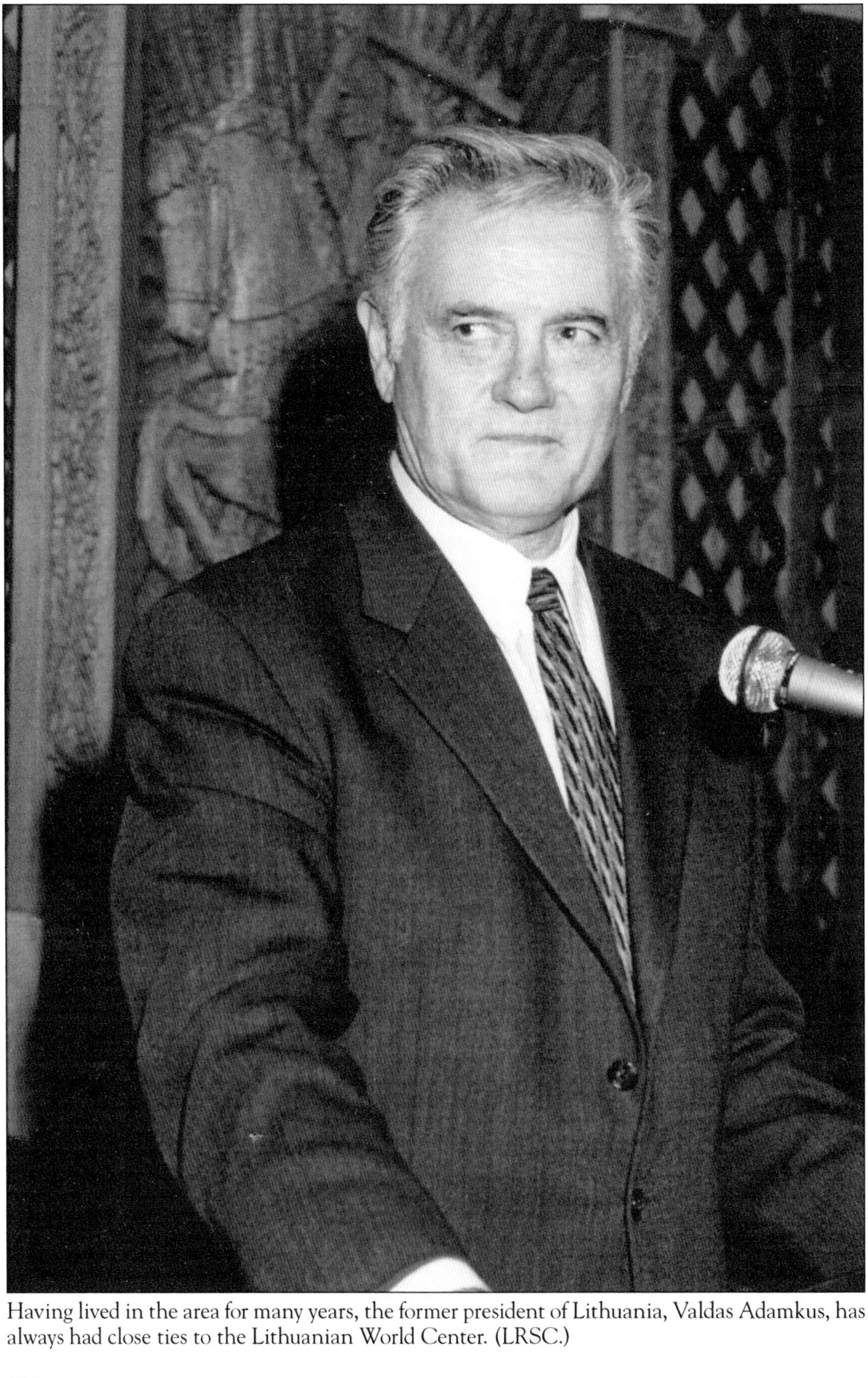

Having lived in the area for many years, the former president of Lithuania, Valdas Adamkus, has always had close ties to the Lithuanian World Center. (LRSC.)

BIBLIOGRAPHY

Aliunas, Leo. *Lithuanians in the United States*. San Francisco: R&E Research Associates, 1978.

Baškauskas, Liucija. "The Lithuanian Refugee Experience and Grief." International Migration Review. Vol. 15. No. ½.: 276-291. 1981.

Budreckis, Algirdas M. *The Lithuanians in America: 1651–1975*. Dobbs Ferry, NY: Oceana Publications, 1976.

Fainhauz, David. *Lithuanians in Multiethnic Chicago Until World War II*. Chicago, IL: Lithuanian Library Press and Loyola University Press, 1977.

Headley, Kathleen J. *Chicago Lawn and Marquette Manor*. Chicago, IL: Arcadia Publishing, 2001.

Kezys, Algimantas. *A Lithuanian Cemetery: St. Casimir Lithuanian Cemetery in Chicago, Illinois*. Chicago, IL: Lithuanian Photograph Library, 1976.

Kucas, Antanas. *Lithuanians in America*. Boston, MA: Encyclopedia Lithuania, 1975.

Petcavage, Margaret. *Sisters of St. Casimir: A Journey Faith, 100 Years*. New York, NY: Booklink, 2007.

Riskus, Justin G. "The Lithuanians in Chicago." *Lithuanian Heritage Magazine* (March/April 2006): 14–19, 30–31.

Riskus, Justin G. "Lithuanians in America: 1870–1940." *Immigrants in American History: Arrival, Adaptation, and Integration*. Santa Barbara, CA: ABC-CLIO, 2012.

——— "Lithuanians in America: 1940–Present." *Immigrants in American History: Arrival, Adaptation, and Integration*. Santa Barbara, CA: ABC-CLIO, 2012.

Subacius, Giedrius. *Upton Sinclair: The Lithuanian Jungle*. New York, NY: Rodopi, 2006.

Swist, Jeannette. *Back of the Yards*. Chicago, IL: Arcadia Publishing, 2007.

Van Reenan, Antanas J. *Lithuanian Diaspora: Königsberg to Chicago*. New York, NY: University Press of America, 1990.

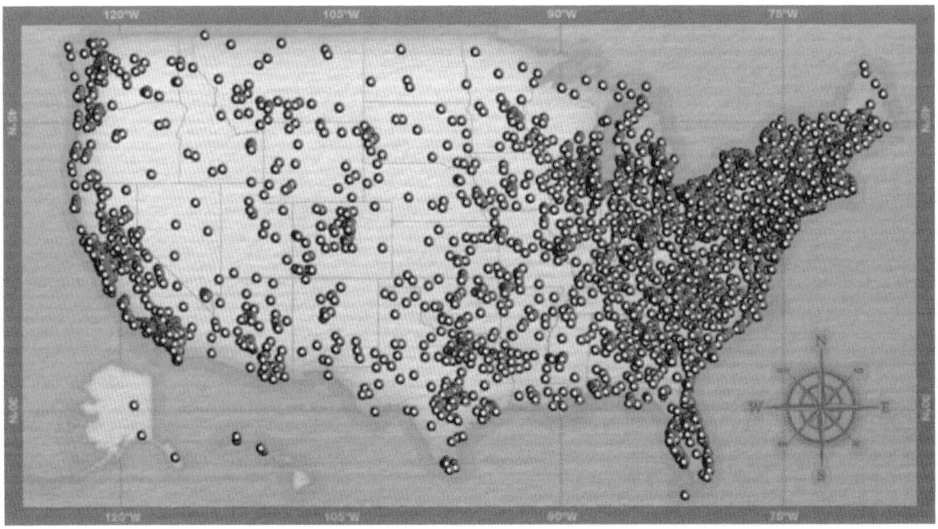